INSTRUCTOR'S MANUAL

to accompany

BUSINESS RESEARCH METHODS

Fifth Edition

Donald R. Cooper
Florida Atlantic University

IRWIN
Chicago • Bogota • Boston • Buenos Aires • Caracas
London • Madrid • Mexico City • Sydney • Toronto

© Richard D. Irwin, Inc., 1976, 1980, 1985, 1991, 1995

All rights reserved. The contents, or parts thereof, may be reproduced for classroom use with *Business Research Methods,* Fifth Edition, by Cooper and Emory, provided such reproductions bear copyright notice and the number reproduced does not exceed the number of students using the text, but may not be reproduced in any form for any other purpose without written permission of the publisher.

Printed in the United States of America.

ISBN 0–256–14938–0

3 4 5 6 7 8 9 0 WCB 1 0 9 8 7 6

BUSINESS REPLY MAIL
FIRST CLASS MAIL   PERMIT NO. 17   HOMEWOOD, IL

POSTAGE WILL BE PAID BY ADDRESSEE

RICHARD D. IRWIN
1333 Burr Ridge Pky.
Burr Ridge, IL 60521-0084

ATTENTION: R. Hercher

(fold)

(fold)

IRWIN

Instructor's Manual to accompany *BUSINESS RESEARCH METHODS*, Fifth Edition by Donald R. Cooper

Please use this postage-paid form to report any errors that you find in this material. Be as complete as possible noting specifically which changes should be made. We will address them in subsequent printings and future editions. Thank You.

NOTE: Extra copies of this form appear at the end of this manual.

Attention: R. T. Hercher

Name _____   School _____

Office Phone _____

Please fold and seal so that our address is visible.

Instructor's Manual BUSINESS RESEARCH METHODS 5/e

TABLE OF CONTENTS

Introduction	Course Design	1
Chapter 1	Research in Business	16
Chapter 2	Scientific Thinking	24
Chapter 3	The Research Process	35
Chapter 4	The Research Proposal	47
Special Section	Ethics in Business Research	57
Chapter 5	Design Strategies	59
Chapter 6	Measurement	71
Chapter 7	Scaling Design	81
Chapter 8	Sampling Design	91
Chapter 9	Secondary Data Sources	102
Chapter 10	Survey Methods	113
Chapter 11	Survey Instruments	119
Chapter 12	Observation	130
Chapter 13	Experimentation	139
Chapter 14	Data Preparation and Preliminary Analysis	149
Chapter 15	Hypothesis Testing	166
Chapter 16	Measures of Association	184
Chapter 17	Multivariate Analysis: An Overview	201
Chapter 18	Presenting Results: Written and Oral Reports	208

COURSE DESIGN

Business research methods courses are as diverse as the people who teach them. The probable reason for this is that, except in the case of marketing, the courses serve a wide range of academic objectives and are offered by professors with a variety of academic interests. However, two major approaches can be discerned. One is oriented toward projects while the other has more emphasis on case study.

The thrust of *Business Research Methods* 5/e is toward the project approach. The premise underlying the book is that students need a single, concise, but relatively complete reading resource which covers the fundamentals of the research process. We further contend that the best way to reinforce theory is to demonstrate the practice through actually planning and doing research. Research is a creative process and the development of skills is best promoted through the design and conduct of research studies by students under faculty guidance.

A Sample Course Syllabus

Exhibit 0-1 presents a course structure which has been used with success in an MBA program. It is for a one semester course with 30 class sessions of about 80 minutes each. The class time is allocated as follows:

Number of Class sessions	Process
19	Discussion of the various materials in the text. Chapters 14, 15, and 16 require two sessions. Other chapters can *usually* be treated in one session.
2	Examinations
4	Project presentations
5	Project work. This is compensatory time off given to the students for research work. The professor uses these sessions to consult with individuals and teams on their specific projects.

The syllabus includes three special project assignments. Alternate assignments are also presented in this section.

1. An individually executed design project and presentation
2. An individual library search or industry analysis project and presentation
3. A field research project (usually in small groups)

In the authors' experience, students can be kept under project assignment throughout the course. Students begin courses slowly and an early project assignment helps smooth out the semester work load. If the project is a long one, it should be broken into interim steps that can be completed and submitted for approval at various points throughout the semester.

Student evaluation. This is a topic on which instructors hold differing views, but it may help to indicate one evaluation scheme which has generally been satisfactory. In the course illustrated in Exhibit 0 - 1, 40 percent of the student's grade is determined by performance on two examinations. Normally no comprehensive final examination is held for the course because of the workload that students face in completing their term projects. Individual design and library research projects early in the semester account for 25 percent credit, while the team field research project is given the remaining 35 percent credit. One may wish to use peer evaluation reports to adjust individual student's grades for team projects.

Projects

Projects may commence on the first day of class, but it is wise to wait a day or so to pick up stragglers. As many as three projects can be used in a semester course if one of them is quite short. Other options are suggested that are not included in the sample syllabus.

Briefings and presentations. Many students feel that they do not get enough experience in making presentations to groups. A short assignment that gives them a week or so to get ready can provide an interesting way to get the course off in a positive manner. One example, the design project, is found in the Close-Up of Chapter 5. An alternative to the design project is found in Exhibit 0 - 3. This exercise could be started earlier but seems to work well after exposure to Chapters 3 and 5.

When the class has no more than 10 students one can conduct all of the presentations within a single class session. When classes are larger it is best to break into groups of about 6 to 8 students and have each group meet separately to make their presentations. The instructor should attend all sessions. While these added sessions are burdensome for the instructor, they are well accepted by students and are worth the effort.

Students should be given briefing evaluation forms and requested to use them to analyze each presentation made. This is an excellent way to provide standardized feedback to the speakers as well as involvement and listening motivation to students. One form is shown in Exhibit 0 - 4. The completed forms can best be given directly to the speakers through the instructor after each presentation. Generally no attempt is made to grade these first efforts.

If the professor wishes to lighten the workload, the presentation(s) supporting the design or library projects may be omitted.

An introductory assignment. The Research Article Critique works well to emphasize the applicational focus of the course. Shown in Exhibit 0 - 2, this assignment is based on Chapter 1's criteria for "good research." Students select a recent article from one of the journals in their specialization. Their efforts are directed at applying the materials from the first few weeks of class to synthesizing the characteristics of good research in a concrete application. The discussion of their findings provides an important opportunity to correct misconceptions of the criteria, the differences between empirical research and think-pieces, and the goals of the course.

A library search project. Many students do not know how to fully exploit the resources of a research library. Alumni feedback suggests that this particular learning experience was quite useful for other courses and later in their careers. A research project which draws on a wide range of library information sources can be valuable. A memorandum to students for one such project is shown in Exhibit 0-5. The emphasis here is on the use of a variety of the bibliographic sources and the sharpening of oral presentation skills.

If the choice of topic is left to the student it is a good idea to have each person submit a topic for approval. Through this process one can exert some control over the appropriateness and value of the exercise as well as guarding against excessive topic duplication. Another approach is to provide a list of topics.

An alternate library search project: industry analysis. Another way to promote the use of library resources is to use a project which calls for the student to investigate an industry and a company within that industry. This exercise can be proposed as a possible prelude for seeking a position with the company. It can be of great interest and perhaps even direct employment benefit to a student. A memorandum which has been used for such a project is shown in Exhibit 0-6. In conducting the briefings it is again often necessary to break the class into small groups which meet several times to complete their presentations. This can be time consuming but it is appreciated by students who normally receive limited opportunity to make oral presentations of data and findings.

In these and other research projects it is a good idea to insist that each student in the audience evaluate the performance of his colleagues. This can be done in many ways but the evaluation form shown in Exhibit 0-4 can be used.

Field research project. The major project of the semester is a research study involving secondary data and primary data collection. A variety of formats are available. If the class is small (say, 5 to 10) it may be desirable to conduct a single class project. The authors' experience with larger classes is that a single class project is not as satisfactory as smaller projects using teams of two to five students. Persons can be assigned to work together or they may wish to choose their team members. One workable rule is to have self selection in small teams and assigned selection for larger teams.

There are good reasons for encouraging students to form teams for a full scale project. First, the interactions that take place during the team's work provide an excellent learning experience. Each team member can contribute to the education of his/her teammates in the development of the study. The result is a quality that generally surpasses projects by individuals. This self education feature is not necessarily operative when classes are so large that the professor can not closely supervise each project.

The quality and scope of student projects is partially a function of the number of personhours available for the task. With more team members there are more resources, but this must be balanced against another consideration. The advantage of small team projects compared to the large team, single class project is that with small teams each student can be involved in every phase of the study. In larger

Introduction *Course Design*

groups there is a tendency for students to work only on narrow portions of the project.

Sources for research studies are legion and topics range widely. Many students will wish to test hypotheses or questions that grow out of their studies in other subjects. Another excellent source of project topics are various organizations, both on and off campus. There are many social, civic, educational, governmental, religious, and business organizations that welcome an offer of research. Surveys and observational studies are especially popular with such groups; experimental studies are not so common but should not be ignored. Exhibits O-8 and O-9 contain handouts for the field research project. Exhibit O-9 shows a more traditional set of components and may not be completely satisfactory for what you have in mind. Use it as a guide and revise it to meet your specifications.

Several problems may occur when an organization is involved as a client. There may be some expenses which are burdensome for the students but organizations are usually are willing to pay out-of-pocket costs for research projects. Of greater concern is the occasional case when an organization wishes to exploit the university connection. This comes more often from student enthusiasm than from the organization's insistence. For example, students may wish to use university letterheads, post office address, and either state or imply that the university is sponsoring the study. Identification with the university should normally be restricted to those cases where the university is actually the sponsor. Otherwise the professor may have a public relations problem with the university administration. It is reasonable, however, to state that they are students at the university and that the study is a class project.

Occasionally, a problem occurs when a firm perceives the project in a way that is not in keeping with the course objectives. For example, a firm may have the survey instrument developed, and what they want is to have some students do the interviewing and the analysis. This is hardly an acceptable project. In such cases the best approach is to insist that the students must have full responsibility for the design and conduct of the study, subject to client review. If this is not acceptable it is probably wise to drop that project. A second problem is that clients usually want the students to conduct many more interviews or observations than is practical in terms of their limited time. A brief experience in observation or conducting interviews is desirable, but any extensive time at these tasks has only limited educational value in most cases.

The ideal project is one in which the client presents a management problem to a research team and seeks their help. The team, in consultation with professor and client, determines the research question which they can study, designs a project to do this study, conducts a moderate amount of data gathering, analyzes the data, and presents the results to the clients. The clients can accept the results in the light of the small number of observations or they can secure additional observations by hiring field workers to gather more data. Often the project will serve as an exploratory study to be expanded later.

Supervision of field research. It is not easy to provide close supervision for several groups of students, each with a different research project. One way to improve supervision is to establish a schedule of interim reports that will help in monitoring the development of each team's project. One approach calls for the students to submit four reports that are sequenced over the semester. A memorandum which illustrates this approach is shown in Exhibit 0 - 7.

On our sample syllabus, the first report is a small-scale research proposal which is due on the fourteenth class session. We recommend using the sections listed in Chapter 4, Figure 4 - 3 under the category Student Term Paper. This will result in a tentative problem statement, research objectives, and bibliography. (If you are requiring only one project for the semester, the first field report should probably be due no later than the second week and a modified report schedule will need to be prepared.)

The second report is more substantial and requires a proposal which should contain (Figure 4 - 3): a problem statement, research objectives, literature review, research design, expected nature and form of results, support and facilities, bibliography, and appendixes (if necessary). This may run up to 10 pages although the average will probably be about 5 - 7. This is due by the seventeenth class session.

The third report is an oral presentation to be given about the last week of classes. It should be a skillfully executed briefing with a generous use of visual aids. Normally, all team members should have a communication responsibility in the briefing. If teams are going to meet high standards of presentation it is necessary that they practice several times. After some practice there should be a rehearsal that includes the instructor. At this time, it is appropriate to critique the team presentation and suggest improvements. In our experience these rehearsal sessions will probably last an hour or so each.

If the project is being done for a client the oral presentation should be made at the client's offices. This is a very motivating experience for the students. The team should aim for a presentation of perhaps 20 minutes or so plus question and discussion time. Each of these sessions will typically take an hour, and should be attended by the professor. If a project is not done for a client, the oral presentation can be made to the class.

The fourth report is the written results of the study. It should be substantial in length, with appropriate appendices and careful attention to proper style. Special emphasis must be placed on the format of the report because few students will have had experience in writing up a research study. They tend to approach the task like writing an essay when what is desired is the carefully organized telegraphic style of a research report.

Often team members are assigned to prepare different sections of the report. In the past this has often led to poorly organized reports which suffered from badly executed transitions, inconsistency of style, poor graphics, and other difficulties. If one team member serves as an editor (or perhaps co-editors are selected) many of these problems can be alleviated. Word processors greatly improve presentation quality and should be encouraged.

Finally, too much attention is typically given to what the researchers did rather than what was found, concluded, and recommended. If professors have strong feelings about the nature of the format they should stress exactly what is desired.

Exhibit 0 - 1   Sample Course Syllabus

---

30 Sessions of 80 Minutes Each

Session	Topic	Reading	Assignment
1	Introduction to Course	Ch. 1	Article Critique (optional)
2	Scientific Thinking	2	
3	Research Process	3	
4	Research Design	5	Design Project (assigned)
5	Oral Presentation: Design	18	Design Project Due
6	Ethics in Research	Spec. Section	Cases for in-class discussion
7	Measurement	6	
8	Scaling	7	
9	Sampling	8	
10	Library Session	9 App. A	Library Search or Industry Analysis Project (assigned)
11	Oral Presentation	-	Industrial Analysis Presentations or Library Project Due
12	Surveys	Ch. 10, 4	Term Project and Research Proposal (assigned)
13	Instruments	11	
14	Observation	12	Proposal Report 1 (due)
15	Experimentation	13	
16	Midterm Exam	1 - 13	
17	Project Day	-	Proposal Report 2 (due)
18	Data Analysis	14	
19	Data Analysis	14	
20	Project Day	-	
21	Hypothesis Testing	15	
22	Hypothesis Testing	15	
23	Project Day	-	
24	Measures of Association	16	
25	Project Day	-	
26	Multivariate Analysis	17	
27	Examination	14 - 18	
28	Project Day	-	
29	Term Project Presentation	-	Term Project Reports (due)
30	Term Project Presentation	-	

Exhibit 0 - 2   Research Article Critique

FROM: Professor _____
TO: Students in Business Research Course
SUBJECT: Project 1

For your first research project please investigate one of the journals listed below for an article of interest to you. Choose one that has sufficient content that you can write a report to me (approximately 2 double spaced pages).

The object of your critique is to describe how the study followed or failed to follow the criteria for good research described in Chapter 1. Speculate on which of the writer's conclusions were warranted and which were not. In addition to Chapter 1, Chs. 2 and 3 may be helpful in getting you started.

Some journals are listed below. Select an article from a recent issue (during the last year):

1. Academy of Management Review
2. Administrative Science Quarterly
3. Business and Society Review
4. Decision Sciences
5. Financial Management
6. Harvard Business Review
7. Industrial and Labor Relations Review
8. Journal of Accountancy
9. Journal of Applied Behavior Science
10. Journal of Applied Psychology
11. Journal of Banking and Finance
12. Journal of Finance
13. Management Review
14. Personnel Journal
15. Public Administration Review
16. Training and Development Journal

Other journals may be considered.

Introduction   Course Design

Exhibit 0 - 3   Alternate to Design Project: Article Evaluation
---

FROM: Professor _____
TO: Students in Business Research Course
SUBJECT: Journal Article Evaluation

   Please investigate one of the journals below for an article of interest to you. Choose one that has sufficient content that you can write a report (not to exceed 2 to 3 double spaced pages).

   In addition, be prepared to give a 5 to 8 minute briefing of the article to a group of your peers on the date assigned. This oral report should follow the suggestions which have been given to you in class plus the advice in chapters 5 and 18 of the text. For purposes of this report your visuals should all be on 8-1/2" x 11' paper, using something like a Pentel pen or magic marker. Please use plain white paper or graph paper.

   You are requested to submit your visuals along with the written memorandum report at the end of the class period. The journals from which you may secure the research are as follows:

   1.   Academy of Management Review
   2.   Administrative Science quarterly
   3.   American Journal of Small Business
   4.   Business and Society Review
   5.   Business Economics
   6.   Business Horizons
   7.   California Management Review
   8.   Columbia Journal of World Business
   9.   Decision Sciences
   10. Financial Management
   11. Harvard Business Review
   12. Industrial and Labor Relations Review
   13. Industrial Marketing Management
   14. Journal of Accountancy
   15. Journal of Applied Behavior Science
   16. Journal of Applied Psychology
   17. Journal of Bank Research
   18. Journal of Banking and finance
   19. Journal of Business Research
   20. Journal of Business Strategy
   21. Journal of Industrial Economics
   23. Journal of Marketing
   24. Journal of Retailing
   25. Management Review
   26. Personnel Journal
   27. Production and inventory Management
   28. Sloan Management Review
   29. Training and Development Journal

Exhibit 0-4 Briefing Analysis Form

Rating	Content
_____	1. Clear purpose (How well did you understand *at the start* what was going to be said?)
_____	2. Logical organization (How well did topics connect and/or relate to each other?)
_____	3. Good balance (How well was breadth of topic coverage balanced against detailed elaboration?) Where faulty?(_____)
_____	4. Clarity of explanation (How well did you understand what was said?) (Where not clear?_____)
_____	5. Adequate summary (How well were major points summarized?)

Presentation

_____	6. Voice (Too loud? soft? clear? tone? variable emphasis?)
_____	7. Speaking Speed (Too fast? too slow? variation in speed?)
_____	8. Verbal distractions ("Ah," overworked words, phrases?)
_____	9. Use of gestures (Many? few? good? distracting?)
_____	10. Physical distractions or mannerisms?
_____	11. Eye contact
_____	12. Handling of aids (e.g.. notes, visual aids) _____)

Visual aids

_____	13. How readable were they?
_____	14. How well did they help your understanding?
_____	15. Did they adequately cover the topic? (too few? too many?)

_____ **TOTAL SCORE**

Speaker_____

Rater_____

Rating Scale
1. Requires considerable improvement
2. Requires some improvement
3. Satisfactory
4. Superior

Introduction *Course Design*

Exhibit 0 - 5   Library Search Project

From: Professor _____
To: Students in Business Research Course
Subject: Library Search Project

Your library search project will use various reference tools. There are two objectives for this project:

1. To develop skills with library resources through practice in a exercise format. This will help to prepare you for your term project and develop or refine your skills for use in other courses and research contexts.

2. To provide you with an opportunity to prepare and deliver an oral presentation of research results in a simulated management situation.

The project itself will consist of the following four aspects:

1. The development of a set of bibliography cards, properly annotated and in correct form. See Chapter 9 for specifics.

2. The actual gathering of information from secondary sources using all four of the major information source types as follows:

    CD-ROM: *Infotrac, Newsbank, UMI Dissertation Abstracts, ABI/INFORM, Business Periodicals ON-DISK. Also online: Internet, ABI/INFORM, Dow Jones News/Retrieval, Lexis, etc.*

    Periodicals: BPI, ASTI, and PAIS as well as others if appropriate. It is expected that periodicals will often be the major source.

    Books: university card catalogs, one of the book bibliographies such as CBI

    Government documents: the monthly catalog of the Supt. of Documents

3. The presentation of a 10 minute oral briefing to an "executive group which has requested the study." Details of the presentation will be given in class at a later date.

4. A typed outline of your presentation that should not exceed three pages.

Exhibit 0 - 6	Alternate to Library Search: Industry Analysis Project

From: Professor _____
To: Students in Business Research Course
Subject: Industry Analysis Project

You are to conduct a research study and present your findings in an oral briefing to the class. The project goal is to give you experience in analyzing a company and the industry of which it is a part. You are assumed to be seeking a career within the industry you are analyzing. The study will be similar to one where a candidate for merger is assessed. Choose an industry that is well enough known that you can find substantial published information.

Procedure:

1. Do the study on an individual basis, although you may confer with others in the class.

2. Determine the information which you feel should be gathered for such a project. Submit an outline of this by (date). Secondary data sources will be the major sources.

3. Determine how and where you will secure this information.

4. Do the data collection and analysis.

5. Prepare an oral presentation, complete with visual aids, to be given on (date).

6. Rehearse the presentation until you can give it skillfully within a 15 minute time frame.

7. Prepare a typed outline of the presentation for submission at the time of presentation.

8. Suggestive of the range of topics which should be in the report are the following:

    A. Industry makeup, including information on concentration.
    B. Geographic dispersion.
    C. Industry growth - past, present, and future.
    D. Current problems and opportunities—market, competition, government, technological.
    E. Cost patterns and profitability patterns.
    F. Other dimensions as necessary.

9. At a minimum the following library sources should be reviewed:

    A. CD - ROM databases
    B. U.S. Census publications and others including Current Industry Reports
    C. BPI, PAIS, ASTI
    D. U.S. Government Monthly Catalog
    E. Wall Street Journal index
    F. Various book indexes

Exhibit 0 - 7 Research Report Schedule

Date   Report

_____ 1. A listing of team members (from 3 to 6). The first report is a small-scale research proposal. The report will contain a tentative problem statement, research objectives, and bibliography.

_____ 2. The second report is a well-developed proposal which should contain a problem statement, research objectives, literature review, research design, expected nature and form of results, support and facilities, bibliography, and appendixes (if necessary). This may run up to 10 pages although the average will probably be about 5. The report should also cover briefly the progress that has been made to date on the project as well as a rough time schedule of future steps which the team expects to take.

_____ *

_____ 3. The third report is an oral presentation to be given about the last week of classes. It should be a skillfully executed briefing with a generous use of visual aids. Normally, all team members should have a communication responsibility in the briefing. The briefing will either take place in a client's office or in the classroom.

_____ 4. A final written research report follows the general format suggested in Chapter 18. Specific format details, bibliography, and style requirements to be provided by the instructor.

*Instructors may wish to require additional interim reports to stay informed on the progress of pilot testing, coding, data analysis, and other activities.

Exhibit 0 - 8 Field Research Project

The Field Research Project is intended to be a mini research study. Its purpose is to integrate the various units of the course and provide a platform for applying the skills and knowledge that you have obtained. The following procedures describe the direction of the project.

1. Select a problem of work, university, or community significance. Keep the scope of the problem small! It must be researchable in a 7-10 week period. Create research questions that capture the essence of the problem and investigation questions that reflect the various facets of the problem expressed by the research question(s).

The nature of the topic will largely determine the type and amount of secondary data available to you. Highly applied topics will fall on the scarce end of the resource continuum for secondary data whereas studies involving existing theory --and on which previous empirical work has been done – will be on the other end. Ideally, you will want to be somewhere toward the middle. In short, you don't want to do an exhaustive review of all the available literature on a topic like capital budgeting or resort to a few newspaper clippings.

2. Go to the library and scan the background information. Use on-line, CD-ROM and other electronic sources to reduce your time. If information is not available in published form, you will want to get access to letters and memoranda from relevant archives, public offices, and files.

3. Secure written permission to gather data from and/or use human subjects in an experiment. Keep these documents on file for your protection and provide them as an appendix to your report.

4. Develop a proposal for the conduct of your research. We will discuss the format in class. It should include a problem statement, preliminary literature review, your design choice, how you plan to sample, the proposed data collection instruments and procedures, and the statistical analysis you intend to use.

5. Be prepared to present your proposal to the class at the time shown on the syllabus. Class members will be asked for ideas to assist you with your project. The instructor will make recommendations and have approval authority for the topic and methodology.

6. Some class sessions may be used for field data collection, analysis, consultation with the professor or on other aspects of the project that may be giving you difficulty.

7. A final oral presentation of your results will occur at the end of the term when your written report is due.

8. Write you paper in the format suggested by the text and handouts provided in class. The Turabian or APA style manuals should be used for proper format.

Exhibit 0 - 9 Components of the Field Research Project

I. The Problem and its Setting

    A. Statement of the problem

        1. Research question(s)
        2. Investigative questions

    B. Hypothesis (if appropriate for the design)
    C. Assumptions (if necessary)
    D. Delimitations
    E. Definition of terms
    F. Importance/benefits of the research

II. Review of Related Literature

    A. Begin your discussion of related studies from a comprehensive perspective (like an inverted pyramid -- broad end first) and then deal with more specific studies relating to your problem. Tie the literature review to your investigative questions.

        1. This part of your project does not call for an exhaustive historical review but rather the most pertinent studies bearing on your problem.
        2. Avoid nonessential details: emphasize major findings, conclusions, and implications. Look for methodological hints and justifications that you can use for your study.
        3. Show the relationship between the studies you have reviewed and your own.

    B. Summarize all that you have written in a final summary section of the literature review and interpret your conclusions in terms of your investigative questions. Those questions that have not been answered by secondary sources are candidates for primary data collection.

III. Methods and Procedures

This is usually the most carefully read section of a research proposal or term project. Up to this point the researcher has told in glowing terms what s/he hopes to accomplish and what it will mean theoretically or practically. The methods section brings this down to earth in operational terms.

In most papers, this section will need adaptations to this outline to describe adequately specific approaches to the problem. Adapt this set of instructions judiciously so that the key ingredients are properly covered. For example, if the design calls for a survey, the sections on sample, design, and data collection can be arranged in a single description of how and where you will gather data. In an experiment, it would be wise to emphasize how the experimental situation will be structured, which variables are controlled and how, sources of contamination, preparation of subjects, and the environmental conditions under which the data are being collected. Elaborate on those aspects appropriate to the type of design you have selected.

A. Population and sample: the level of description in this section gives the reader a good idea about generalizability.

   1. Sampling plan: include information about the reasons for choosing a particular form of sampling and the nature of the strata, clusters, etc., if used.
   2. When a complex plan is used, provide a graphic (chart or table) that shows your approach.
   3. A rationale should be provided if the total population is used in lieu of a sample.

B. Design: that fact that this term is used suggests a carefully controlled plan for obtaining required data. Select one of the designs we discussed in class. Review the characteristics of design to be certain that the one you are identifying corresponds with how you will collect data and what goals you have specified as outcomes (reporting, description, explanation, prediction).

C. Data and instrumentation: describe the data that are needed for each investigative question and their location.

   1. What are the procedures for data collection and how have you provided for control of anticipated sources of unwanted variation?
   2. Describe the measures (and scales) used for collection.
   3. Instrumentation: Show how your instruments are acceptable definitions of the variables and how they have proper measurement characteristics for your intended purpose. Explain what is known about the reliability and validity of the measures. Empirical evidence to support your statements should either be general knowledge (as with a commonly used test), a specific citation in the literature, or provisions should be made for providing confirmation as a result of the data you collect.

D. Analysis: state carefully and unequivocally how the data were treated. What techniques were selected and why? What hypotheses were tested? What inferences were made?

IV. Discussion and Conclusions

This two part section allows you to describe the findings from the statistical analysis and plug them back into the investigative questions. Which questions were answered authoritatively, tentatively, or not at all? How do your findings amplify or contradict previous studies you have cited in the literature?

The conclusions section shows how the findings meet the original objective of the research (in the problem statement), how the research question is satisfied, and what the practical outcomes are. What benefits do your findings have for decision makers who supported the study? What theoretical improvements are implied by the findings?

V. Bibliography and appendices

A. The bibliography must follow the style manual format.
B. Include a copy of the measuring instrument.
C. Letters of permission for collecting data go here.

CHAPTER 1

RESEARCH IN BUSINESS

There are three learning objectives in this chapter. They are: (1) Define the nature of research by discussing what constitutes research, and by describing application areas, research approaches, and objectives; (2) Learn the qualities that identify a good research effort and how they may be distinguished by reviewing either research proposals or research reports; and (3) Explain the value and importance of research to management and some of the problems which complicate the successful integration of research and management objectives.

On the first day of class there are always administrative details to get out of the way before turning to research issues. Lecturing is often necessary when this chapter is used since many students will not have read it. If there are sufficient books present in the classroom it may be possible to assign various students to read quickly and summarize various parts of the chapter such as the distinction among the various types of studies conducted and examples of each. Also see the sample assignment at the end of this unit.

Class Discussion Suggestions

An alternative approach is to use some of the questions at the end of the chapter for discussion and lecturing. For example, students often seem unable to think of applications of research approaches until specific situations are pointed out to them. Question 4 at the end of the chapter provides a good vehicle for this discussion and can be organized around the fourfold classification of research objectives.

Other discussion topics of interest are:

1. What is research? Discuss this question first by distinguishing between pure and applied research. The case examples in the text provide a good introduction to the fourfold classification scheme. (It is a five-part classification if control is used separately rather than as an extension of prediction.)

2. Another topic concerns the relationship between research, the manager, and the researcher. It is important to point out that managers have the responsibility to gather information and that they can either do this or delegate it to a specialist. Questions 2, 3, and 5 address various facets of this question.

3. Question 6 may be used to stimulate a discussion about the characteristics that identify good and bad research. It is sometimes desirable to connect these characteristics to a preview of the course so that students get the big picture at the outset rather than acquiring it inductively along the way.

Chapter 1 — Research in Business

Exhibit 1 - 1   Article Critique Instructions to Students

From: Professor _____
To: Students in Business Research Course
Subject: Article Critique Assignment

For your first research project please investigate one of the journals listed below for an article of interest to you. Choose one that has sufficient content that you can write a report to me (approximately 2 double spaced pages).

The object of your critique is to describe how the study followed or failed to follow the criteria for good research described in Chapter 1. Speculate on which of the writer's conclusions were warranted and which were not. In addition to Chapter 1, Chapters 2 and 3 may be helpful in getting you started.

Some journals are listed below. Select an article from a recent issue (during the last year):

1. Academy of Management Review
2. Administrative Science Quarterly
3. Business and Society Review
4. Decision Sciences
5. Financial Management
6. Harvard Business Review
7. Industrial and Labor Relations Review
8. Journal of Accountancy
9. Journal of Applied Psychology
10. Journal of Banking and Finance
11. Journal of Finance
12. Management Review
13. Personnel Journal
14. Training and Development Journal

Other journals may be considered.

Exhibit 1 -2   Sample Student Article Critique (by Jo Ann Jolley*)

This is a descriptive study of the perception of service delivery in the public sector compared to that in the private sector. The design of this study is not complex, and it reports fairly simple statistical data. As in most descriptive research, it does not attempt to answer the question why, but lays a foundation for future research of that question.

Statement of the Research Problem

The researchers state that while there is a widespread assumption that service delivery in the private sector is superior to that in the public sector a 1991 study by Miller and Miller found "generally favorable assessments... for most local government services" (Poister and Henry, 1994, p. 157). Poister and Henry's study was designed to examine Georgia residents' assessment of the quality of local public and private sector services. The survey responses were compared to determine how the assessment of the quality of public services compared with that of private sector services. In addition, perceptions of the general public were compared with those of recent consumers.

Poister and Henry provide an adequate literature review on service quality, including several studies on quality in the public sector. The scope of their study was limited to Georgia residents. They did not provide precise meanings of significant words, but this is probably not unusual in descriptive research. Their definition of this research question was adequate.

17

Chapter 1 *Research in Business*

Description of Research Procedures

The researchers provided information on their method of collecting data. It was sufficient to allow evaluation of their method, and permit duplication of their study. The mention of a "computer assisted telephone interviewing system" (p. 156) was somewhat unclear. Was the system only used to select respondents and assign them sets of questions or was the interview actually conducted by the computer? Even with standardized responses the possibility of interviewer bias exists through inflection and prompts. This would not be a factor if the interview was conducted by a computer.

Flaws in Procedural Design

The researchers did discuss the difficulty of attempting to parallel public and private services. While agreeing that direct comparisons in many types of services were impossible, they attempted to compensate for this by "solicit[ing] ratings across broad slates of public and private services" (p. 158).

Poister and Henry discussed the wide variation in quality ratings of both sectors. They emphasized that their findings should only be viewed in an overall context and not as a direct comparison of any one service.

Analysis of Data

As previously mentioned, the sample characteristics of the Georgia study favorably compared to the population characteristics. results paralleling the Miller and Miller findings tend to support the reliability of the Georgia study. The findings of the ratings of recent users verses those of the general public are also supported by the studies of Katz *et al.* (1975).

A minimum of information is given on the statistical findings. The mean, standard deviation, and significance are given in an easy to read table, an provide the basic necessities for evaluation.

Limited and Justifiable Conclusions

Poister and Henry posed their central question as: "How does the public's assessment of the quality of specific public services compare with that of private sector services?" (p. 156). The specific conclusion of this study is that "Georgia residents exhibited no particular tendency to rate the quality of local public services as better or worse than other services provided by businesses in their local communities" (p. 158). This study supports only this specific conclusion.

Researcher Reputation

As is typical of journal published research, limited information is provided on the background of the researchers. Such information, including employment and books published, is usually adequate for general interest purposes. A list of publications would always be helpful in assessing experience and reputation, although space limitations usually preclude this.

* Used by permission of Ms. Jolley.

Answers to Chapter Questions

1. Research is defined on page 11 in the text as a "systematic inquiry aimed at providing information to solve problems." Business research is further defines as "a systematic inquiry that provides information to guide business decisions." Distinctions can be made between applied and pure or basic research, but both are research. Questions arise when various people begin to provide their own definitions which in some way restrict the meaning of "research" to specific approaches, to specific topics, or to the use of specific

procedures. The present authors are no exception in this. While it is difficult to say what is always right and what is always wrong, it is important to recognize that different definitions have values, and that what is appropriate depends upon the circumstances. Notwithstanding these limits, one can define what is properly called business research and what can, in given cases, be judged either to be good or bad research.

2. If the manager elects to conduct the research herself, a "make" situation, she must be technically capable of defining her research needs, developing an appropriate design, and selecting the proper tools. She must also have the time and facilities to collect the data or supervise its collection by others, and be able to analyze and present her findings. Too often the manager's skills or training are not adequate for these tasks, or else the demands of her managerial positions are such that she does not have the time to carry out these research activities.

If she calls on others to gather information, a "buy" situation, she still must be able to define her information needs; the task is even more difficult because of the problems of trying to communicate the flavor of the situation and one's needs to others. She must also judge research proposals as to appropriateness of methods as well as evaluate the finished research product and techniques. If she is not able to make these judgments she forfeits part of her vital decision making role to the researcher. In either case there is a need for managers to have a clear understanding of business research design, methods, and techniques.

3. If the information gathered by the research suggests a policy which disrupts the status quo, there may be a conflict between the individual's role of investigator and manager. The manager is likely to favor findings which speak well for the continuation and possible expansion of the operation, or changes in ways which conform to the manager's preconceived thoughts and wishes. As a researcher, however, one is called upon to gather and objectively weigh all information and report the results of findings regardless of the course of action favored by the findings. The manager can be honest and well intentioned with a desire to be totally objective in this case, but the problem of full objectivity is still in doubt.

4. Any number of research ideas might be proposed for each of these. Some of them are:

   A. Manager at national chain

   Reporting - An inventory study to determine what items are out of stock.

   Description - An observation study of shoppers in the department as to age, whether shopping alone, in pairs, etc.

   Explanation - Survey of persons who shop but do not buy as to why they did not buy.

Prediction - Analysis of department traffic patterns to determine staffing needs for the next day.

B. Auto plant manager

Reporting - Development of an accident statistics summary.

Description - Analysis of quality control, defects discovered at final inspection station, by shift and assembly line.

Explanation - Analysis of high absentee employees by demographic and other measures to determine the "cause" of absenteeism.

Prediction - Determination of the effect on assembly line output of the elimination of convertibles from the product mix.

C. Admissions director

Reporting - Weekly summary of inquiries and applications to the university.

Description - Analysis of applicant rates and acceptances by SAT scores.

Explanation - Survey of admitted students who decline admission to determine why they declined.

Prediction - Analysis of weekly application growth rates for purpose of forecasting total applications volume.

D. Investment analyst

Reporting - Periodic report of price and volume movements in a selected portfolio of common stocks.

Description - Comparison of individual stock price and volume movements relative to major price indexes.

Explanation - Analysis of operating results published for a company in effort to determine causes of profit declines.

Prediction - Company profit projections for next year.

E. Director of personnel

Reporting - A report on employee turnover by department.

Description - Employee turnover report, classified by department, seniority, marital status, and so on.

Chapter 1   *Research in Business*

Explanation - An experiment to determine the effect on climate of two different styles of management.

Prediction - A forecast of staffing needs for the next five years.

F. Product manager

Reporting - A report on monthly warehouse withdrawals of product.

Description - Demographic profiles of users of various major brands of toothpaste.

Explanation - Test marketing of strategies that employ different advertising weights and price levels.

Prediction - Projection of test marketing results to national sales volume estimates.

5. Many different studies might be helpful in this situation. Probably the two major lines of investigation should be on (1) the firm's operating inefficiencies and (2) its future prospects in the industry. In the first case the president might request research to determine whether the inefficiency is caused by internal production problems, poor organization, ineffective cost controls, weak sales management, and so on. It might be in the form of a company management audit. The examination of the industry and the firm's future in it would probably be directed at possible trends in consumption patterns and distribution systems. With this database the president might then consider possible changes in company operations that could help them adapt to these trends.

6. The criteria discussed on pages 12-14 should provide a good base for the discussion of this question, where needed, the instructor should elaborate or qualify each of these points.

True - False Questions

T   1) At a basic level, research is an inquiry carried out to secure information.

F   2) For research to be "scientific" it has to be something more than purely descriptive.

T   3) History shows that science typically has had its beginnings in the pragmatic problems of real life.

F   4) Descriptive research represents the highest order of possible research objectives.

Chapter 1   Research in Business

F   5)   A descriptive study deals with the discovery of answers to the "who, what, where, when, how, and why" questions.

T   6)   A measure of the development of science in any field is the degree to which prediction and explanation have replaced reporting and description as major research objectives.

F   7)   Research opportunities are largely restricted in a business organization to research and development and marketing.

T   8)   Many research studies in a business organization cut across the normal business functional areas such as marketing, finance, etc.

F   9)   There is broad public support and wide publication of results within the field of social research when compared to research in the physical sciences.

F   10) Business research will improve when both managers and practitioners utilize the same specific techniques presently being used by the natural science researcher.

F   11) The major contribution of applied research is that it advances our knowledge.

F   12) Managers should not be expected to do their own research.

T   13) Business research is problem-oriented research whose main function is to assist the manager in making better decisions.

F   14) When a researcher takes an assignment from a manager-client, the latter generally should guard against volunteering much information to the researcher.

T   15) Increased interest in business research grows out of both (1) an increased need in business for better information and (2) the availability of ways to provide such information.

F   16) The major reason why science in business research has grown so slowly, compared to the natural sciences, is that environmental conditions in a business research setting can not be controlled.

F   17) Relationships in a social setting are much more complex than those found in a physical science setting and this is a major reason why scientific research in social science is not as far advanced as in physical sciences.

Chapter 1   *Research in Business*

Multiple Choice Questions

1. Which of the following types of research is conducted to evaluate specific courses of action or forecast current or future values ?
   - A) Reporting studies
   - B) Explanation studies
   - C) Description studies
   - * D) Prediction studies

2. Which of the following is not an example of research?
   - A) An experiment in product taste preferences.
   - B) A statistical analysis of errors in the recording of inventories.
   - C) A test of cognitive dissonance theory and major investment decisions.
   - D) A simulation of the information flows in an organization.
   - * E) A decision to change the firm's method of accounting.

3. Are any of the following not a good reason for managers to be well grounded in basic research? To allow them to:
   - A) do some research for themselves.
   - B) make competent decisions on whether to "buy" research from researchers outside the firm.
   - C) define their own needs and form researchable questions for the specialist.
   - D) judge the logic of a research approach.
   - * E) All are good reasons.

4. Applied Research:
   - A) Has little direct impact on policy decisions.
   - B) Is problem directed but not decision directed.
   - * C) Is problem directed and closely related to action or policy needs.
   - D) Calls for a hypothesis to initiate the research.

23

CHAPTER 2

SCIENTIFIC THINKING

There are three primary learning objectives for Chapter 2. The first objective is to build a more precise understanding of what may be called good scientific research. Second, we would like to introduce the student to a number of important concerns that can be summarized under the term "scientific method." We introduce this subject by exploring some basic ideas involved in how we think, the characteristics of the thought process, induction and deduction, and the connection between reflective thinking and the scientific method. The less cognitive side of scientific inquiry, the attitude of science, is also presented here and connects to a later emphasis on the exploratory and discovery aspects of research. The second learning objective also seeks to achieve some minimum understanding among readers of the basic inference processes -- the foundations of all thinking -- and their applicability to research thinking.

The final learning objective is for students to grasp the components of theory and how, when combined, they help us explain and predict. Such elements as concepts, constructs, operational definitions, hypotheses, are critical to clear thinking about any subject but are especially critical to research.

The topics in Chapter 2 are unfamiliar to many students and the abstractness of the materials make it desirable to discuss them in class in some detail. Normally, a single session of 1 1/2 hours is not enough to cover these topics adequately; two sessions could be used profitably. For additional discussion on constructing operational definitions, see Bruce Tuckman, *Conducting Educational Research*, p. 57 ff. Many examples of operational definitions can be found in research publications such as the *Academy of Management Journal, Journal of Applied Psychology,* and *Journal of Marketing Research*. The supplemental readings at the end of the chapter are especially useful.

Because this chapter tends toward philosophical rather than technical topics, some instructors may find that it connects well with materials in the Ethics Special Section. Please see that part of the Instructor's Manual for suggestions.

Class Suggestion Discussions

Treatment of the topics in Chapter 2 may be organized into the following four major sections.

1. Most of the material in chapter 2 appears to be so remote from "doing research" that is is useful to begin with a question like, "What is good research?" The discussion on thinking styles that should follow might stress the idea that high quality in research is reflected in many different paradigms. Examples of colleagues' work in organizational behavior, finance, marketing, economics, and so forth will quickly reveal to students that research is conducted from diverse perspectives and with diverse methods. (See discussion questions 2 and 5). Furthermore, point out

Chapter 2 Scientific Thinking

that such questions as (1) definition of research purpose, (2) design of procedures, and (3) analysis of data, are critical to research and to answer them well we should begin with some basic questions about our perspective before conceptualizing, operationalizing, hypothesizing, and theorizing. In this way we can build a justification and rationale for exposing the students to the abstract material in the remainder of Chapter 2 and build a bridge to Chapter 3. The Research Article Critique assignment discussed in Course Design is a useful assignment at this point in the students' experience.

2. A second major effort in class should be to assure that the students can propose concepts and constructs and provide operational definitions for them. One might begin by asking students to offer concrete examples of concepts that are quite observable and to define them operationally. For example, ask them to define the concept of chair and distinguish it from other pieces of furniture such as tables. Carry this on to the simple concrete problem of operationally defining various types of chairs so that someone new to our culture could conduct a detailed chair inventory in your building. (Be sure to include office type seating). Questions 5 and 7 are helpful in this regard.

3. A third area for coverage should be hypotheses. Question 7 is useful for moving from definitions to hypothesis formulation. Question 8 can also be used with success, especially if assigned in advance. Since this question does not call for the student to specify the implications of the hypotheses advanced, this additional step should be brought out in class. It is a good way to introduce the topics of induction and deduction and their combination into the double movement of reflective thought. Experience suggests that the discussion of the logical nature of induction and deduction, alone, can take substantial class time with little apparent reward. When these are incorporated into the format of actual inference problems most students appear to grasp their essential nature more quickly and easily. (Also, see discussion question 3).

4. The fourth topic, theory, can be dealt with on two different levels. If time is short and you are placing your emphasis elsewhere you might want only to point out that theory and fact are not opposites and are not incompatible. We all operate on the basis of various behavioral theories. A hypothesis is a simple type of theory. When we combine a number of independent and moderating variables into several interrelated explanatory hypotheses we are building better theories with which to explain facts. It is possible to tie question 6 into this discussion.

With more time, you may want to extend this topic by asking students to develop a theory. For example, construct a theory which will explain the differentials in academic success that various students achieve in a B-school:

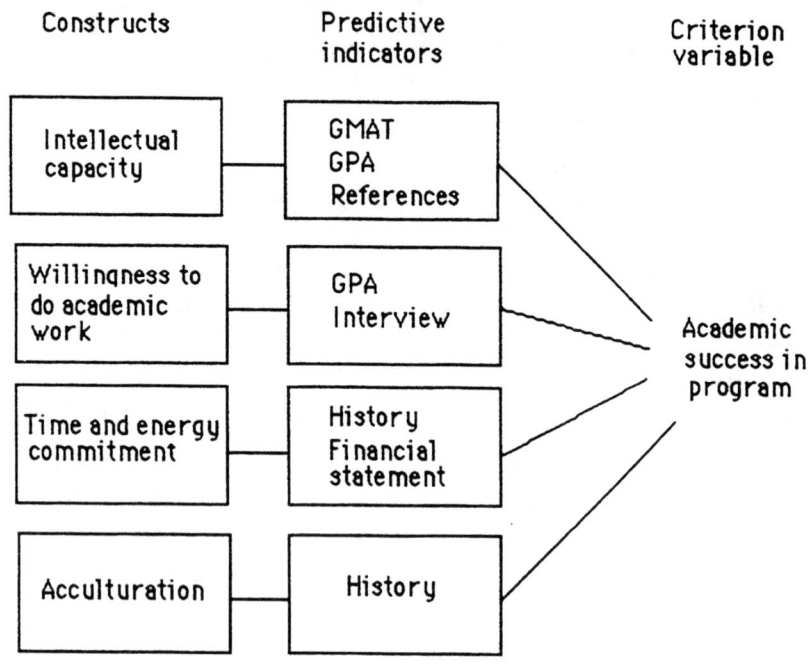

Answers to Chapter Questions

1.   A. Concepts and constructs are both abstractions, the former from our perceptions of reality and the latter from some invention which we have made. Constructs tend to be more abstract and complex than concepts. Both are critical to thinking and research processes since one can think only in terms of meanings we have adopted. Precision in concept and constructs is particularly important in research since we usually attempt to measure meaning in some way.

    B. Both deduction and induction are basic forms of reasoning. While we may emphasize one over the other from time to time, both are necessary for research thinking. Deduction is reasoning from generalizations to specifics that flow logically from the generalizations. If the generalizations are true and the deductive form valid, the conclusions must also be true. Induction is reasoning from specific instances or observations to some generalization which is purported to explain the instances. The specific instances are evidence and the conclusion is an inference which *may* be true.

    C. Dictionary definitions are those used in most general discourse to describe the nature of concepts through word reference to other familiar concepts, preferably at a lower abstraction level. Operational definitions are established for the purposes of precision in measurement. With them we attempt to classify concepts or conditions in an unambiguous manner and to use them in measurement. Operational definitions are essential for effective research, while dictionary definitions are more useful for general discourse purposes.

D. Concepts are meanings abstracted from our observations; they are used to classify or categorize objects or events that have common characteristics beyond a single observation (see A). A variable is a concept or construct to which numerals or values are assigned; this operationalization permits the construct or concept to be empirically tested. In informal usage, a variable is often used as a synonym for construct or property being studied.

E. A proposition is a statement about concepts which may be evaluated as by its truth or falsity when compared to observable phenomena. A hypothesis is a proposition which has been configured for empirical testing. This further distinction permits the classification of hypotheses for different purposes, e.g., descriptive, relational, correlational, causal, etc.

F. A theory is a set of systematically interrelated concepts, constructs, definitions, and propositions that are advanced to explain and predict phenomena or facts. Theories differ from models in that their function is to explanation and prediction whereas a model's is representation. A model is a representation of a system which is constructed for the purpose of investigating an aspect of that system or the system as a whole. Models may be used with equal success in applied or theoretical work.

G. The characteristics of the scientific method are confused in the literature primarily because of the numerous philosophical perspectives one may take when "doing" science. A second problem stems from the fact that the emotional characteristics of scientists do not easily lend themselves to generalization. For our purposes, however, the scientific method is a systematic approach involving hypothesizing, observing, testing, and reasoning processes for the purpose of problem solving or amelioration. The scientific method may summarized with a set of steps or stages but these only hold for the most simple problems. In contrast to the mechanics of the process, the scientific attitude reflects the creative aspects that enable and sustain the research from preliminary thinking to discovery and on to the culmination of the project. Imagination, curiosity, intuition, and doubt are among the predispositions involved. One Nobel physicist described this aspect of science as doing ones utmost with no holds barred.

2. The scientific method emphasizes (1) direct observation of phenomena, (2) clearly defined variables, methods, and procedures, (3) empirically testable hypotheses, (4) the ability to rule out rival hypotheses, (4) statistical rather than linguistic justification of conclusions, and (6) the self-correcting process. A more formula-based approach to the scientific method is found in the section entitled Reflective Thinking and the Scientific Method.

3. A. 1. If money supply is the basic economic variable, then economic condition changes will parallel it with a lag.

    2. Economic condition variations lag money supply by 6-12 months.

Induction

Chapter 2   *Scientific Thinking*

      3. Therefore; money supply is the basic economic variable

  B. 1. If smoking causes lung cancer, heavy smokers will have a higher lung cancer rate than non-smokers.

      2. Heavy smokers do have a higher lung cancer rate.

     Induction

      3. Heavy smoking causes lung cancer.

  C. 1. If a person goes to church regularly, this person is a reliable worker.

      2. "Bob" goes to church regularly.

     Deduction

      3. "Bob" is a reliable worker.

  Note: 3 is a valid deduction from the major premise (1). The truth of the major and minor premises may be challenged: church attendance and reliability in the workplace must be unequivocally connected and "Bob" must be a person, not my dog.

4. Marketing, management, organizational behavior and other studies where the human input is the central focus tend toward empirical solutions to problems and theory-building. Management science, operations research, production, and associated areas tend toward rationalist approaches. A quick survey of the current issue of the top two or three journals in each field will reveal a lot about preferred methodologies. From this you may wish to construct a piechart on the board showing the range of research approaches for each discipline.

5.   A. First Line Supervisor

  Operational definition - for purposes of a given study a first line supervisor is anyone who is shown on the company roster as having a job level of "M-1".

  B. Employee Morale

  Operational definition - Degree of mental satisfaction among employees as represented by their score on the XYZ morale inventory.

  C. Assembly Line

  Operational definition - An assembly line is any work arrangement that meets the following tests:

    1. The work consists of performing specific tasks in a fixed sequence of

successive work stations.

2. The work at a given station is repetitive.

3. Materials upon which work is performed moved through the sequence to various work stations rather than machines or workers moving to the material.

D. Overdue account

Operational definition - All accounts receivable which remain unpaid by the 5th day after the invoice date.

E. Line Management

Operational definition - Line management consists of all supervisors listed in Company A's organization tables who are in the direct chain of command between the company's president and the production worker, sales worker, or finance worker. Supervisors in units whose major functions are to assist other organization units in their performance are not line management.

F. Leadership

Operational definition - An act of leadership shall be recorded when any member of the small groups under observation is :

1. Recognized by group members as their leader by their submission to his/her assignments to specific roles in one of the exercises, or

2. Agrees to his/her suggestion as to how to proceed in making assignments.

G. Price-Earnings Ratio

Operational definition - The ratio found by dividing a company's common stock price (average of the year's closing daily bids or final transaction prices on the New York Stock Exchange) by the company's net profit after taxes as reported for the calendar year or fiscal year ending before July of the following year.

H. Union Democracy

Operational definition - The condition of union governance in which the rank and file members exercise the power in the union as measured by responses to the following three tests:

1. Are there free and open elections of leaders in which opposition slates are allowed free access to the members?

2. Is there open and free discussion and vote by rank and file members on any contract approval?

3. Is there an effective rank and file committee board or other type of organizational arrangement by which effective worker oversight of union officials is exercised?

I. Ethical Standards

Operational definition - The ethical standard of the respondent will be measured by his or her score on the SEST (Student's Ethical Standard Test).

6. The statement that "theory is impractical and thus no good" illustrates a misconception of the true meaning of theory. The second quotation is more to the point: there is nothing so practical as a good theory (Kurt Lewin) because of the power it gives us to explain and predict the target phenomenon.

We all use theory constantly as we explain why certain events occur or why one procedure succeeds and another does not. The real problem is that our theories are often too simplistic and even these are not made explicit and challenged.

7. There are an almost infinite variety of answers to this question. One example might be:

A. *Concepts* - diligent, maintenance worker, much, rural or urban background, completed job, and score.

Constructs - job completion index, work ethic, Protestant ethic, and standard hour.

B. Maintenance workers who come from rural backgrounds are much more diligent than similar workers from urban backgrounds.

- More diligent = has higher average performance score on the job completion index (JCI).
- Much more diligent = an average at least 10% higher on the JCI index.
- JCI score = the sum of standard times for all jobs completed in a week, divided by the number of hours actually spent on the jobs.

8. Hypothesis 1 - As a result of the firing incident the workers are sabotaging production.

The above hypothesis can be induced from the situation described in the problem. From the hypothesis we must be able to deduce some other factual conditions implied by this hypothesis. For example:

Fact 1 - The timing of the trouble with the employee and the onset of stamping problems must coincide in the predicted manner.

Fact 2 - A trusted operative or foreman must also have stamping problems when they attempt to do the stamping job.

Fact 3 - Careful observation of stamping processes will indicate worker actions that can be identified as causing stamping problems.

Hypothesis 2 - Some change in the sheet metal material has occurred and this is adversely affecting the forming of the fenders.

Fact 1 - A check with purchasing or other appropriate sources will show that a change in specification or supplier has occurred at this time.

True - False Questions

F   1)   Science should be viewed as a body of systematized information that includes connected principles, theories, and laws.

T   2)   The dynamic view of science is that there is a body of generally accepted rules by which one deals with knowledge.

F   3)   Empiricism emphasizes reason as the primary source of knowledge.

F   4)   The only perspective for conducting business research is the empirical perspective.

T   5)   If the reasons in an inference imply a conclusion, and represent proof, then the inference must be a deduction.

F   6)   A valid deduction must also be a true deduction.

T   7)   Deduction is a form of inference which purports to be conclusive.

T   8)   The scientific method uses both induction and deduction.

T   9)   Concepts are symbols we attach to bundles of meanings that we hold.

T   10) A concept is normally only a part of the reality for which it is a label.

F   11) "Central heating" is more likely to be classed as a construct than as a concept.

F   12) A construct is typically less complex and less abstract than a concept.

F   13) A concept is an image or idea specifically invented for a given research and/or theory building purpose.

F   14) Hypothetical constructs differ from constructs in that they are directly

Chapter 2 Scientific Thinking

observable.

T 15) In a deduction the reasons imply the conclusion. In an induction the reason supports the conclusion.

T 16) An operational definition is stated in terms of specific testing criteria.

T 17) To believe a statement because we think it logically follows from another is to make an inference.

F 18) An example of an operational definition of a suit is, "a series or group of things forming a unit or constituting a complement, as in a suit of clothing."

T 19) Of all types of definitions, it is the operational definition which is of greatest value in research.

T 20) Operational definitions should have both good precision of meaning and good linkage.

T 21) Operational definitions are even more critical for treating abstract ideas than dealing with relatively concrete concepts.

F 22) A concept is really just a variable which reflects the presence or absence of a property.

T 23) An independent variable is a presumed cause or the manipulated variable.

T 24) In an asymmetrical relationship there is at least one independent and one dependent variable.

F 25) An intervening variable is a factor which affects the observed phenomenon and can be seen.

T 26) Propositions are combinations of concepts in the form of statements which can be judged true or false if they refer to observable phenomena.

F 27) Hypotheses are of two types - propositional and descriptive.

F 28) An example of a descriptive hypothesis is "young men eat more candy than do older men."

F 29) While hypotheses are useful in pure research, they have only limited value in applied research.

T 30) "If A then B" is an example of an explanatory hypothesis.

F 31) A correlation should imply a cause-effect relationship.

Chapter 2　　　　　　　　　　　　　　　　　　　　　　　　　　　　　　Scientific Thinking

T　　　32)　A good explanatory hypothesis must first of all explain the facts that give rise to it.

T　　　33)　Hypothesis A is superior to hypothesis B if the former explains more facts with less assumptions than does B.

T　　　34)　Theory and facts are not only quite compatible, but also often found together.

T　　　35)　One relates elements of a theory to empirical reality by operational definitions.

T　　　36)　A model is to a theory as a representation is to an explanation.

Multiple Choice Questions

1.　Which of the following are concepts?
　　A)　Shoe
　　B)　Chair
　　C)　Store
　　D)　Pain
*　E)　All of the above

2.　Which of the following is most true about a construct?
　　A)　it must always be directly observable.
　　B)　it usually is directly observable.
*　C)　it usually is not directly observable.
　　D)　it can be sharply differentiated from a concept.

3.　Which, if any, of the following is not an operational definition? A good student is:
　　A)　One who passes this course.
　　B)　One whom we agree to be a good student.
　　C)　One who ranks in the top one-half of his/her class.
*　D)　One who is a superior student.
　　E)　More than one of the above are not operational definitions.

4.　Which of the following is an explanatory hypothesis?
　　A)　Forty percent of Company Y stockholders favor the dismissal of their company president.
　　B)　American consumers feel that cars manufactured before 1980 are safer than those manufactured today.
*　C)　Warning labels on cigarette packages concerning the dangers of smoking have led to a decrease in the growth of smokers in this country.
　　D)　Vice President McGill has higher than average verbal skills.

33

Chapter 2 — Scientific Thinking

5. Which is the most correct statement?
   A) Most of us seldom use theories.
   B) Constructs are used only in explanatory hypotheses.
   *C) In induction we observe facts and draw conclusions from them.
   D) While operational definitions are very useful, there are many good research studies which do not use them.

6. Which is true concerning the differences or similarities between a theory and a hypothesis?
   A) Both tend to be simple, two variable propositions involving concrete instances.
   *B) Theories tend to be more abstract and involve more variables than does a hypothesis.
   C) Both tend to be abstract and involve multiple variables.
   D) Both tend to be very abstract, but a hypothesis is typically a two variable proposition.

7. Which is not a useful way in which a theory serves research?
   A) It narrows the range of facts the researcher must study.
   B) It suggests which approach to a problem is likely to yield the greatest meaning.
   C) It suggests a system for the researcher to impose on data in order to classify it meaningfully.
   *D) It suggests a framework from which the researcher can search for data which supports his own beliefs.

8. For a deduction to be correct thereby implying a conclusion and representing a proof it must be:
   A) true but not necessarily valid
   B) valid but not necessarily true
   C) valid and the conclusion must necessarily follow from the premises.
   *D) valid and the premises given for the conclusion must agree with the real world.

9. The double movement of reflective thought is
   A) A process of deduction
   B) A process of induction
   C) A process of construct building
   *D) None of the above is an adequate explanation

10. Which of the following is correct?
   *A) Only deductive arguments can be proved.
   B) Only inductive arguments can be proved.
   C) Both inductive and deductive arguments can be proved.
   D) Neither can be proved.

CHAPTER 3

THE RESEARCH PROCESS

Chapter three has three learning objectives. First, to stimulate student thinking in terms of specific research studies which are grounded in the management decision process. Second, to establish problem formulation through a "hierarchy of research questions" approach. The question hierarchy is an organizing principle which we return to several times throughout the book. The third objective is to introduce the research process. To fulfill this objective, we attempt to provide an overview of the entire process of conducting empirical research -- the outline of which largely guides the organization of the remainder of the book. Appendix B provides a decision theory example to illustrate the section on valuing research information. This is best used with more advanced students.

Sellitz et al., and Fox all have good descriptions of the various sequential steps of a research study. The Tull and Hawkins reference has a more detailed discussion of Bayesian analysis if the instructor wishes to pursue this topic.

Class Discussion Suggestions

It is desirable to address all three of the above objectives. However, depending upon the preparation of the students or constraints of time, you may not wish to cover decision theory. It is placed in Appendix B because it illustrates only one aspect of the research process model and is not necessary for every curriculum. Although it is an interesting topic, we do not drawn upon it further in the course. Its value for this course lies largely in the project assessment logic which it presents and as a comparison to sampling theory statistics (found later in Chapters 14-17).

Assuming that you assign the entire chapter, it should take 1-1/2 hours in class to cover the three objectives adequately. One approach might be the following:

1. Briefly show that applied research grows out of management information needs. A convenient way to do this is to use question 1 at the end of the chapter to suggest management problems that can profit from the use of research. Select several of the management problems mentioned by the students and ask them to suggest research questions.

2. This discussion process may be continued on into the research question hierarchy. Take a couple of the better research questions and ask the students to elaborate them into investigative questions, and even on into measurement question examples if they can. There is a need for guided development of the question hierarchy because the process of question fractionation is an unaccustomed one. See Exhibit 3-1 or consider question 6 as a class exercise.

3. While the question hierarchy and fractionation process is an important way to look at project development, the more traditional approach is outlined in

Chapter 3   The Research Process

Figure 3-1, p. 53 of the text, and described step by step throughout the chapter. There is little need to do more than summarize these steps at this point because they will each be treated in detail in later chapters. Discussion questions 3 and 6 are good vehicles for discussing how a project sequence unfolds, although the Chapter Close-Up may be adequate for this task. The question hierarchy example below may be turned into a lecturette to help students visualize the process of taking abstract management questions and progressively making them more and more concrete. We find that the more examples, the better.

If you opt to touch on the valuation issue in research it is desirable to make some brief comments on the difficulty of measuring the contribution of research, especially ex ante. In addition, you may want to stress the importance of the valuation problem even if we are not yet able to solve it. If you have chosen to treat Appendix B on decision theory more fully at this time, it is probably wise to begin with a brief review of the basic concepts. Then either review the example in the appendix or go directly to another one of your choosing.

Exhibit 3 - 1   Question Hierarchy Example

Glenn Detrick had just finished revising a job satisfaction study for a local retailer when the phone rang. It was Ed Byldor, a local contractor, whom Glenn had met at the Rotary Club meeting recently. Ed is active in the development of subdivisions in Northridge, an old town now becoming a high-growth suburb. He and his partners had purchased substantial acreage there for future development, but now the local planning board is threatening to rezone the land. If rezoning goes through, it will virtually eliminate any chance for profitable development. Ed is preparing to fight the planning board proposal and feels a need for some quick research help. Glenn made an appointment to meet him the next day to talk it over.

Glenn was experienced enough to anticipate the major concerns Ed would have. Clients usually expect to learn immediately what research needs to be done, how it should be done, how much it will cost, and how quickly it can be completed. Instant answers to these questions are generally not possible, but useful answers should be in the research design statement that results from following an orderly research procedure.

The Problem as the Client Sees It

Ed and his associates have purchased a substantial quantity of land for future development. He now faces a possible rezoning of this land that will virtually eliminate his existing plans for profitable development. In cooperation with several other builders, Ed is beginning to mount a broad campaign against the planning commission's position. The commission has proposed that current zoning, which calls for residential development on lots of 7,500 to 10,000 square feet, be changed to require a minimum of one acre and sometimes two acres for each building site.

The first task that Ed suggests is the development of an economic argument showing how much more municipal revenue the greater building density will bring, how many more stores and shopping centers will be developed, and how many jobs will be generated with the increased population. In addition, Ed feels the need to show that the people who are living in his other developments like the area and want to stay there.

After further exploration, including some in-depth interviews with Northridge residents, Glenn arranged another meeting with his client. By this time, he had determined that an economic argument could be developed from published studies and data available from local planning commission.

The Problem as Glenn Sees It

The general nature of the commission's position suggests a need for research among the people of the area to test the major points that the planning commission is making. None of the commission's five members is considered an expert in planning. A majority of them believe that the present development of the city is inadequate. They are backed in this view by a few long-time residents living on large estates directly in the path of the population movement. Further analysis of the commission majority's argument indicates that an entirely different research direction is called for.

The argument presented by the planning commission and its backers is that existing development of the area is leading to three deficiencies:

1. Aesthetic - Residential development is creating a definite problem of unsightly urban sprawl. Commercial development is being accomplished by area strip zoning, which brings about further urban ugliness.
2. Social - The area is primarily a working-class neighborhood. The city must attract more affluent people to provide future civic leadership. One way of doing so would be the provision of acre-or-more land plots on which more expensive homes could be built.
3. Economic - The school system, although growing rapidly, is chronically overcrowded. Further dense housing development would continue to put pressures on the school system. A decrease in the density of residential development would lessen school population pressures.

An analysis of these arguments suggests that a study of residents should provide useful information concerning the first two arguments (the third is answered by an economic analysis). The investigative questions are stated in terms of the following descriptive hypotheses.

1. The population of the city represents a broad cross section that includes many college-educated, concerned citizens who are potential civic leaders.
2. A large share of the population is composed of young families who have been attracted by the lifestyles and environment in the city leaders.
2. A large share of the population is composed of young families who have been attracted by the lifestyles and environment in the city.
3. These satisfied residents see the city as their permanent home and do not expect to leave the area, even if they buy larger homes.
4. While the residents desire environmental improvements, they do not want any drastic changes in present plans for residential use.

The research hypotheses are translated into specific research requirements. For example, hypothesis 2 concerns attitudes of people toward their area as a place to live and raise a family. To test this, the researcher has to learn the basis for the residents' original attraction to the area; their opinions about schools, churches, shopping, and convenience to work; their satisfaction with their specific neighborhood and neighbors; and their views on the adequacy of their homes and lot size.

The exploratory in-depth interviews with residents give the researcher a better understanding of the types of people and their responses. From these interviews, a questionnaire is developed. Glenn tests it, revises it, and tests it again. Dummy tables are drawn up to suggest the ways in which the final data will be analyzed. These tables and their probable contents are then compared against the specific research requirements to be certain the objectives will be met.

Sampling reliability is determined to be a critical matter. At the same time, the research budget suggests that the sample size must be limited. These restrictions, plus the fact that the area of study is clearly defined and geographically limited, lead to the use of probability sampling methods. All addresses in the study areas are listed and a random sample drawn.

After the successful pilot test, the project is released to a field interviewing organization, which places a substantial number of interviewers in the field. They complete their study in a few days. The results are then tabulated and analyzed and the final report presented to the client.

Chapter 3   *The Research Process*

Answers to Chapter Questions

1.   A.   The production manager of a shoe factory

    1. Management problem: How can we improve our plant productivity by 10% next year?

        Research question: How does productivity in this factory compare to industry norms, by major input and output factors?

    2. Management problem: Is there a way to improve employee performance?

        Research question: Is there an employee morale problem in the plant, and if so, what are its major dimensions?

    B.   The president of first National Bank

    1. Management problem: What five year growth target shall I set for our bank?

        Research question: What are the major factors which will impact the growth of bank deposits in the next 5 years?

    2. Management problem: What must our industry do to secure branch banking in this state?

        Research question: How have shifts to branch banking been brought about in other states?

    C.   The vice president for labor relations for an auto manufacturer

    1. Management problem: What should be our bargaining strategy for the up-coming labor negotiations?

        Research question: What are the present attitudes of union members toward a long strike?

    2. Management problem: Should we propose a location pay differential policy to reflect local plant environments?

        Research question: What are the typical wage rates in each of our plant cities?

    D.   The chief of police in a major city

    1. Management problem: What must we do to develop a system of computerized dispatching of police officers?

        Research question: How have other police departments developed and introduced computerized dispatching?

2. Management problem: How can we make our crime prevention program more effective?

Research question: program are working as planned and which are not?

2. There are many reasons why a research project will not make an adequate contribution to a management problem. Some likely ones are: Poor rapport between manager and researcher due to a distrust by the former or his inability or unwillingness to communicate fully to the researcher. Failure of the researcher, for whatever reason, to ground his/her research approach in the basic management problem. Another source of difficulty may be political considerations in the organization which complicate the process of defining or conducting effective research. There is also the problem of research obsession with a particular technique which may not be appropriate for the problem. Other reasons for failure include a lack of researcher competence in planning and conducting the study, poor standards of research used by the manager in buying the project, or the occurrence of unpredictable events which distort or negate the research findings.

3. A. The statement by the vice president may be correct, but we need to know more about the problem. What are the indicators of the problem? When were they first noticed? Is there a history of turnover in this department? It is possible that a survey such as the vice president suggests is the appropriate action to take, but on what grounds was this decision made? While it may be politic to do what the vice president wants, let's assume that you have a good rapport with the VP and that she will listen to your advice on how to do the study. In this case you might make some suggestions along the following lines:

B. Do some exploratory research first. Gather some day data about the nature of the company turnover of computer programmers. Try to develop a historical perspective on the company's experience. At the same time do some secondary data research to learn more about general turnover problems, with special interest in computer programmers and similarly technically trained persons who may be in a tight labor market. As the third exploratory step, talk with representatives of key area companies to ascertain what their turnover rates are. By this time you may have uncovered the major elements in your company's retention difficulties. If a survey then appears to be the most feasible action you should recommend it. In this event your exploration will have shown you where to look for answers and what they may be.

4. In addition to the obvious political ramifications, the chief difficulty is uncertainty. For example, results often come too late to guide current research decision; neither costs nor benefits easily estimated in advance; the uniqueness of certain projects is such that managerial experience does not provide insight for proposal evaluation; the benefits side of the equation is difficult

Chapter 3   The Research Process

to estimate; and, evaluations alternatives are not always made explicit which invalidates later measurement.

5. In considering whether a topic is researchable it is wise to point out that the answer is one of degree. Research can shed some light on most topics, but there are two situations where research can not provide much help. In the first case there are questions of value for which fact gathering can not contribute much. For example, we may be considering making a merger offer to company X and might ask the question, "Do we really want to grow in this way?" Or, "Will we be happier making this offer rather than an offer to company Y?"

A second situation where the value of research is limited concerns those questions where data gathering could be helpful but our present techniques or procedures are inadequate. In the merger case, for example, we might ask the question, "Will the stockholders of Company X welcome our merger offer?" This is the type of question which research might be able to answer if there were some way that we could get the data before we make the offer, but we may have no method by which to make this assessment short of asking them or making the offer. Or again, the question, "Will the U.S. Department of Justice fight our merger plan?" This too can be learned in due course but we probably have no legitimate techniques by which to secure such information before the fact of making the offer.

The problems poses by ill-defined problems are related to both of these responses and present the researcher with definitional and methodological dilemmas.

6. The editor of *Gentlemen's Magazine* has asked you to carry out a research study. The magazine has been unsuccessful in attracting advertising revenue from shoe manufacturers. The shoe manufacturers claim that men's clothing stores are a small and declining segment of the men's shoe business. Since *Gentlemen's Magazine* is sold chiefly to men's clothing store managements, the manufacturers have reasoned that it is therefore not a good advertising medium for their shoes.

The editor disagrees about the size and importance of shoe marketing through men's clothing stores. Neither side has much direct evidence on the matter, so the editor asks you to carry out a study to determine the facts about these stores as a channel of distribution for men's shoes. You agree to do so and proceed with the first structuring of the problem.

1. *Management Question.* The problem facing the magazine management is that of trying to expand their advertising revenue. There are a number of ways that this might be done, and research might help in many of them. In this case, however, the management has already decided that the management's problem is to secure more advertising from the shoe industry. The researcher accepted the problem definition as stated.

2. *Research Question.* The research question was defined as "Are the actu-

al or potential sales of men's shoes in men's wear stores large enough to represent an advertising opportunity to shoe manufacturers?"

3. *Investigative Questions.* Three major investigative questions were proposed:
   a. Are shoe sales important to men's wear stores?
   b. Have shoe sales been growing in importance in men's wear stores and are they expected to grow in the future?
   c. Does the situation in men's wear stores present an advertising opportunity for shoe manufacturers?

It was agreed that the only feasible research design which could be carried out within the available budget was a national mail survey. Because of the limited scope of the study and the problems of population estimation from a mail survey, it was agreed that the research study would be concerned chiefly with the first two questions. The third question would be approached within the limits of the research design, but a full answer to this question would require information not available to the researcher.

To answer the major investigative questions posed above it was necessary to secure information on a number of much more specific points. These represent investigative sub questions which we must know to answer the three major questions. Parenthetical statements attached to them suggest the rationales for including the questions in the study.

A. Are shoe sales important to men's wear stores?
1. What percent of men's wear stores carry men's shoes? (One important measure of this channel of distribution and an indicator of the importance of shoes to retailers.)
2. What percent of men's wear store sales come from shoes? (A measure of the importance of shoes to total store operation.)
3. How do shoe gross margins compare with total store gross margins? (Another measure of shoe importance to the store and an indicator of whether or not shoes are likely to secure store management attention.)
4. How do space/sales ratios compare between shoe departments and the total store? (Another measure of the contribution of shoes to the total store volume. Also a measure of how secure shoes might be as a part of the store product mix.)
5. How important are shoes as traffic builders, extra sales, or extra business from those who do not buy other merchandise at the time? (Another measure of the value of shoes to store success and an indicator of the mix security of shoes.)

B. Have shoe sales been growing in importance in men's wear stores and are they expected to grow in the future?
1. What percent of the stores have added, expanded, dropped, or reduced shoe operations in the last five years? (A measure of the changes in importance of shoes in men's wear stores in recent years.)
2. Have shoe sales grown or declined in absolute dollars in recent

Chapter 3   *The Research Process*

                    years? As a percent of total store sales? (Measures of the changes that have taken place in men's wear stores concerning shoes.)

            3. What are store managements expecting in the next few years concerning shoes? Add or drop? Reduce or enlarge? (A measure of store operator expectations concerning shoes.)

    C. Does the situation in men's wear stores present an advertising opportunity for shoe manufacturers?

        1. What percent of the men's shoe volume is sold through men's wear stores? (A very crude measure of the importance of this channel to the manufacturer. This estimate will be carefully hedged since there is little hope that the survey can provide an unbiased estimate of total sales of men's shoes.)

        2. How important are leased departments in men's shoes operations in men's wear stores? (A measure of the need for shoe manufacturers to contact individual store managements to secure distribution, or whether the approach of a few central buying firms might suffice.)

        3. What price lines are carried, and what are their relative importance? (A measure of the type of demand for men's shoes represented in this channel.)

        4. What is the importance of casual shoes versus dress shoe sales? (Another measure of the type of shoe demand that prevails in this channel.)

        5. What brands are carried and what are their relative importance? (A measure of the penetration by various manufacturers as well as a measure of the product characteristics that are popular in this channel.)

   3. *Measurement Questions*. The 13 investigative questions listed under the three major questions were translated into about 20 specific measurement questions that were finally asked of the respondents. There were six additional classification-type questions. They differed from the investigative questions chiefly in wording and format so as to aid the respondent in replying with a minimum of difficulty and a maximum of reliability.

7.   This question addresses the issue of shortsightedness in planning. The use of exploration, even under budgetary restraints, may make the difference between terminating the project early or spending a substantial sum to rediscover what is already known. The use of published data and experience surveys, for example, may permit answering the question, changing the question, refining the question, or selecting an optimal methodology-- all of which are cost saving. Whereas exploration avoids costly mistakes on the front end of the problem, pilot testing identifies methodological misapplications and measurement problems before data collection. Both activities add to the cost of the project but without them the information may be completely without value: the failure to do some exploration may result in studying the wrong problem and the failure to pretest may threaten the validity of the study.

Chapter 3 — The Research Process

Appendix B Questions

B1. Using such concepts as maximin and expected monetary value, suggest appropriate decision rules and variables in each of the following cases:
a. Whether to switch to a new supplier of raw materials.
b. Whether to invest in project A or B.
c. Whether to make a product or buy it from another company.

  A. Switch to new supplier

   1. Maximin: Choose the supplier who will do the best job under the most adverse conditions (states of nature) expected.

   2. EMV: Choose the supplier who has the lowest expected average price over all anticipated conditions.

  B. Invest in project A or B

   1. Maximin: Invest in the project with the smallest loss or best gain under the most adverse conditions expected.

   2. EMV: Invest in the project whose EMV is highest.

  C. Make or buy situation

   1. Maximin: Make or buy, depending on which is the more economical under the expected worst condition situation.

   2. EMV: Make or buy depending on which alternative has the lowest expected average cost weighted over all states of nature.

B2. You are considering whether to product and market a new product. Your choices are:
A_1 - Produce and market the new product.
A_2 - Do not product and market it.
A_3 - Market test the product to determine whether it should be marketed.

You are uncertain about what to do, but the research department has proposed a market test. They estimate that it will cost $75,000 but will predict the product's chances for success. On the basis of your experience, you estimate that the product could be very profitable; if it receives strong market acceptance, the company should make about $500,000 in incremental profits over the product's life. However, if the acceptance is poor, there would be an incremental loss of $300,000. You best judgment now is that there is a 40 percent chance that acceptance will be poor and a 60 percent chance that it will be strong.

a. Assuming you use the *EMV* criterion, should you launch this product even if you do not test market?

Chapter 3 The Research Process

b. You are confident of you conditional profit and loss estimates but question your outcome probability estimates. How low could your success probability estimate be and still produce a positive *EMV*?
c. Would research be a worthwhile action, assuming that it gives a perfect success-failure prediction?
d. Suppose research of this type is accurate in its prediction only 80 percent of the time. Would it then be worth doing?
e. Howe might your answers to the above questions be affected by the fact that your company's net worth is $1 million?

The major question in this case is whether to make a market test (use research) or not. The decision variable proposed is "expected incremental dollar profits." The decision rule is: "select the course of action which yields the greatest expected incremental profits (EMV)." Decision tree analysis follows the answers to the various parts of the question.

A. Yes, go ahead and launch the product. It has an EMV, without research, of $180,000 over the alternative of not launching the new product.

B. As long as the probability of a successful outcome (O_1) is large enough to provide a positive EMV the product should be marketed, assuming the existing decision rule. As long as the probability of O_1 (success) exceeds .375 there is a positive value for EMV.

EMV = 0= P(O_1) (500,000) + (1 - P(O_1))(-300,000)

800.000 P(O_1) = 300,000

P(O_1) = .375

C. The value of the research is estimated to be $120,000 under the assumption that the market test is a perfect predictor. If the research costs less than $120,000 it is worthwhile according to the existing decision rule. (See decision tree).

D. With imperfect (80%) information the research would still be worth doing if it cost less than $37,280. (See decision tree).

E. We would not recommend an EMV decision rule because such a venture would probably be too risky for that size company. We would use some expected utility scale that requires greater certainty or a much higher profit to loss ratio. We may even set some upper limit on the amount of resources which we would risk in any single venture.

Chapter 3   The Research Process

True - False Questions

T   1) Conceptually, the value of applied research is easy to determine but in practice it is usually quite difficult.

T   2) The concern for technique and an available pool of information are sources of misguided research priorities.

F   3) There is no such thing as a question which is not researchable.

F   4) In the research hierarchy, an investigative question is usually divided up into several research questions.

T   5) Exploratory research is often used to clarify concepts and to establish priorities for further research.

F   6) Once a research question is set, there is no need to adjust it after exploration.

T   7) In the design stage, several competing designs should be considered rather than following the literature.

F   8) Research proposals are seldom required when dealing with managers since their knowledge of the problem is substantial.

T   9) Pilot testing is useful for providing proxy data for selecting samples.

F   10) Primary data have at least one level of interpretation inserted between the event and its recording.

F   11) Ex post facto evaluation of research is of little value.

Multiple Choice Questions

1. Which of the following is not a part of the research process hierarchy of questions?
   A) Investigative questions.
   B) Management problem.
   C) Measurement questions.
   * D) Exploratory questions.

2. Which of the following is typically not a part of the formal research plan?
   A) Definition of the major concepts and constructs.
   B) Specification of research techniques/methods.
   * C) Coding and tabulating instructions.
   D) Time and cost budgets.

Chapter 3 The Research Process

Appendix B True - False Questions

T   B1) A decision rule and a decision variable must be jointly used to express a criteria for option evaluation.

F   B2) A decision tree is a decision flow diagram in which the problem is structured in reverse chronological order, the most distant decision is placed at the left side and the most immediate decision is placed on the right hand side.

T   B3) Expected monetary value is an example of a decision variable.

F   B4) The maximin criterion is a decision rule that is usually not as conservative as the expected monetary value criterion.

Appendix B Multiple Choice Questions

B1.   Which of the following is a decision rule?
    A) Contribution to marginal cost.
*   B) Provides lowest probability of loss.
    C) Level of contribution to profits.
    D) Difference between final and initial overhead costs.

B2.   Action course "A," if successful, will net you a $10,000 profit, but if it fails you will lose $3,000. You believe there is a 60% chance it will succeed. Your alternative course "B" is to "do nothing." This is an example of:
*   A) using subjective probability
    B) using classical probability
    C) using imperfect information
    D) decision making under conditions of certainty

B3.   Action course "A," if successful, would net you a $10,000 profit. but if it failed you would lose $3,000. You believe that there is a 60% chance it will succeed. Your alternative course '"B" is to "do nothing." What is the maximum you should pay for research which will perfectly forecast success or failure?
    A) $7,800
    B) $6,000
    C) $1,200
*   D) $2,800

CHAPTER 4

THE RESEARCH PROPOSAL

At about this point in the course -- particularly project-oriented courses -- there is a need for students to decide on a problem for their term project (or have one assigned). Having recently finished units on reasoning, scientific inquiry, the question hierarchy, and the research process, application of this information to a concrete problem is desirable. This chapter offers practical information on construction of a proposal. A proposal is suggested as part of the term project assignment. Alternatively, a short assignment may be constructed to emphasize the research process.

There are two major learning objectives for this chapter. First, is to demonstrate the value of research proposals and second to expose students to various types of proposals and their composition. Many institutions have their own formats for papers and proposals; others simply require a style manual such as Turabian, MLA, or APA. In situations where there are few guides for the student, this chapter is more relevant. As a result of reading this chapter, the student should be able to organize research proposals of different types. It is helpful for the instructor to have several examples of student, internal, and external proposals available for students to examine.

This chapter is not intended to be prescriptive. Figure 4-2 on page 80 shows the level of complexity of proposal types. This figure also shows a continuum in which various proposal types can be placed. Variations exist. Figure 4-3 on page 82 shows proposal modules included in different proposal complexity levels. This figure is a *general guide;* often colleges, schools, corporations, or governments will have different requirements. Nevertheless, the figure provides a base on which instructors can explain their requirements.

Class Discussion Suggestions

The material in Chapter 4 can easily be covered adequately in one class session when built on the objectives mentioned above. Alternatively, instructors may wish to assign the chapter for background and allow the students a class period to discuss their research proposals with the professor.

1. If the chapter is being used as a stand-alone unit, a good lead-off discussion could use Figure 4-1 of the text, the iterative process of proposal development. Then, the instructor may select a management problem (perhaps from the previous session) and ask for brief proposals from groups of students. Upon re-

Chapter 4 — The Research Proposal

viewing one proposal, the instructor can clarify the problem and ask for a revision of the proposals. Students learn the value of working with management to elicit clearly defined terms and goals. A brief discussion of other benefits is sufficient to fix the value of the proposal. The chapter Close-Up provides an example that we refer to throughout the text. This example connects with the vignette series starting in Chapter 1 through Chapter 13 (concluding in Chapter 18). If you want to bridge from the examples to a proposal assignment, see Exhibit 4-1 and 4-2 at the end of this section for handout materials.

2. Emphasis of proposal types can be done briefly by question and answer. Discussion question 1 is helpful. Move from this to the proposal modules, what they contain, when they are used, and why they are included.

Answers to Chapter Questions

1. A solicited proposal is usually in response to a request for proposals (RFP). The proposal is likely competing against several others for the contract or grant. As such, it will concentrate on a known problem and propose an innovative research design to address the problem. The problem statement will be brief and to the point. The research objectives will be already known to the client and will be briefly reviewed. Most of the proposal will concentrate on the research design and the distinguishing characteristics of the proposal (qualifications, schedule, budget, and resources).

   An unsolicited proposal has the advantage of not competing against others but the disadvantage of having to speculate on the ramifications of a problem facing the firm's management. As such, more time will be spent developing the problem statement and the research objectives. In addition, the qualifications of the researchers will be emphasized. The results section will be strongly worded to convince the recipient of the necessity of the information.

2. Any number of journal reports can be chosen for this one. Each should be evaluated on its own merits. A useful exercise is for small groups to critique proposal outlines. The proposals are distributed without identification and the group works as a team to prepare a critique for each of 4-5 proposals.

3. One possible form would include the following items:

    I. Problem Statement
        A. Discussion with management
        B. Describe the management problem

C. List subproblems if any
II. Research objectives
   A. Develop research questions related to problem statement, above
   B. Describe target population for each research question
III. Literature review
   A. Description of related research
   B. Listing of relevant statistical sources
IV. Research Design
   A. Listing of possible research designs, check appropriate design
   B. Discuss why particular design is appropriate
V. Describe results
   A. Discuss with management types of results
   B. Return to II if results do not meet expectations
VI. Budget - include sign-off from financial department
VII. Schedule - review with management

A form like this simplifies the early stages of research proposal writing and provides an easy to understand list for the sponsoring manager. This facilitates management - researcher communications. In addition, it ensures that management knows exactly the type of research that is being commissioned. In this way, the results obtained will be beneficial in solving the management problem.

4. A. This is a small study. The information about other companies' plans will be available through an outside contractor. The proposal would typically be in the form of a memo to the president detailing the following:

   1. Problem Statement - restate presidents request
   2. Research Objectives - in operational terms, how you interpret the presidents request include:
      a. definition of comparable firms
      b. definition of health benefits
      c. time period for comparison
      d. other related items
   3. Research Design - descriptive
   4. Results anticipated
   5. Schedule

   B. Equivalent to a Masters Thesis proposal. See Figure 4-3.

   C. An External Exploratory Study. Since the bank contacted you, it is inappropriate to include a strong "importance of the study" section. Include the following:
   1. Executive Summary

2. Problem Statement, as it was described to you
3. Research Objectives, translate the problem statement into a set of research questions
4. Literature Review, although not shown in Figure 4-3, it is appropriate to show the client from where you intend to get your population figures.
5. Research design - descriptive
6. Qualifications of researchers
7. Budget
8. Schedule
9. Special resources (access to computerized census data, for example)

D. This is equivalent to an External Small-Scale Contract. See Figure 4-3 on page 82.

5. Student imagination can provide many examples which the authors have not included below.

A. *Desktop Publishing:* Desktop publishing makes it easy to provide professional looking proposals at a small cost. Graphic possibilities improve the ability for the proposal to show the nature of the results. In addition, word processors make it possible for a "boiler-plate" proposal to be developed. Having all the standard modules, the boiler-plate proposal would be used whenever a new proposal needs to be written, ensuring that the proper form and style are used and that all of the relevant information is included. Such a proposal authoring tool would dramatically reduce the amount of time it would take to develop proposals.

B. *Multimedia computer authoring and display:* This would allow a brief to be developed for the client so that actual interviewing situations could be explored. This would most probably be used for the client who has already contracted the researcher and is deeply involved in the design of the project. Although multimedia computer systems are currently being used primarily in training and education, new uses such as traveling displays, full graphic presentation techniques, and motion picture reproduction are being developed. Their advantage over traditional video is that powerful personal computers can be equipped with multimedia capabilities and still remain portable.

C. *Video taping and display:* This may be used to show a potential client the types of specialized facilities you have. In addition, it may be used to demonstrate the proficiency of your interviewing staff or to graphically demonstrate the problem statement or importance of a study.

6. This list of criteria may take many forms. Examples of acceptable answers are presented below.

   A. *Market Research*

       1. Problem Statement/Research Objectives/Benefits
           50 points
           a. the background of the problem is understood
           b. the research objectives are clear and correct
           c. the complexities of the research are understood
           d. the benefits match/exceed managements expectations

       2. Design/Analysis/Results
           20 points
           a. the design is explained adequately and is appropriate
           b. the researcher has the proper analysis tools at his/her disposal
           c. results will be in a usable form

       3. Budget/Schedule/Special resources/Qualification
           30 points
           a. project is within budget and on schedule
           b. special resources are available
           c. researcher qualification is appropriate

   B. *Advertising effectiveness:* same as Market research except more weight given to design, less to problem statement, research objectives, and benefits.

   C. *Employee opinion surveys:* An internal study, large in scale. Each of the major modules would be included in the evaluation. A typical point scale may range between 5 and 20 points for each section, with more weight given to the research design, results, and project management than to the literature review, importance, and bibliography.

   D. *Credit card operations:* same as Market Research except no special resources are needed. Design/Analysis/Results would carry a heavier weight, 40 points; Problem Statement/Research Objectives/Benefits would carry a lower weight, 30 points. This is because the problems are relatively well understood and analytic in nature whereas the design and analysis are important to insure that the results are usable by the department store.

   E. *Computer service effectiveness at the individual store level:* Probably an external study, of moderate size. Considerable attention would be given to the problem statement and the research objectives to ensure that the correct problem is being researched. As in Employee Opinion Surveys, each of the modules would be included, and the weights would be split between them.

True - False Questions

T   1. The more inexperienced a researcher is, the more important it is to have a well planned and adequately documented proposal.

F   2. To avoid upsetting clients, proposals should not include potential problems that may be encountered along the way.

T   3. A poorly planned, poorly written, or poorly organized proposal damages your reputation more than the decision not to submit a proposal for a prestigious project.

T   4. The proposal provides a document that the sponsor can evaluate based upon the current organizational, scholastic, or scientific needs.

T   5. The research sponsor to assesses the researcher and the proposed design when reading a proposal.

F   6. The proposal is used for selecting a research contractor and then is not used again.

F   7. It is the sponsor's responsibility that the management question is translated into research questions and objectives that can be studied.

T   8. One of the benefits of an unsolicited proposal has is not having to compete against alternative designs.

T   9. An exploratory study done within a firm's research division may only need a memo outlining the objectives, approach, and time allotted to the project for a research proposal.

T   10. The difference between student and internal or external proposals is that more emphasis placed upon the literature review and bibliography in student proposals.

T   11. In the small scale proposal, the literature review and bibliography are consequently not stressed and can often be stated briefly in the research design.

Chapter 4 | The Research Proposal

F   12. An executive summary is appropriate only when the proposal is being sent to a corporation's executive(s).

T   13. The executive summary of an external proposal may be included within the letter of transmittal.

T   14. The research objectives module addresses the purpose of the investigation.

F   15. The literature review section should not include old citations.

F   16. The importance/benefits of the study section is particularly important to the solicited external proposal.

T   17. The research design section shows the sponsors exactly what it is that they are "buying."

T   18. If projects require special facilities or resources, they should be described within the body of the proposal.

Multiple Choice Questions

1. One of the main reasons for doing a research proposal is:
   A. To present the problem to be researched and its importance.
   B. To start the final research report early.
   C. To allow the client to choose the proper research design
   D. To force the client to choose which data analysis tool will be used

2. Which of the following is something that a proposal will NOT tell the reader:
   A. What will be done.
   B. Why it will be done.
   C. What the results will be.
   D. What is the benefit of doing it.

3. If parts of the problem can not be researched empirically, the researcher should do which of the following?
   A. Propose an alternative design, such as a policy analytic study
   B. Refuse to make a proposal on the work
   C. Make a proposal, including those parts of the problem which can be studied empirically and excluding those which cannot be researched
   D. Propose to research the problem and leave the design to a later p h a s e of the project.

Chapter 4 — The Research Proposal

4. The most complex proposals are usually created for what type of client?
   A. Corporate sponsors
   B. Contract research
   * C. Government sponsors
   D. Internal clients
   E. Universities

5. A proposal which is created by a research department or division for client who is in another department of the corporation is called a
   A. unsolicited proposal
   B. solicited proposal
   C. external proposal
   * D. internal proposal

6. In corporations, the most simple business proposal is for a(n)
   A. small scale study
   B. memo proposal
   * C. exploratory study
   D. internal study

7. Some of the most important sections of the external proposal are the
   * A. objectives, design, and qualifications
   B. literature review, appendix, and anticipated results
   C. anticipated results, budget, and data analysis
   D. objectives, glossary, and qualifications

8. The executive summary allows a busy manager or sponsor to understand quickly the thrust of the proposal. Therefore, the goal for the summary is to have the executive:
   A. agree to sponsor the research programs at the university.
   * B. pass the proposal on to his/her staff for a full evaluation.
   C. request a meeting with the researcher for further discussion.
   D. ask the research department to undertake a similar study.

9. The problem statement section of the proposal
   A. states the problem
   B. states the problem's background
   C. explains the problem's concrete consequences
   D. repeats the management question
   * E. all of the above

10. A complete section on the methods used for analyzing the data is appropriate for what type of proposal?
* A. Large scale contract research projects and doctoral theses
  B. Small and large scale contract research projects
  C. An exploratory study and student projects
  D. Unsolicited external proposals

The following resources are provided for student handouts.

Exhibit 4 - 1 Presentation Outline for Proposal Review

1. Overview of your research problem and what you expect to accomplish.

2. Statement of the problem:

       1. Research question(s)
       2. Investigative questions
       3. Hypothesis (if appropriate for the design)
       4. Assumptions (if necessary)

3. Importance/benefits of the research.

4. What you discovered from your preliminary look at the literature.

5. The methods and procedures you anticipate using (highlights).

6. How you will analyze the data.

Exhibit 4 - 2 An Abbreviated Student Proposal with Comments

Problem

A large volume of literature exists concerning feedback and its effects. Many of the studies are laboratory experiments whose results have been directed toward the fields of administration and management. In the laboratory setting, all variables can be controlled and therefore the results of these experiments cannot be directly applied to the daily organizational situations with the same level of effects demonstrated in experiments. This research is designed to supply some empirical evidence from a field setting.

Section heading.

Introduction should contain a broad overview of the problem. This is an overview of the problem without much context.

Statement of the Problem

This research proposes to address how sources of feedback influence employee satisfaction and performance in the work setting.

Research Questions:

1. What are the sources of feedback that influence employee satisfaction and performance?
2. What importance do individuals attach to sources of feedback?
3. How are satisfaction and performance measured in the work setting when various sources of feedback are used?

The "sources" and nature of feedback could be informally defined so that logical linkages could be made.

The lack of definition affects the clarity of the RQs. No IQs are presented. The third question is an operational problem for the researcher not a question.

Importance of the Study

This research is important because although work has been done in the field, additional attention needs to be given to the application of this information in the work setting. With an increase in knowledge workers, one should find it advantageous to know how to effectively increase motivation and performance levels in employees through the use of effective feedback sources. Both intrinsic and extrinsic forms of feedback need further investigation. If managers can determine what types of feedback is most effective in their work setting, they can increase performance and satisfaction levels in their organization.

There is no evidence in this paragraph that the writer's assessment of work setting applications of feedback research is correct. Feedback has been researched to death and much is known in both intrinsic and extrinsic categories. The rationale for this study does not have a sound foundation nor is it logically argued.

Special Section *Ethics in Business Research*

ETHICS IN BUSINESS RESEARCH

As we said in the text, the major objective of this special section is to stimulate a dialog about values and research constraints early in the course. The ideas presented in the section have a wide range of applications that are relevant throughout the text. Following our applied focus, the themes of the chapter are organized around the ethical treatment of respondents, clients, and other researchers. Page 105 has a resource table for ethical awareness you may want to use for topical lecturettes.

We also recommend the *Annual Editions: Business Ethics 94/95* (Dushkin Publishing Group, 800-243-6532) for a collection of articles on business ethics and corporate responsibility. William D. Hall's *Making the Right Decision: Ethics for Managers* (John Wiley and Sons, 1993) presents ethical dilemmas from a businessperson's point of view.

Finally, Cynthia Crossen's article "How 'Tactical Research' Muddied Diaper Debate," (*WSJ*, May 17, 1994, p. B1), discusses the public policy research on disposable diapers of which Arthur D. Little company's study was one. You may wish to copy and distribute the article for reading prior to the class session -- perhaps as a transition from Chapter 2's discussion of how we legitimately view different realities and how those perspectives affect our values -- and consequently, how we conduct research. The ethical ramifications of a corporate-sponsored, research-driven policy duel are exciting for graduate and undergraduate students alike. The discussion establishes an important foundation for subsequent debate about ethics.

Other Class Discussion Suggestions

Another approach uses the cases at the end of the section for discussion. Students should be asked to identify principles like deception, informed consent, privacy rights, confidentiality, safety, and others in assessing the conflicts posed in the cases. Some suggestions for discussion follow.

Case Questions

Case 1: A Competitive Coup in the In-Flight Magazine

A. If the adage, "all is fair in love and war" is particularly true of market intelligence, why should the manager be constrained by ethical guidelines intended for traditional functional areas?

B. Does the draft status of the company's *Business Conduct Guidelines* change the manager's responsibility to her firm?

C. To what extent should professional standards (of associations or industry groups) exceed those currently in place for this automotive manufacturer? What's the value of standards without enforcement?

D. Is a description of new products contained in a proprietary study any different from "spy photos" found in industry magazines or an industry analyst's future predictions? Should this be a consideration of the manager's decision to return the document?

Case 2: Free Waters in the Miro Beach: Boaters, Inc. Versus City Government

A. What are the ethical ramifications of asking the university professors to develop a research template (under the guise of requesting a proposal) for the purpose of having the staff do the work themselves?

B. Why should administrative staff be required to conduct an impartial study rather than seeking only information that supports their case? How are the rights to quality research of the city's citizens violated?

C. Discuss privacy and confidentiality issues in the hiring of a PI and unauthorized use of background checks.

D. Is the tactic of flooding the city with public records requests a responsible tactic?

Case 3: The High Cost of Organizational Change

A. What should the researcher do in response to the VPs request? What are the consequences of your proposed course of action?

B. Discuss the politics bred by an organization's culture and their effect on managements desire for preferred versus objective answers to the employee survey.

C. How are deception and violation of confidence used by management in this case? What other behaviors do you find questionable?

D. If this firm has government contracts, how might its behavior be considered illegal as well as unethical?

CHAPTER 5

DESIGN STRATEGIES

There are three major learning objectives for this chapter. The first is to make the student aware of the nature of research design and the dimensions used to classify various design approaches. Most discussions of design mention only a few of these dimensions. The student should understand that every research design involves to some degree the eight decisions listed on page 114 of the text.

A second objective is to lead the student to understand in some depth the two classification dimensions of greatest concern at this stage of the course. These are exploratory versus formalized and descriptive versus causal research.

Our third objective is to provide a foundation in causality. How is causation inferred? How confident can we be of it? How can variables be related? How must these relationships be established to provide strong inferences?

Class Discussion Suggestions

The material in Chapter 5 can usually be covered adequately in a 1-1/2 hour class session when built on the objectives mentioned above.

1. Discussion of the 8 dimension classification of research designs is a good lead-off, but should take only a small portion of the total class time. Discussion questions 1 and 4 at the end of the chapter may be of value in discussing this topic.

2. In discussing the exploratory-formal research dichotomy one should stress the values of the 2 - stage approach in all non-routine research design. Question 3 is useful for discussing how to carry out exploratory research.

3. In this chapter, the Close-Up is a design analysis exercise which may be considered for in-class use, or with some modification, as an out-of-class assignment. Depending on the specialities represented among the students, you may prefer to select journals and topics different from the general management themes we used. This exercise may be used after suggestions 1 and 2 or in place of them. See Exhibits 5-1 through 5-3 for details.

4. Students have more difficulty understanding causality than most others sections of the chapter. Questions 5 through 8 provide useful discussion material in this area.

Exhibit 5 - 1 Sample Design Critique Instructions

FROM: Professor _____
TO: Students in Research Methodology Course
SUBJECT: Project ___

For your second research exercise please select one of the journals listed below for an article of interest to you.

The purpose of your paper is to critique the design of the chosen article using the criteria established in Chapter 5. Consider the following characteristics in writing your paper.

Expectations for "B" work:
Stated the purpose of the critique
Listed the criteria to be used in performing the critique
Defined the characteristics of the criteria used
Developed reasonable arguments for decisions on each criterion
Cited ample specific instances from the article to support conclusions
Summarized the findings of the critique

Expectations for "A" work (in addition):
Provided sufficient contextual information about the article (in abstract form, overview, or by incorporation into critique)
Provided additional criteria (of her/his own) to judge the design
Described weaknesses/strengths of the design

Some journals are listed below. Select a *recent* issue (during the last year):

Academy of Management Review
Administrative Science Quarterly
Business and Society Review
Decision Sciences
Financial Management
Harvard Business Review
Industrial and Labor Relations Review
Journal of Accountancy
Journal of Applied Behavior Science
Journal of Applied Psychology
Journal of Banking and Finance
Journal of Finance
Personnel Journal
Training and Development Journal

Other journals may be considered.

Chapter 5 — Design Strategies

Exhibit 5 - 2 Sample Student Design Critique (by Susan R. Seaber*)

The article *The Commitment of Social Workers to Affirmative Action*, from the Journal of Sociology and Social Welfare, is an attempt to study the relationship of several variables concerned with affirmative action. The Texas chapter of the National Association of Social workers (NASW/Texas) was selected as the population for the study. Surveys were mailed to 474 members, and 193 responded, creating a response rate of 46.3 percent.

Three general study variables were selected, from which the authors analyzed the data collected from the study participants. The first variable concerns the respondent's commit to affirmative action. The participant's knowledge of affirmative action is another variable. Finally, the respondents were asked if their experiences with affirmative action were negative or positive. By dividing the participants into certain groups (sex; age; ethnic background; political party; age; job level; public or private institution; and community size) the researchers were able to determine which of these factors had an effect on the respondents' experience with affirmative action.

The purpose of this critique is to determine which criteria for proper research design are utilized in this particular study on affirmative action experiences. The criteria are outlined in Business Research Methods by Emory and Cooper (1991) on page 139. The basic elements of design criteria and the use of them in this article are described below.

First, the degree of problem crystallization must be addressed. The study may be exploratory or formal. An exploratory study loosely structures the research with the objective of learning what major research tasks are required. The purpose is to develop hypotheses and questions to aid in subsequent research efforts. Formal research begins with a hypothesis or question, and the goal is to test the hypotheses or answer the research questions. This study is a formal study, although the statement of the goal is rather vague. on page 124 of the article, a central question is stated which reads: "to what degree and under what circumstances do social workers in Texas support the concept and implementation of affirmative action policies?" The purpose of this research question.

The method of data collection can be monitoring or interrogation. Monitoring is observational, and the researcher only views the activity or material to be studied. Interrogatory studies occur when the researcher actually questions the subjects and collects data about the responses. This article is an example of interrogation: 474 questionnaires were mailed to randomly selected members of NASW/Texas, and the researchers gathered data concerning certain characteristics of the respondents and certain attitudes toward affirmative action.

The third criterion for research design concerns the researcher control of the variables; this can be experimental, where the researcher attempts to manipulate the variables, or it can be ex post facto, where the researcher has no control over the variables and cannot manipulate them. This particular study is an example of an experimental design, since the researchers are attempting to determine certain characteristics which may create certain attitudes, and certain variables are used to determine an effect on other variables. An ex post facto study would merely report that a particular condition existed, not a potential reason for the condition.

The next criterion involves the purpose of the study. Descriptive studies are used to determine who, what, where, when, or how much. Causal studies are used to determine why and to explain relationships. This article is summarizing a causal study - again, the characteristics of the individuals responding to the questions are expected to determine the response indicated. An individual possessing these characteristics would be expected to reply to the questionnaire in a certain manner.

Time dimension can be cross sectional, when a "snapshot" is taken from one point in time, and the study is only conducted once, or it can be longitudinal, when the study is repeated over a period of time. The affirmative action study is a one-time occurrence, taken from a randomly selected group of people, and is therefore a cross-sectional study.

Chapter 5 *Design Strategies*

The next criterion is the topical scope. This can be either statistical, which is an attempt to determine characteristics of a population by analyzing data which is collected from a representative sample, resulting in quantitative tests of the responses. The topical scope can also be a case study, which emphasizing a full analysis of a limited number of events or conditions. Qualitative data is relied upon, making it difficult to support or reject a hypothesis. This article describes a statistical study - a random sample of social workers was selected, and the results were quantitatively calculated by statistical means, resulting in generalizations about the population. The Results section (p. 120) and the Measures of Association section (p.130) describe the particular statistics utilized to analyze the data collected from the survey.

The research environment is the next criterion: field studies take place under actual environmental conditions, and laboratory studies take place under other conditions which are not the natural environment and which may be simulated. The affirmative action study is a field study, which was conducted in the natural environment of the respondent.

The final criterion for research design involves the subjects' perceptions of the study. When people in the study perceive that the research is being conducted, t may affect the results of the study. The subjects are capable of influencing the outcome of the results by having knowledge of being studied. In this study, the respondents obviously are aware of the fact that they are being studied, and although there is no evidence that this will bias the results, it is possible that this particular outcome could occur.

The previous criteria are directly from the textbook <u>Business Research Methods,</u> but obviously there are other criteria which may serve to describe a research design. In this particular case, the question can be asked: "Can this study be generalized to other locations or is it likely to be specific only to Texas?" In my opinion, this study cannot be generalized to a population in other states. For instance, the minority population in Texas may differ greatly from other states, resulting from the state's proximity to Mexico. Also, affirmative action may be approached in a different manner in other states for various reasons.

Another criterion which may be useful would be to determine whether the study focuses upon factual, non-negotiable responses by participants or by opinions of the respondents. This study is a combination of the two: the factual characteristics are described, and are then used to determine the effect on other variables. In some cases, though, it may be important to use only factual data, while the majority of studies will rely on respondents' opinions.

This critique has so far determined the specific characteristics of the study conducted using social workers and their attitudes toward affirmative action. The article indicates that this study was designed with the purpose of describing certain characteristics of individuals in the Texas social workers population and to determine whether or not they (1) have knowledge of affirmative action; (2) have a commitment to affirmative action; and (3) have been negatively or positively impacted by affirmative action.

The results indicate that surprisingly, having knowledge of affirmative action is not significantly associated with commitment to affirmative action. In other words, educational efforts to improve commitment to affirmative action would not be effective, according to this survey. Also, a negative commitment usually corresponded with negative experiences, and positive commitment usually corresponded with positive experiences. Furthermore, those respondents with negative or positive experiences are more likely to have higher scores in the area of knowledge of affirmative action.

Commitment to affirmative action was described as follows: women scored higher than men; and racial or ethnic minorities scored higher than non-minorities. Commitment was also affected by political party affiliation and job position. Variables which did not affect commitment included public or private employment, community size, or level of education.

One weakness of this article was the limited response of the selected population. According to Rubin and Babbie in <u>Research Methods for Social Work</u> (1989), a 50 percent response rate is considered merely "adequate" for analysis and reporting. While a 50 percent response rate was quoted as "adequate," this survey generated only a 46.3 percent response rate. Also, although a general research question was stated, the actual predictions and desired outcomes were very vague, resulting in some confusion concerning the actual reason for the study. Another possible weakness is that, while the NASW/Texas membership consists of 74.5 percent females and 25.5 percent males, the actual response rate was 62.1 percent female and 37.9 percent male. This indicates a possible problem concerning representativeness of the sample.

Despite these potential weaknesses, the authors did indicate that this particular study is preliminary and "designed to identify key issues and to design instruments which would be applicable with a larger nationally representative sample" (p. 134). They acknowledge that possible weaknesses exist, and encourage other researchers to expand on the study in order to develop more information which may be helpful in determining the problem and solving it.

References

Emory, C. William and Donald R. Cooper (1991). Business Research Methods. Boston: Irwin.

Rubin and Bobbie (1989). Research Methods for Social Work: Belmont, CA: Wadsworth.

Stout, Karen D. and William E. Buffum (1993). *The Commitment of Social Workers to Affirmative Action*. Journal of Sociology and Social Welfare, 123-134.

* Used by permission of Ms. Seaber.

Chapter 5   Design Strategies

Exhibit 5 - 3 Research Design Paper: Evaluation Form (Graduate Students)

Student _____

In the research design critique, the student:

	Level of Attainment
	Low High

Expectations (based on class example):

Stated the purpose of the critique	1	2	3	4	5
Listed the criteria to be used in performing the critique	1	2	3	4	5
Defined the characteristics of the criteria used	1	2	3	4	5
Developed reasonable arguments for decisions on each criterion	1	2	3	4	5
Cited ample specific instances from the article to support conclusions	1	2	3	4	5
Summarized the findings of the critique	1	2	3	4	5

Additional Criteria Beyond the Expectations for this Assignment*

Provided sufficient contextual information about the article (in abstract form, overview, or by incorporation into critique)	1	2	3	4	5
Provided additional criteria (of her/his own) to judge the design	1	2	3	4	5
Described weaknesses/strengths of the design	1	2	3	4	5

Comments:

Grade:

Grading scale:
    A   Scholarly work   B   Good work
    A-   Superior work   B-   Deficient in some areas
    B+   Very good work   C+   Deficient in most areas

Chapter 5 — *Design Strategies*

Answers to Chapter Questions

1. See definition discussion on pages 114 - 117 of the text.

2. Inductive conclusions, unlike deductive conclusions, have no "necessary" connections between facts and conclusions. Thus the conclusion of an induction may be simply *one* explanation for an observed fact whereas the conclusion of a deduction is *the* explanation, if the deduction's requirements have been met. This means that when dealing with causal relationships we require other more rigorous devices to assure ourselves that our probabilistic statements contain the least possible margin for error. Methods such as experimentation and statistical tests help to improve our confidence in ascribing cause to inductive conclusions.

3. A good first step would be some exploratory research following the pattern presented on pages 117 - 121 of the text. From this the researcher would develop a proposal for a formalized study if one is needed. It may be an in-depth case study which is a cross sectional, field, ex post facto, descriptive survey. This project might concentrate on those few companies uncovered in the exploratory research as having successfully dealt with a similar problem. Obviously, other acceptable designs are possible.

4. A. An exploratory investigation to determine what kind of research situation exists. Such a study might involve field observation of conditions in the company, study of secondary sources, and the like.

   B. A longitudinal analysis of various indicators related to performance may be available from company records. Such an observational case approach would use turnover data, grievance records, absenteeism reports, and the like for the study.

   C. A formal cross-sectional survey of persons in various departments, gathering descriptive data on worker attitudes, would also provide good insight into the alleged problems in the division.

5. A. *Stimulus-response:* When you are challenged to justify your position during a management meeting your pulse rate increases rapidly and you speak out strongly in defense of your position.

   B. *Property-disposition:* You are a member of a minority ethnic group and this makes you very sensitive to ethnic type comments by others.

   C. *Disposition-behavior:* You have strong opinions about the degradation of our physical environment by some industries; as a result you are highly

   selective in choosing the companies with whom you interview for career opportunities.

   D. *Property-behavior:* You have grown up as a member of the upper-lower social class and now follow the typical consumption practices of that class.

Chapter 5   *Design Strategies*

6. There are literally an infinite number of extraneous variables which may confound a causal relationship. Many are unanticipated and unidentified. We also have a limited ability to control more than a few variables. By randomization we can, within specific limits of variance, expect to equalize out the influence or potential influence of these many extraneous variables. We can, however, control for a few variables that are expected to be most important. By so doing we can assure that they do not confound our study results.

7. A. While the relationship between consumer confidence and the business cycle may be interdependent, the most frequent form has the consumer confidence as the independent variable and the business cycle as the dependent variable. In fact, consumer confidence is usually viewed as a leading indicator of the business cycle. We might have as moderating variables the level of employment, actions taken by the federal government in tax policy, and others. Extraneous variables might include such things as inflation rate, development of exciting new automobile models, the price of gold, and changes in the role of the family in society. Note that the designation of moderating and extraneous variables is often a matter of choice.

8. A. These two approaches are similar in their objective of trying to show IV-DV or causal relationships, basically by means of:
    1. Studying covariation patterns between variables.
    2. Determining time order relationships.
    3. Attempting to eliminate the confounding effects of other variables on the IV-DV relationship.

    They often use the same data collection and data manipulation methods. For example, either may use interviews or observation, use certain statistical methods, and the like.

    B. They differ in their ability to measure causal effects. In experimental design we can set up situations, manipulate variables, assign subjects to exposure or control groups, and control other variables. With ex post facto research we must accept what is, or what has been, uncover comparative groups who have been exposed and others who have not been exposed to the "causal" factor, attempt to learn the time order effect after the fact, and attempt to "control" other variables by various after-the-event statistical or classification procedures. Given these problems it is easily apparent as to why experimental design is the more powerful of the two methods for causal analysis.

True - False Questions

T   1)   The major concern in exploratory research is the discovery of ideas and insights into the problem.

T   2)   Exploratory research can be used to establish priorities for further research.

Chapter 5 — Design Strategies

F   3) The major difference between an exploratory and a formal study is the degree to which the researcher can affect the variables under study.

T   4) Exploratory research is typically the first stage in a research study.

T   5) Exploratory research is often used to clarify concepts and to establish priorities for further research.

F   6) In longitudinal studies the researcher must examine the same people over a period of time.

F   7) Descriptive studies should be seen as fact gathering expeditions, and any information that seems to be relevant to the study should be collected.

F   8) An example of a causal study is a research project aimed at predicting the number of college students who are likely to go on to graduate school.

F   9) Exploratory research is most useful when the researchers have a clear idea of the problems that they will face in the course of the study, but they can't decide upon the final research methodology or design.

F   10) Typically, exploratory research takes three forms: literature survey, experience survey, and experimentation.

F   11) In a good exploratory research study a probability sample of the population is imperative.

T   12) Formalized research studies are typically well structured and have unambiguously stated hypotheses or investigative questions.

T   13) The essential element in the theoretical concept of cause is that A "produces" B or A "forces" B to occur.

T   14) In the statement, "A good advertising campaign always increases sales," the increase in sales is the dependent variable.

T   15) One can differentiate between a moderator variable and a control variable by recognizing a moderator variable as one which actively affects the IV-DV relationship.

T   16) An intervening variable is a conceptual mechanism through which the IV and MV all affect the dependent variable.

F   17) The major relationships of interest to the research analyst are those which are symmetrical.

T   18) A stimulus-response relationship is the most direct causal type of connection between two variables.

Chapter 5　　　　　　　　　　　　　　　　　　　　　　　　　　　　　　　　Design Strategies

T　　　19) A basic assumption of experimental designs is that experimental and control groups can be established in such a way that they are equal.

F　　　20) Experimental designs are inferior theoretically to the ex post facto design but are often used because of practical considerations.

Multiple Choice Questions

1. The research experiment is superior to the ex post facto research design when the researcher:
   A) Must avoid influencing the variables under study and therefore avoid biasing the results.
 * B) Needs to cause variables to be changed or held constant in keeping with specified research objectives.
   C) Is limited to holding all factors constant by selection of subjects according to strict sampling procedures and statistical manipulation of findings.
   D) Decides to use the design more common to research in the social sciences and business.

2. The basic method by which we determine equivalence between study and control groups in an ex post facto study is by
 * A) Matching
   B) Definition
   C) Induction
   D) Random assignment

3. The basic method by which equivalence between experimental and control groups is determined is
   A) Matching
   B) Definition
   C) Frequency control
   D) Cross-classifying
 * E) Random assignment

4. Which of the following statements is false with respect to the two-stage research approach to a management question. The two-stage approach:
   A) often uncovers evidence that a major study is unnecessary in the first stage.
   B) is particularly useful when the research is to be done on a fixed cost basis.
   C) is particularly useful when the complications and problems that will be encountered are difficult to anticipate.
 * D) is less expensive and less in-depth than a one-stage research approach.

Chapter 5 — Design Strategies

5. Which of the following can be classified as a causal research study? The researcher is attempting to find out:
   A) What percentage of the population believes consumer products are of the same or better quality today than 10 years ago.
   B) Which manufacturers in the U.S. contribute the highest percentage of their net income to private non-profit organizations.
   C) How the murder rate in Detroit fluctuates with the economy and population trends.
   * D) Why unemployment is higher in Chicago than Houston.

6. Research designs may be viewed as being
   A) Exploratory or experimental
   B) Laboratory or ex post facto
   C) Cross-sectional or case
   * D) Descriptive or causal
   E) Longitudinal or statistical

7. In an exploratory study the first step usually should be
   A) Defining a hypothesis
   B) Seek "insight-stimulating" interviews
   C) Develop the research design
   D) Estimate the cost of the study
   * E) Do a literature search.

8. The interactions between two sets of variables may reflect relationships which are
   A) Symmetrical
   B) Reciprocal
   C) Asymmetrical
   * D) All of the above

9. "The introduction of a four day week leads to increased productivity particularly among young workers by improving job satisfaction." In this statement, improving job satisfaction is the:
   A) Independent Variable
   B) Dependent Variable
   * C) Intervening Variable
   D) Moderating Variable

10. Which of the following is not a good basis for classifying research designs?
    A) Degree of research problem crystallization
    B) The time dimension
    C) The nature of the relationships among variables
    * D) The importance of the problem being studied.

Chapter 5　　　　　　　　　　　　　　　　　　　　　　　　　　　Design Strategies

11. The statistical study differs from the case study in that:
    A) The statistical study has greater depth than the case study,
    B) The case study has both greater depth and breadth over the statistical study.
  * C) The case study places more emphasis on the full analysis of a limited number of events and their interrelations.
    D) The statistical study places an emphasis on both a full analysis of the complete range of events and is greatly concerned about analyzing interrelationships.

12. Which of the following is not a type of symmetrical relationship?
    A) Disposition - behavior
    B) Property - behavior
    C) Property - disposition
    D) Stimulus - response
  * E) Stimulus - property

13. The major relationships of interest to the research analyst are those which are
  * A) Asymmetrical
    B) Exclusive
    C) Independent
    D) Reciprocal
    E) Symmetrical

CHAPTER 6

MEASUREMENT

There are three learning objectives for this chapter. First, it is important that the student learn that measurement is a complex process involving a number of different scale types; and, that each scale has its own meaning, applications, and powers. The student should grasp the rudimentary concepts of validity and reliability, as well as be able to apply them to measurement situations. The third objective is to learn to develop a measurement index. This latter topic is usually the most difficult and should be used based on the level of students in the class. Additional materials in this area are listed in the Suggested Readings.

Class Discussion Suggestions

The materials in this chapter are somewhat abstract and the student's ability to understand and work with them is enhanced by plenty of class discussion that connects to everyday experiences. One session of 1-1/2 hours should suffice to cover the following topics:

1. What is measurement? Two points need to be reinforced in this regard. One is that we do not measure objects, nor even properties of objects, rather, we measure indicants of properties of objects. Thus, we measure the profitability of a company (property of an object) by an indicator in the form of the net profit figure for the year as stated in the company's annual report. In truth, a look at the company's accounting records and federal income tax return will probably give two other figures on net profits, and all three are ethically and legally acceptable, although numerically different. The second point which needs emphasis is that measuring involves the process of *mapping* these indicators from one conceptual domain to another so that we can compare, compile, or statistically manipulate the data to meet our needs. For example. we measure a company's success in terms of net profits defined in some operational terms (a mapping process). We may then develop an index of investment attractiveness (e.g., ROI) by which we classify various companies into attractive or unattractive investment groups (another mapping). Question 1 is a useful discussion vehicle for this topic.

2. The discussion of scale types is usually brief and simple. The classification system based on order, distance, and origin is easily understood. The implications for statistical manipulation are also relatively easy concepts if the students have had a statistics course. If not or if their memory is faulty, Chapter 14's Close-Up starting on page 395 provides a good review of descriptive statistics. Question 2 at the end of the chapter addresses these points directly.

3. A larger share of the class time is usually needed for discussing how one characterizes "sound measurement." It might be useful, first, to position the instrument as only one of several important error sources. Then the discussion can move directly into the problems of measuring as expressed in validity and reliability terms. Three common forms of validity -- content, criterion, and construct -- are

Chapter 6 — Measurement

discussed in the text. Questions 5 and 6 at the end of the chapter are useful here.

Reliability and its relation to validity should be made clear. Another way to describe these concepts is in terms of the types of variance they address. A measure could have great bias (systematic variance) and still be reliable if it is consistent in its scoring. High reliability indicates only limited error variance is present, but says nothing about systematic variance. A valid measure is also reliable, but in addition a valid measure has little or no systematic variance as well as not having error variance.

4. The fourth section of the class should be concerned with index construction. This is another creative topic and one which students seem reluctant to embrace. The four step process can be illustrated with the case example on the development of the interest in work innovation index.

Answers to Chapter Questions

1. In measuring we attempt to note and record certain observable indicators of properties of the subject under study.

   A. Laundry detergent - Some of the obvious but non-functional properties we might measure are weight, volume, texture, color, odor, cost, etc. Functional properties might include dirt removing power, effect on colors, speed of cleaning action, and skin irritation power.

   B. Employees - Non-functional properties include age, sex, hair color, marital status, and the like. Functional properties of employees include motivation, reliability, job skill, and productivity.

   C. Factory output - We might be interested here in measuring properties such as volume of output, costs, salability of product, seasonal nature of output, and identification of what is produced.

   D. Job satisfaction - Here we might seek to measure attitudes toward work, attitudes toward the job environment, perceptions of fair treatment and compensation, and absenteeism.

2. A. This is summarized well in the figure on page 143. Nominal scales differentiate among scale values only on the basis of being alike or different from other scale values. Ordinal scales incorporate this feature of differentiability plus the concept of order (i.e., a subject may exhibit more, less, or the same amount of a property as another subject). Interval scales incorporate both of the features of the ordinal scale plus the added one of distance between scale points. For example, the distance between 1 and 2 is the same as between 2 and 3. Finally, ratio scales include all of the interval scale features plus the added feature of having a zero origin. This allows us to say that 4 is twice as large as 2 and to multiply scale values.

   B. Parametric statistics assume at least interval measurement scales and the statistical measures of arithmetic mean, standard deviation, etc. should technically be used only with these scales. Nonparametric scales are the nominal and ordinal scales. When people use parametric statistics for ordinal or nominal scales they are literally adding information to what actually exists. This position is technically incorrect, but when a normal distribution underlies the variable(s) in question it may not be a problem.

3. There are relatively few pure interval scales found in business research. Almost all text discussions of this scale refer to the example of temperature scales. However some attitude scales such as the Likert and Semantic Differential are claimed to approach interval characteristics. In addition, many claim that approximate interval scales can be developed from paired comparisons and rank orders of objects.

A. Store customers

Nominal - Class them by race, ethnic background, married or single status, etc.

Ordinal - Rank them as very frequent buyers, frequent buyers, infrequent buyers.

Interval - Some scale of attractiveness in which the scale is presumed to be interval.

Ratio - Average size of monthly purchases.

B. Voter attitudes

Nominal - Classed as Republican, Democrat, Independent, and Other.

Ordinal - Rank of candidates in order of preference.

Interval - Likert - type scale

Ratio - Count of votes for various candidates in each district.

C. Hardness of alloy

Nominal - Identification of alloys that include nickel and those that do not.

Ordinal - Ranking of hardness by determining which alloys scratch which others.

Interval - Use of an interval scale designed to rate alloy hardness.

Ratio - Amount of nickel per pound of steel in various alloys.

D. Common stock preference

Nominal - Industry classification of preferred stocks.

Ordinal - Rank order of five stocks as to your preference for them.

Interval - Rating of preference for the stock by converting the results of a paired comparison rating into presumed interval scale.

Ratio - Six month changes in price of various preferred stocks.

E. Division profitability

Nominal - Classification of sources of division profits, e.g., manufacturing, assembly, trading, price changes, etc.

Ordinal - Ranking of divisions by the size of their dollar profits in 199X.

Interval - Use of Semantic Differential scale in evaluating the profit performance image of various divisions.

Ratio - Dollar profits for each division in 199X.

4. In research we hope that any measurement represents a true portrayal of the property being measured, but we recognize that it often does not. Errors can be of either a random or systematic type, but it is the latter which represent the greater threat to the measurement process. Most systematic error in a survey, for example, flows either from the respondent, from some factors in the situation, from the researcher, or from the instrument being used. Assume, for example, that we are interviewing persons about economic topics and include a question about their annual income. The respondents themselves may be a source of error for they may not actually think of every source of income which is included in the research definition. Respondents may also bias results if they tend to exaggerate or understate.
The situation under which the interview takes place may distort the measurement, especially if the study is being done in the presence of someone else, even a family member. Other situational biases arise if the interview conditions do not foster carefully reasoned answers or provide access to records. The interviewer can affect results, if he/she fails to achieve rapport with the respondent and therefore appears as a threat. Careless recording, coding, and tabulating are other researcher sources of error. Finally, the measurement instrument itself can be an error source. The question may confuse the respondent or be phrased in a way to lead to one answer more than another. The question may, in addition, just not cover all of the possible income sources. (For example, in one major national survey more than a dozen questions were used to establish a family's total annual income.)

5. A. A measurement tool that is valid is also reliable, but a reliable tool may not be valid. If we have an instrument which measures what it claims to measure (validity) it will also be reliable.

B. Probably not true in most cases. We usually determine content validity in a judgmental way and if we agree that a study has content validity then, for our purposes, it does. Predictive and construct validity, on the other hand, may be much more difficult to develop.

C. True - See A. above.

D. False - Stability is concerned with personal and situation fluctuations and is achieved if we get consistent results with repeated measurements of the same person with the same instrument. Equivalence is concerned with consistent results over different investigators or different samples of items.

6. Assume that the instrument has about 20 scale items and is administered to students at the end of the semester. Each item calls for a reply ranging from "5" strongly agree to "1" strongly disagree.

A. Stability (or test-retest reliability) would be measured by repeating the administration of the questionnaire to the same students about 2 weeks later and then correlating the results of the two administrations to measure the stability.

B. We might develop two parallel versions of the same test and correlate the results.

C. Here we are interested in homogeneity of the items. Even and odd or randomly selected half may be used with the Spearman-Brown formula. The KR20 and Cronbach's alpha have better overall utility for multi-item scales.

D. The measure of content validity is largely judgmental. Using the research question hierarchy to organize the topic is one good way to try to include all aspects of the topic in the instrument. It is probably desirable to use a panel of judges to determine whether the content coverage in an instrument is adequate.

E. Good criterion-based validity is difficult to show since there are no clear pragmatic measures of course quality. If the instrument predicts how students vote in a "quality of course" poll, or if it predicts how faculty would rate the courses as to quality then it has predictive validity.

F. Construct validity requires that the results of the measurement compare well with other measures which purport to indicate course quality. For example, we would expect high quality courses to be particularly popular with academically strong students and less popular with weak students. Entirely different methods of attempting to evaluate courses (e.g., accreditation agency evaluation, a faculty poll, recognition of the quality of the course from syllabus analysis by experts, and the like) should all correlate well with the results from using the instrument. If these results do correlate well with our results we would have an example of convergent validity, a subtype of construct validity.

Chapter 6   Measurement

7.   This is the book by Robert Levering, Milton Moskowitz, and Michael Katz, *The 100 Best Companies to Work for in America*. They use the following five dimensions by which to measure the companies: pay, benefits, job security, chance to move up, and ambience.

8.   A. There are many concepts and constructs which might be suggested and operationalized here, but for purposes of illustration we restrict the discussion to two definitions: full-time student and student morale.

B. Full-time students will be defined as those who are taking at least 12 semester credit hours of work and are studying either for a bachelor's or a graduate degree. Morale may be divided into three major dimensions: academic, living conditions, and social life.

C. For measuring student status we classify all students as full-time students if they report when asked, that they are currently registered for at least 12 semester hours study and are working for a degree. For measuring morale we develop four statements concerning each of the three morale dimensions and ask students to show their degree of agreement with these statements on a 1 to 5 agreement scale. (How to develop and choose these scale items will be discussed in Chapter 7).

D. The simplest way might be to sum the answers to the four items and average for each of the three dimensions. These can, in turn, be combined in the same way to secure an overall index. In some cases we might wish to use a weighting system in compiling the index.

E. Reliability can be determined by using several versions of the scales to determine morale and calculating coefficient alpha. We might also administer the scales several times over a short period of time to the same students to determine if they give stable results. We can test for validity by looking for other indicators of a person's morale. We might, for example, talk with friends of the students or query professors, advisors, or parents.

True - False Questions

T   1) Researchers cannot measure objects or properties of objects. They measure indicants of the properties of objects.

F   2) Interval scales indicate no order or distance relationship.

T   3) Some purists argue that the use of nominal scales does not qualify as true measurement.

T   4) The use of an ordinal scale implies a statement of "greater than" or "less than" without our being able to state how much greater or less.

F   5) The appropriate measure of central tendency for both nominal and ordinal scales is the median.

Chapter 6 — Measurement

F 6) Researchers in the behavioral sciences agree that parametric significance tests are appropriate with ordinal measures.

T 7) The arithmetic mean is the proper measure of central tendency for an interval scale.

F 8) Centigrade and Fahrenheit temperature scales are good examples of ordinal scales.

T 9) The question of scale type affects both the interpretation of results and the form of statistical analysis which may be used.

T 10) Ratio scales incorporate all the powers of interval scales, plus the concepts of absolute zero.

F 11) Only with ratio scales can the standard deviation be used as the measure of dispersion.

T 12) The four major sources of measurement error are the respondent, the situation, the measurer, and the measurement instrument.

T 13) Measurement error can be classified as either random or systematic.

F 14) The number of years the respondent has been in school receiving an education is an example of an interval scale.

F 15) Brand names of televisions sold is an example of an ordinal scale.

F 16) When suffering from transient factors such as fatigue, boredom, or anxiety about some other matter, the respondent's ability to respond accurately and fully is limited. This is an example of situational factors acting as a source of study error.

T 17) Poor sampling of the universe of items of concern is one major way in which the measurement instrument can distort a research study.

F 18) There are three major considerations we should use in evaluating a measurement tool: validity, reliability, and stability.

T 19) The external validity of research findings refers to their generalizability across persons, settings, and times.

T 20) Internal validity is the extent to which differences found with a measuring tool reflect true differences among those being tested.

F 21) There are basically three types of internal validity: content, concept, and construct.

Chapter 6 — Measurement

T 22) The extent to which a measuring instrument provides adequate coverage of the topic under study is a measure of content validity.

T 23) Predictive and concurrent validity differ primarily in a time perspective.

T 24) Construct validity of a measuring instrument can be inferred if the measurements on the devised scale correlate in a predicted way to an associated set of propositions.

F 25) Reliability is a necessary and sufficient condition for validity.

T 26) Reliability is concerned with estimates of the degree to which a measurement is free of random or unstable error.

F 27) A measure that has been used many times and has always produced similar results is valid.

T 28) A measure is said to be stable if we can secure consistent results with repeated measurements with the same instrument on the same individual.

T 29) One perspective on reliability is equivalence. It is concerned with variations at one point in time among observers and samples of items.

T 30) A valid measure is reliable.

T 31) Reliability and validity refer to the scientific requirements of a project while practicality refers to the project's economy, convenience and interpretability.

T 32) Researchers often must make a trade-off between increased validity and practicality.

Multiple Choice Questions

1. In the most literal sense what does one "measure"?
   A) Objects
   B) Properties
   C) Things
 * D) Indicants

2. For one of the following types of scales the mode is the most appropriate measure of central tendency which technically should be used.
   A) Ordinal
   B) Ratio
   C) Interval
 * D) Nominal

Chapter 6 — Measurement

3. In order to improve our measurement of worker attitudes we devise a 20 item attitude scale. We then divide the 20 items randomly into two scales with 10 items in each and administer these two scales to a group of people. This is an example of:
   A) Concurrent validity testing
   B) Construct validity testing
   C) Stability testing
   * D) Equivalence testing

4. A measurement instrument can distort research results in several ways. One of the most important of these is:
   A) The interviewer distorts responses by recording.
   * B) There is a poor sampling of the universe of content.
   C) There is a danger that a second person will distort results
   D) None of these
   E) More than one of these

5. One type of scale is defined as having "both order and distance, but no unique origin." Which is it?
   A) Nominal
   B) Ratio
   * C) Interval
   D) Ordinal

6. Which of the following describes a form of criterion related validity?
   A) Face validity
   * B) Concurrent validity
   C) Content validity
   D) Construct validity

7. If we use a scale setting up 5 categories of ethnic origins what type of scale would this represent?
   * A) Nominal
   B) Ratio
   C) Interval
   D) Ordinal

8. Which of the following is a hierarchical listing of measurement scales in terms of increasing power?
   A) Nominal, interval, ordinal, ratio
   B) Ordinal, nominal, ratio, interval
   * C) Nominal, ordinal, interval, ratio
   D) Nominal, ordinal, ratio, interval
   E) None of these

Chapter 6 — Measurement

9. Which of the following statements best expresses the relationship between reliability and validity?
A) A measurement can be valid and not reliable.
* B) A measurement can be reliable and not valid.
C) A reliable measure is relatively free from systematic error, while a valid measure is free of random error.
D) Of the two, the more powerful measurement concept is reliability.

10. Three common forms of reliability are:
A) Accuracy, precision, stability
B) Accuracy, stability, equivalence
C) Equivalence, precision, stability
* D) Stability, equivalence, internal consistency

11. Measurement should also meet the test of practicality. Practicality is typically defined in terms of:
A) Economy, accuracy, and interpretability
* B) Convenience, economy, and interpretability
C) Economy, consistency, and interpretability
D) Convenience, consistency, and interpretability
E) Convenience, economy, and consistency

12. In forming a measure of public speaking competence we decide to look for 3 things: voice presentation, diction and language use, and physical presentation. Which of the steps in the process of measurement tools development are represented above?
* A) Concept development
B) Dimension specification
C) Selection of observable indicators
D) Combination of indicators into an index.

CHAPTER 7

SCALING DESIGN

This chapter has two primary learning objectives. The first is to understand the nature of scales and the scaling process. Included is the presentation of a scaling classification system using six approaches. Two of these approaches (response methods and scale construction techniques) form the basic organization structure for the chapter. The second set of objectives is for the student to learn the major scale construction techniques, to be able to point out their strengths and weaknesses, to know when they should be used, and to be able to explain how they should be constructed.

For additional material on the various unidimensional scaling methods both the Edwards and Kerlinger books are excellent. The Miller book has a large collection of existing scales that have been developed for social and business research. Usually the background of the scale is given along with information on validity and reliability. The Sage Publications quantitative analysis series contains several fine monographs on various multidimensional techniques.

Class Discussion Suggestions

The topic of scaling can easily take two class sessions if much attention is given to working with the more complex unidimensional scales, or if the instructor wishes to carry the discussion of multidimensional scaling beyond the treatment given in this chapter.

1. If limited time is allocated to this topic most of it should probably be spent discussing scale types and the most common forms of scaling and how they are carried out. For example, questions 1, 2, 3, 5, and 6 at the end of the chapter all lend themselves to discussing the basics. Thus, the distinction and comparison of rating vs. ranking scales, Likert vs. differential scales, and unidimensional vs. multidimensional scales can be covered. A class exercise, which uses a Semantic Differential scale, appeals to students and has good integration potential. The classic semantic differential scale is useful because many students are skeptical that pairs of adjectives, such as "heavy-light" will apply to a variety of concepts.

2. If additional time is available the material in this chapter lends itself to exercises in class which illustrate the construction and use of scales. Such a demonstration might use discussion question 7 on Likert scales or the one shown in Exhibit 7-1. Another exercise with the semantic differential scale which has consistently given interesting results in class has been to ask students to complete such a scale for the subject "cigarette smoking." A person's scale position on this topic is generally a pretty good predictor of whether that person is a smoker or not. An SD scale might be also used to evaluate well known political figures.

Chapter 7 *Scaling Design*

Exhibit 7 - 1 In - Class Scaling Exercise

Instructors often want a hands-on exercise that brings the details of the chapter together with a practical experience. Semantic Differential scales allow students to examine a scaling application using a topic familiar to them (the attitude object can be their *MBA program,* current class or other topic of your choice). Likert, graphic, or other rating scales typically require more preparation or item analysis work than you can spare for a brief in-class illustration. Although SDs may not be frequently used in general business research, they allow a good conceptual transition to multidimensional scales for instructors with advanced students.

Student Instructions:

1. Using the semantic differential scale below, record your impressions of your "current educational program" by placing a small "X" on each adjective continuum.
2. Score your responses by assigning a 7 to the positive end of each continua and a 1 to the negative adjective end. Note that some scales are reversed.
3. Which of the adjective pairs are evaluative? potency? activity?

Instructors may wish to provide a scoring key on the board after the ratings are made: 7s are good, strong, active, complete, fast, hot, meaningful, and heavy.

Sample scale form:

```
      good  __:__:__:__:__:__:__  bad
      weak  __:__:__:__:__:__:__  strong
    active  __:__:__:__:__:__:__  passive
  complete  __:__:__:__:__:__:__  incomplete
      fast  __:__:__:__:__:__:__  slow
      cold  __:__:__:__:__:__:__  hot
meaningful  __:__:__:__:__:__:__  meaningless
     heavy  __:__:__:__:__:__:__  light
```

Answer to item 3 of student instructions:

evaluation	activity	potency
good-bad	active-passive	strong-weak
complete-incomplete	fast-slow	heavy-light
meaningful-meaningless	cold-hot	

Instructor: show group scores in a scatterplot on the blackboard. Students submit scores, anonymously, on a scrap of paper. It is interesting to compute sub-scores for evaluation, activity, and potency and interpret them.

Optional: If time permits, compare the results for the "ideal program" to the previous findings. Examine the dimensions that contribute most to the differences.

Chapter 7 — *Scaling Design*

Answers to Chapter Questions

1. A. Rating scales have the advantages of requiring less time, being interesting to use, and having a wider range of application than ranking methods. They can also be used with a large number of properties or variables. The major disadvantage of rating scales is that they assume that a person can and will make good judgments. The human element in rating scales makes the scale subject to the common errors of leniency, central tendency, and the halo effect. These errors are discussed individually in the section entitled "Problems in Using Rating Scales." Ranking scales do not have the wide application of rating scales nor can they be used with a large number of properties or variables. However, ranking scales permit the respondent to express his/her attitude in an unambiguous manner. In addition, there is a body of opinion which holds that interval scales can be developed from ranking comparisons.

   B. Likert scales are relatively easy to develop compared to differential scales. They are most useful when it is possible to compare the person's score with a distribution of scores from some well defined group. If constructed in the classical manner, each item that is included in the scale has met an empirical test for discriminating ability. Since respondents answer each item it is probably more reliable than a differential scale in which only a few items are chosen. Also, it is easy to use this scale both in respondent-centered and stimulus-centered studies.

   The disadvantage of the Likert scale is that a total score can be secured by a wide variety of answer patterns, thus there are questions as to the meaning of the total score.

   Aside from the relative merits and demerits of differential scales that can be inferred from the above comments, a couple of statements are in order regarding differential scales. The cost and effort required to construct differential scales has limited their use. Also, this approach has been criticized on the grounds that the values assigned to various statements by the judges may reflect their own attitudes and thus be biased.

   C. Unidimensional scales are usually easy to construct and are not difficult to understand. Conceptually, however, there is a question of whether we are truly measuring a single dimension. The Guttman technique is one effort made to assure that a so-called unidimensional scale is actually unidimensional. Multidimensional scales are a way of recognizing that many concepts are not characterized by a single dimension. However, these techniques are difficult to use and to understand. The classical SD scale is the first major multidimensional form which has received much attention. Currently there are many developments in multidimensional scaling using computer based procedures which are attracting widespread interest, especially in marketing research.

2. A. The *Thurstone scale* would be a set of statements about the economic system. Each statement would have been rated as to its degree of favorable-

ness along some assumed dimension. For example, the statement, "The U.S. economic system is generally superior to the systems found in other countries," might be presented among a list of 10 statements. This one might have been appraised as a "7.6" on a scale of 1 to 10. The respondent would be expected to select one or more statements with which he agrees.

B. A *Likert scale* would consist of a series of statements about the economic system, each with a 5 point scale (may also be 3 or 7 point) to express degree of agreement or disagreement. If the classical Likert approach is used the items on the scale would have been chosen by a pretest using an item analysis approach.

C. A *semantic differential scale* of the classical type would use a set of bipolar adjective scales with the subject being something like "U.S. economic system." Similar scales might be used for other subjects such as the "Japanese economic system." An ad hoc SD scale would be similar to that shown in Figure 7-4 of the text, except that the adjective pairs would be chosen to fit the subject. These adjective pairs are normally chosen on an arbitrary basis.

D. A *scalogram* would involve a limited number of statements of varying degrees of favorableness that have been chosen through the traditional Guttman techniques. The statement shown in the Thurstone example might well be one of these statements.

E. The most common form of *multidimensional scaling* is non-metric in nature and one form of it involves the comparison of a number of items. These comparisons are then mathematically manipulated to develop a map of meaning similarities involving two or more dimensions. In this example we might compare the economic systems of, say, the nine leading nations of the world and secure a set of relationships similar to those illustrated in the multidimensional scaling section in Chapter 17.

3. The five methods of scale construction are arbitrary, consensus, item analysis, cumulative, and factor sales. The sixth or "other" category in the text refers to specialized measurement devices. The scales differ with respect to the manner in which the scale items are selected.

Arbitrary scales are constructed by collecting a number of items which the researcher believes to be unambiguous and appropriate to a given topic. Some of the items are selected to be included in the instrument, but no testing of the relevance of each item is conducted.

In the *consensus scaling* approach we use a panel of judges to select items. The panel determines
    1) whether the item belongs in the topic area.
    2) its ambiguity, and
    3) the level of attitude that the scale item represents.

In the *item analysis* procedure, each particular item is evaluated on the basis of how well it discriminates between those persons whose total scores for all items are high and those those scores are low. It is inferred that each item that discriminates well between high and low scorers has met an empirical test for discriminating ability.

Cumulative scales are chosen on the basis of their conforming to some ranking of items with ascending and descending discriminating power.

Finally, *factor scales* may be constructed on the basis of intercorrelation of items that indicate that a common factor accounts for the relationships between items. Factor scales attempt to deal with two problems which are not treated by the other scale construction techniques. They are
    1) how to deal more adequately with the universe of content which is multidimensional, and
    2) how to uncover underlying (latent) dimensions which have not been identified.

These differences are of real importance, because they distinguish between the relative ability of each scale to explain that what it purports to explain. The greater the amount of confidence that the researcher can have as to the appropriateness of the items in the scale, the greater the trust he/she can place in his/her findings.

4.   A.

	Koak	Zip	Pabze	Mr. Peepers
Koak	X	50	115	35
Zip	150	X	160	70
Pabze	85	40	X	45
Mr. Peepers	165	130	155	X
TOTAL	400	220	430	150
RANK ORDER	2	3	1	4

    B.

	Koak	Zip	Pabze	Mr. Peepers
M_p	.625	.40	.662	.312
Z_j	.32	-.254	.42	-.49
R_j	.81	.24	.91	.00

5.   A. These choices may be criticized because there is no way for a respondent to express an "undecided" response or a "don't know" response.

    B. A widely used set of response choices and generally acceptable. One problem is the operational definition of the various terms. What is "fair" to one may be "good" to another when both are actually making the same judgment.

C. This assumes that the average must fall between good and fair, while it might be that average should be elsewhere.

D. The central choice of "neither agree nor disagree" does not adequately reflect the situation which might be called "uncertain" or "indifferent."

6. A student exercise. Differences among students will result about which we can only conjecture. Carelessness in reading and interpretation is a factor. Different meanings and connotations will be attached to various words and statements. Various respondents will have different biases or feelings about some of the points made or institutions mentioned.

7.
A. SD = 5
B. SA = 5
C. SA = 5
D. SD = 5
E. SA = 5
F. SD = 5

The responses for each person answering could be totaled to give a measure of each person's attitude toward the program. The purpose would be to measure the attitudes of the respondents for their "total attitude." On the other hand each statement could be tallied separately to determine how the program scores on each point. In this case the emphasis is on different perceptions of the program rather than attitudes of different students toward the program.

8. In the classical SD scale we use the adjective pairs that the research has indicated to express evaluation and other dimensions. In an ad hoc scale we choose adjective pairs which are specifically descriptive of the subject we are studying. The classical scale allows us to tap latent attitudes and relate our findings to the theory which has been developed for this scaling approach. Ad hoc scales allow us to secure manifest responses based on how subjects respond to the dimensions listed. We cannot relate the results to SD theory nor ascertain latent meanings without further factor analysis.

True - False Questions

T   1) Scales are often designed to use the respondents as judges of the objects or stimuli presented to them.

F   2) Comparative scales are used when the respondent's score some object without direct reference to other objects.

F   3) Studies have shown that five-point scales give optimum sensitivity of measurement.

Chapter 7 — Scaling Design

T   4) With a comparative rating scale, the respondent rates the subject against some experience standard.

F   5) Three of the most common tendencies to constant error for any respondent are leniency, central tendency, and the echo effect.

T   6) Raters' reluctance to give extreme judgments accounts for the error of central tendency.

F   7) The systematic bias that the rater introduces by carrying over a generalized impression of the subject from one rating to another is called the learning factor.

T   8) The "Method of Paired Comparisons" is a technique with which the respondent can express attitudes in an unambiguous manner by making a choice between two objects.

T   9) Using the "composite-standard method" we can develop an interval scale from paired comparisons data.

T   10) The Likert scale approach is also identified with the item analysis approach.

T   11) Arbitrary scales can be designed to be highly specific to the case and content of interest.

T   12) Item Analysis relies upon the analysis of actual responses to the items as the basis for determining item acceptability.

F   13) A summated scale consists of a number of statements which express either a favorable or unfavorable attitude toward the object of interest. The respondent is asked to rank the statements by the degree of favorableness.

F   14) The Likert scale is easy to construct but has never become popular among researchers.

T   15) In the development of a Likert scale, test items are classified *a priori* as favorable or unfavorable.

T   16) Summated scales are most useful when it is possible to compare the respondent's score with a distribution of scores from some well defined group.

F   17) The Guttman scalogram is a summated scale.

F   18) A scale is said to be unidimensional if the responses fall into a pattern in which endorsement of the item reflecting the extreme position results in rejecting all items which are less extreme.

Chapter 7 Scaling Design

T 19) The semantic differential scale is a method which attempts to measure the psychological meanings of an object to an individual.

F 20) The Thurstone approach is that which is used for the specific purpose of developing a unidimensional scale.

F 21) Researchers utilizing the semantic differential scale have concluded that "semantic space" is unidimensional rather than multidimensional.

T 22) The semantic differential scale is an efficient and easy way to secure attitudes from a large sample.

T 23) Factor scales are particularly useful in uncovering latent attitude dimensions.

Multiple Choice Questions

1. In classical SD scaling, Suci and his associates found three latent psychological meaning factors which emerged repeatedly in studies. Which of these normally is the most important in terms of extractable variance?
   A) Activity
   B) Dynamism
   * C) Evaluation
   D) Potency or power

2. Six different approaches were suggested by which to classify scales into various types. Of these, which is used as the primary way to organize the discussion in the chapter?
   A) Degree of preference
   B) Study objective
   C) Scale properties
   D) Number of dimensions
   * E) Scale construction methods

3. Which of the following is not a form of scale as classified by the method of scale construction?
   A) Consensus
   * B) Rating
   C) Cumulative
   D) Factor

4. Which of the following scales is classed as a ranking scale?
   * A) Method of paired comparisons
   B) Consequences scale
   C) Graphic scale
   D) Cumulative scale

Chapter 7 Scaling Design

5. One of the problems in using rating scales is that their use often results in a halo effect. This effect describes:
   A) The tendency for certain persons to be easy raters
   B) The tendency for raters to be reluctant to give extreme judgments
   * C) The tendency to give a subject the same score on different scale items
   D) None of the above

6. A major problem with using the method of paired comparison is that
   A) People have difficulty understanding the method when it is used with them.
   * B) If there are many stimuli to judge the method becomes tedious
   C) There is a strong risk of halo effect
   D) The results can not be converted into interval scale results

7. The composite-standard type of scale construction is an effort to
   * A) Convert an ordinal scale into an interval scale
   B) Develop a cumulative scale
   C) Simplify scale construction
   D) Make rating scales more accurate

8. The quality of an arbitrary scale depends largely upon
   A) The form of the scale
   B) Whether it can be viewed as an ordinal scale
   * C) The subjective logic underlying the scale
   D) Whether it is a rating or ranking scale

9. Which of the following is generally viewed as being a consensus scale?
   * A) Thurstone differential
   B) Likert
   C) Guttman
   D) Semantic

10. The Thurstone Differential scale
    A) Is usually developed by using the item analysis technique
    B) Usually is a 5 point scale
    C) Is one of the easiest to construct
    * D) Is claimed to be an interval scale

11. The Likert type scale
    A) Is often developed by the consensus method
    B) Provides less data than does the Thurstone scale
    C) Is claimed to be an interval scale by its advocates
    * D) Is easy to use both in respondent-centered and stimulus-centered studies

12. Factor scales have been developed in an effort to
    A) Deal more adequately with a multidimensional universe of content
    B) Uncover latent dimensions in attitudes
    C) Develop unidimensional scales
    * D) Do two of the above

13. A scaling approach using a seven point scale and pairs of bipolar adjectives is known as a
   A) Semantic Differential scale
   B) Guttman Scalogram
   C) Comparative Judgment scale
   D) Likert type scale

CHAPTER 8

SAMPLING DESIGN

This chapter has four learning objectives. The first objective answers the question: what is sampling? Included are: why is it useful, what are the various types of sampling design, and what are the strengths and weaknesses of each design? The second objective is to teach the student to design a simple random sample including determination of the appropriate sample size. The third objective is to provide a relatively nontechnical introduction to complex probability sampling, particularly for the instructor who wishes to treat the more complex designs. Fourth, the student should be aware of the widespread use of nonprobability samples, their types, and usefulness -- despite our reservations about bias and lack of precision. For more depth the Kish book is recommended. There is also good coverage in the other suggested readings.

Class Discussion Suggestions

Many students find the entire subject of sampling to be a mystery, even after they have had a course in statistics. Therefore, more than the normal amount of explanation and reinforcement as needed for this topic. While students may seem to grasp the individual details of the discussion on sampling, they are often at a loss when asked to design a simple random sample for some real-life situation. The vignette and Close-Up are designed to illustrate that skill. Three hours of class time can be comfortably used to discuss the various topics in this chapter and to work the problems at the end of the chapter.

1. While we can intuitively understand that a sample is easier and cheaper to take than a census, it is useful to stress the points that (a) sampling is acceptable only when it adequately reflects the population from which it is drawn, and that (b) no sample is a perfect representation of its population.

The idea of sampling is based on two concepts. When you take a sample some of the observations understate the value you are trying to estimate but their effect will be balanced out by other observations which overstate the value. The result is to give you a reasonably good estimate of the population parameter unless something causes one side to outweigh the other. This concerns sample *accuracy* and is defined as the degree to which systematic error is absent from the sample. The best way to assure accuracy is through random probability sampling.

The second concept, sample *precision*, is concerned with the random fluctuations that occur as one draws the members of the sample. This also is error but is quite separate from the sample accuracy problem. Precision concerns whether the sample is large enough to limit the effects of random error. Accuracy is concerned that systematic bias is curbed regardless of sample size.

It may help at this point also to note that many samples in business research are not probability samples and why this is so (see the section on Nonprobability

Chapter 8 — Sampling Design

Sampling).

2. In discussing probability sampling one might well begin with the six step process which is presented in the section, Steps in Sampling Design, page 203. The major task is to assure that the students actually understand the basic decisions by which one determines the size of a simple random sample. Since no sample fully reflects a population, the question we face in determining sample size is the degree of precision that we want (recall that drawing a random sample addresses the accuracy question, so the problem left is to determine what precision to seek).

The most difficult points to get across concern the concepts of interval range and significance or confidence levels. The section entitled Sampling Concepts is a good vehicle for this task, particularly Figures 8-1 and 8-2. You may wish to bring out the following:

A. The point estimate of the population parameter is made by a simple sample statistic (X- bar).

B. While we actually take only one sample, the theory of probability sampling is based on the idea that we can take an infinite number of samples (with replacement) and calculate an arithmetic mean or other statistic for each sample. Each of these sample means is a separate point estimate of the population parameter. When we have the results from a number of such samples we can develop the distribution shown in Part B of Figure 8-2. This distribution has two important characteristics: (1) the distribution tends to be normal even if the basic population is not normal; and, (2) the width or dispersion of this distribution is a function of two factors, the size of the sample drawn, and the variance or dispersion in the population. The dispersion of this distribution of sample statistics is measured by the standard error, computed by the following equation:

$$\sigma_{\bar{X}} = \frac{\sigma}{\sqrt{n}}$$

where:

$\sigma_{\bar{X}}$ = standard error of the mean

σ = standard deviation of the population

n = size of the sample

The fact is, however, we do not know and never can know the standard deviation of the population, but we estimate it by the standard deviation of the sample we have drawn.
This results in a revision of the above equation to give:

$$\sigma_{\bar{X}} = \frac{s}{\sqrt{n-1}}$$

where:
s = standard deviation of the sample.

C. While a single sample statistic, such as the arithmetic mean, is the best

Chapter 8 Sampling Design

single point estimate it would only be by chance that it hits the true population mean. However, the sample means would be distributed around the population value as shown in Part B of Figure 8-2, and we can use a measure of their dispersion (the standard error) to stake out an interval within which the population mean almost surely falls. We do this by projecting the standard error points of the distribution in Part A of Figure 8-2.

In practice we reverse the process by first setting an interval estimate within which we wish to find the population value, and then work back to calculate the sample size needed to provide such an interval estimate (standard error). We do this by expressing our desired interval estimate in two ways:

1. In terms of units, such as dollars, in which we might express the desired interval, estimate as a plus or minus $1.50. This would indicate that if the population mean is actually $8.00, the sample mean which we would get should be between $6.50 and $9.50.

2. We also state the interval estimate in terms of standard error units, say, we wish a sample large enough that the standard error of the mean is $1.50. This would mean that we could be confident that, two times out of three, the sample mean would fall within the range $6.50 - $9.50. If we desired to have a higher degree of confidence, say two standard errors (95.45%), we would want a plus or minus two standard errors to encompass the range of plus or minus $1.50.

One standard error would therefore equal $ .75. With this standard error value, plus an estimate of the standard deviation of the sample, we can calculate the size of sample required. Another way to handle this discussion is to use problems 3, 4, 6, and 8 at the end of the chapter.

It is probably more desirable to go through the sample size calculation process using the assumption of an infinite population before introducing the finite population adjustment factor. Problem 7 at the end of the chapter is a good vehicle for introducing this new concept.

3. At a minimum it is desirable to introduce the concepts of complex sampling by discussing the question of stratification and simple clustering. If the instructor wishes to go further, the examples in Kish or Kalton can be used to discuss when stratification is called for, why disproportionate sampling is technically superior to proportionate sampling, how to go about allocating a sample size among strata, and finally how to determine the relative sample efficiency of simple random sampling vs. stratification vs. clustering.

Answers to Chapter Questions

1.   A. A *parameter* is a value of a population, while a *statistic* is a similar value based on sample data. For example, the population mean is a parameter, while a sample mean is a statistic.

       B. A *population* is the total collection of people, cases, or other elements which we define and about which we wish to make inferences. The *sample frame* is the actual pool from which we draw our sample. Ideally it is the same as the population but it often differs due to practical considerations of information availability.

C. *Unrestricted sampling* occurs when sample elements are selected individually and directly from the population at large. *Restricted sampling* occurs when additional controls are placed on the process of element selection.

D. The *standard deviation* is a measure of dispersion of a distribution. When the standard deviation is calculated for a distribution of sample statistics it is known as a *standard error*. For example, the standard deviation of the distribution of sample means is known as the standard error of the mean.

E. *Simple random sampling* is that form of probability sampling which is unrestricted and in which each member of the population has an equal chance of being selected. *Complex random sampling* is a probability sampling procedure in which selection of elements is restricted.

F. *Convenience sampling* is nonprobability in nature: element selection is unrestricted and carried out usually on the basis of convenience alone. *Purposive sampling* is also nonprobability in nature, but involves a deliberate attempt to secure a sample that conforms to some determined criteria.

G. *Sample accuracy* refers to the degree to which bias is absent from the sample. An accurate sample has a balance of underestimates and overestimates among the sample members. *Precision,* on the other hand, refers to the degree to which random error variance is estimated to exist in that sample.

H. *Systematic variance* is that variance due to inaccurate sampling and is indicated by a bias in sample results. *Error variance* refers to the lack of precision in a sample. It is generally thought of as that variance which remains after all systematic variance is accounted for.

I. *Variables data parameters* are normally computed from ratio or interval scale data. Examples are age, length, dollars, scores, etc. The most common measures of variables data are the arithmetic mean and the standard deviation. *Attributes data parameters* are expressed in numbers or proportions of the population or sample which have or do not have certain characteristics. They are necessary for nominal data and are widely used for other scales. The most frequently used measure of attributes is the percentage.

J. The mean of the sample is the *point estimate* and the best predictor of the unknown population mean. The *interval estimate* brackets the point estimate of the population mean and reveals the range wherein any sample mean will fall given a specified level of confidence.

Chapter 8   *Sampling Design*

     K. A *proportionate* sample, particularly within the context of stratified sampling, is one where each stratum is proportionate to its share of the total population. *Disproportionate samples* are departures from proportionate relationships among the strata.

2.   A. If one is interested in assuring maximum precision and accuracy in a sample then probability sampling is the choice. With it we can minimize biases and estimate, in statistical terms, how much random error there is likely to be.

Nonprobability sampling is more appropriate when probability sampling is not feasible, when we do not need a true cross section of population, or when time and money costs required for probability sampling are too high to be justified.

B. A simple random sample is appropriate when there is a complete population list available and there appears to be no justification, either statistically or economically, for stratifying or clustering.

A stratified random sample is recommended when the researcher desires to:
    1. Increase a sample's statistical efficiency,
    2. provide for separate analysis of sub-populations, or
    3. enable different research methods and procedures to be used in various strata.

Cluster sampling is recommended when economic efficiency is a major consideration, i.e., there is some opportunity to reduce costs by sampling in clusters.

C. The finite population adjustment is of value when the sample size required to give a certain degree of precision exceeds about 5 per cent of the population size. The net effect is to reduce the size of sample needed to give the desired degree of precision.

D. A disproportionate stratified sampling design (as contrasted to the proportionate design) is warranted when there is evidence to indicate that within stratum variances differ widely and the costs of sampling within these various strata also differ.

3.   You must determine the size of the acceptable interval range and the degree of confidence you wish to have that the population parameter will be within that range.

4.   This is an exercise in the reading and interpretation of the table of the proportion of area under the normal curve (Table F-1).

    A. Approximately 15.87%, or the area beyond 6.3 + 1s.

Chapter 8   Sampling Design

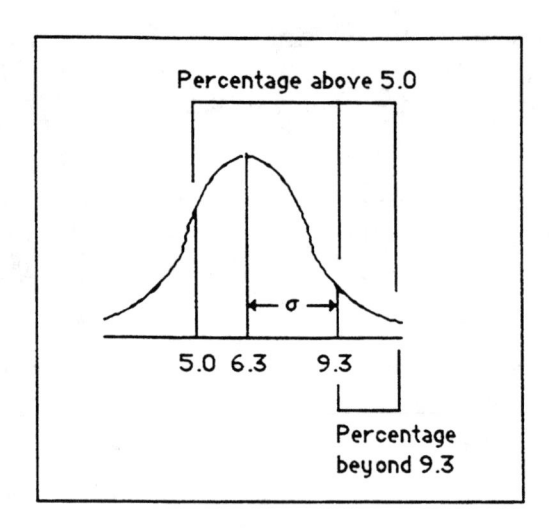

[Figure: Normal distribution curve with "Percentage above 5.0" bracket spanning from 5.0, with mean at 6.3, and σ extending to 9.3. "Percentage beyond 9.3" marked on right tail.]

B. Approximately 66.76%, 6.3 - 5.0 = 1.3

$$z = \frac{1.3}{3.0} = .4333 \, s$$

Entering Table F-1 and interpolating between Z = .43 and .44 we find that .3324 of the lower half of the distribution extends beyond (below) .4333 s. Thus the percent of cases above 5.0 consists of:

- all cases in top half of distribution   = .5000
- plus a portion of bottom half   = .1676
  (.5000-.1324 = .1676)

  Total   .6676

5. A quota sample is appropriate here. Interview in a variety of locations around campus at different times to increase the chances of getting a representative cross-section on variables other than sex and class. Since data are available by sex and class, simultaneously, we would set interview quotas for males and females, by class, in proportion to the importance of each in the total undergraduate student body.

6. In this problem a small sample is used to provide the estimate of the population dispersion (s = 10). In addition, we must make subjective decisions about the size of interval estimate we wish, and the degree of confidence of 95% (a = .05) and an interval estimate of $ .50. Then we need a sample of 1539.

$$\$.50 = 1.96 \, \sigma_{\bar{x}}$$

$$\sigma_{\bar{x}} = .255 = \frac{10}{\sqrt{n-1}}$$

$$n = 1539$$

7. The sample size estimate should be adjusted for the fact that there is a finite population of 2,500. With this adjustment we reduce the needed size of sample from 1539 to 953.

$$.255 = \left(\frac{10}{\sqrt{n-1}}\right) * \sqrt{\frac{2500-n}{2500-1}}$$

$$n = 953$$

8. This problem involves attributes data. The interval estimate of $\pm 5\%$ is given but we need to set a degree of confidence. Assume a roughly 90% degree of confidence (1.65 standard errors). Also needed is a measure of population dispersion. We must either make such an estimate or set the estimate at a pq ratio of .25. This represents the largest possible percentage value for dispersion (p = q = .5). With this dispersion estimate we calculate the maximum size sample needed. The answer in this case is 279.

$$1.65 \, s_P = .05$$

$$\sigma_P = .03 = \sqrt{\frac{.25}{n-1}}$$

$$n = 279$$

True - False Questions

T 1) The basic idea in sampling is that the analysis of some of the elements in a population provides useful information on the population as a whole.

T 2) The "population" is defined by whatever dimensions the researcher's objective dictates.

F 3) A census always provides improved accuracy over a sample, but samples are used more often due to their lower cost.

F 4) If a sample is accurate then by definition it has precision.

F 5) The smaller the standard error of estimate, the higher is the accuracy of the sample.

T 6) Accuracy and precision are the two indicators of a representative sample.

T 7) Probability sampling is based on the concept of random selection, meaning that each population element is given a known nonzero chance of selection.

F 8) When each sample element is drawn individually from the population at large, it is known as a systematic sample.

Chapter 8 — Sampling Design

T   9) A simple random sample is the special case in which each population element has an equal chance of being selected into the sample.

T   10) Typically, the population of interest is apparent from the management problem and the research objectives.

F   11) The sampling frame is the geographic location and setting where the sample is actually drawn.

F   12) The use of the finite population adjustment equation in determining the size of a simple random sample typically results in a larger sample than when the infinite population equation is used.

T   13) The absolute number of people in a random sample is normally more significant than is the sample's size relative to the population size.

F   14) To determine the size sample that will make an acceptable representation of the population one needs only to set the desired size of the interval range around the estimated parameter, set the acceptable confidence level for the estimate, and then calculate the results.

T   15) Population size and variance are the two factors inherent in the population which affect the sample size needed to provide a given quality of representation.

F   16) The "dispersion of individual responses about the sample mean" refers to the standard error of the mean.

T   17) The standard error of the mean varies directly with the standard deviation of the population from which it is drawn.

T   18) The means of random samples drawn from a population are dispersed around the population mean in a distribution that is generally close to normal even if the population is not normal.

T   19) The degree of confidence and the desired interval of estimate are subjective decisions by the researcher when deciding on the size of random sample.

F   20) The sample size needed to give a representative picture of population members is independent of population dispersion.

T   21) With attributes data it is the proportion of the population that has a given attribute that is the measure of concern.

F   22) The standard error of the mean is the proper measure of dispersion for attributes data.

T   23) Sample size calculations typically assume an infinite population.

Chapter 8 — Sampling Design

F   24) Asymmetrical confidence regions occur when the distribution of sample means is not normally distributed.

T   25) In order to select a simple random sample the researcher needs a list which identifies each individual universe element.

T   26) A more efficient sample in a statistical sense is one which provides a given precision with a smaller sample size.

T   27) The researcher desires to choose a probability sample of 400 from a list of 20,000 homeowners. By drawing a random number between 1 and 50 the number 28 is chosen. Then starting with the 28th homeowner the researcher chooses every 50th homeowner. e.g., 28th, 78th., 128th., etc. This is an example of "systematic sampling."

T   28) "Stratified sampling" is possible when a population can be segregated into a number of mutually exclusive subpopulations.

F   29) Stratification is usually less efficient statistically than simple random sampling.

F   30) An area sample is an example of a stratified sample in which the areas correspond to the strata.

F   31) When the clusters in a cluster sample are internally homogeneous the sample has maximum statistical efficiency.

T   32) High statistical efficiency is achieved in cluster sampling when each cluster contains as many diverse element values as possible.

T   33) Nonprobability sampling is theoretically inferior to probability sampling but is often much more practical.

F   34) Purposive and convenience methods of sampling are used with the "Double Sampling" technique.

F   35) Proportionate stratified sampling typically is superior in statistical efficiency to disproportionate sampling.

F   36) Sampling frames cannot be larger than the population of concern.

Multiple Choice Questions

1. Sampling is often claimed to be superior in quality of results to taking a census. Which of the following is *not* a reason why this is so?
   * A) More certain of full representativeness in a sample.
   B) Better quality of interviewing in a sample.
   C) Lower cost and quicker execution in a sample.
   D) More thorough investigation of missing information in a sample.

Chapter 8　　　　　　　　　　　　　　　　　　　　　　　　　　　　Sampling Design

2. A good sample is one in which there is no bias from the sampling process. This is defined as
   A) Consistency
   * B) Accuracy
   C) Precision
   D) Reliability

3. Which of the following represents an unrestricted method of sample element selection?
   A) Systematic random sample
   B) Cluster random sample
   * C) Simple random sample
   D) Quota sample

4. The list of elements from which the sample is actually drawn is called the
   A) population
   B) universe
   C) parameter list
   * D) sample frame

5. Which of the following methods of probability sampling is usually most efficient in a statistical sense?
   A) Cluster sampling
   * B) Stratified sampling
   C) Simple random sampling
   D) Two stage sampling

6. In drawing a simple random sample, and determining how large a sample to take, which of the following factors is *not* considered?
   A) The estimated level of reliability
   B) The variance of the population or sample
   * C) The desired interval range
   D) The desired confidence level

7. The size of the interval estimate is measured in terms of which of the following measures of dispersion?
   A) Standard deviation of the sample.
   B) Variance of the sample.
   * C) Standard error of the sample mean or percentage.
   D) Coefficient of variation of the sample.

8. You plan to draw a sample of names from the city telephone directory for a survey and you would like for it to be a probability sample. Which of the following would usually be the best to use?
   A) Stratified sample
   B) Cluster sample
   C) Simple random sample
   * D) Systematic sample

Chapter 8 Sampling Design

9. You wish to design a simple sample from a national roster of club members and you have the following information:
    Total membership = 20,000
    Estimated population standard deviation = 25
    Desired degree of confidence = 1.5 sigma
    Desired interval range = 3
    Which of the following numbers is closest to the desired sample size?
    A) 10
    B) 70
    * C) 160
    D) 280

10. Which of the following statements about nonprobability samples is most true?
    A) Purposive samples are so biased that they seldom provide useful results.
    B) Convenience samples are generally as dependable as the other nonprobability sample types
    C) Quota samples, using precision controls, are about equal in quality to probability samples.
    * D) None of the above is true.

11. A stratified sample is of greatest statistical efficiency when
    A) The variances within strata are large.
    * B) The variances within strata are small.
    C) The sample is a significant portion of the population.
    D) The sample is large.

12. Suppose you wish to draw a simple random sample of a population of college students. You will ask them whether they favor allocating a portion of their student fees to a certain program. You want to have a sample large enough to be confident, at the two sigma level, that the sample will be within a ± 2% of the true figure. Approximately what size sample would you use?
    A) 312
    B) 625
    C) 1250
    * D) 2500

13. Suppose you wish to study consumption of coffee among 10,000 families and conclude you should use a clustering method with clusters of 8 families each. You study several such clusters and find that the standard deviation of the cluster means is 3 lbs. per year. Suppose you want to estimate population consumption within a plus or minus .4 lbs. at a two sigma level of confidence. Which of the following numbers is closest to the number of clusters you should use?
    A) 10
    B) 20
    C) 60
    * D) 230

CHAPTER 9

SECONDARY DATA SOURCES

There are three learning objectives for this chapter. The first objective is to convince the student that secondary sources of information are valuable for management research and are often the more economical than primary sources if effectively exploited. The second objective, a catalog of the major business oriented public data sources, is met by the sources listed within the chapter, in the notes and in the suggested readings. Appendix A, a supplemental effort for this objective, was originally developed by the staff of the Washington University Libraries and has been revised by Ms. Darlene Parrish, a university business reference librarian, and the senior author. Finally, an example for making an efficient search of secondary sources is presented in the Close-Up.

Class Discussion Suggestions

Generally, there is little need for lecturing on the topics in Chapter 9, but there is value in conducting a few exercises and drills. Many students, even graduate students and some professors, are not knowledgeable about the research tools of good university library. One class period is typically enough for discussing the materials in Chapter 9.

1. The Values of Secondary Data - The class session can be opened with a brief set of comments regarding the time, cost, and effort of using secondary data as well as pointing out that secondary data are sometimes all that is available. The point might also be made that secondary data sources are particularly useful at the exploratory stage of research study. To discuss these topics the instructor might wish to refer to chapter questions 1, 2, 3, and 6.

2. To achieve the second learning objective, understanding the depth and breadth of available sources, it is useful to provide actual exercises for the students. One good way is to hold a class session at the library. Enlist the aid of the librarian to demonstrate a CD-ROM search or online search and then collect reference works and make them available for the class in a separate room or area. Students can be asked to use the materials to answer certain questions which you pose to them. The following library search exercise has proved useful for this purpose. The parenthetical items in this exercise are resources which should be collected and available for students to examine.

An alternative might be to use discussion question 12 as a homework assignment. If you do this, it is still helpful to hold a class session in the library. The session could be devoted to a description of available source and reference materials (by the business librarian) and several trials with the computerized search and retrieval facilities (particularly CD-ROM and on-line databases).

Chapter 9 — Secondary Data Sources

Library Search Exercise.

1. Is there a recent bibliography on corporate mergers and acquisitions?
   (Bibliographic Index or CD-ROM *MLA International Bibliographies)*

2. Where can I find historical statistics on commodity futures prices?
   (Guide to U.S. Government Statistics or CD-ROM *CIS Statistical Masterfile)*

3. What is the name of the latest book by Richard Ofshe?
   (Cumulative Book Index or *Books in Print)*

4. What was last year's rate of unemployment among the 20-24 year age group?
   (Monthly Labor Review)

5. Has the U.S. Senate published any hearings on small business matters in the last year?
   Monthly Catalog or CD-ROM *CIS Congressional Masterfile)*

6. What is the name and address of the association for the peanut industry?
   (Encyclopedia of Associations)

7. Is there a U.S. magazine for the mortuary industry?
   (Ulrich's)

8. What is the nearest university that receives the *Journal of the Oil Chemist's Society* ?
   (Union List of Serials)

9. What was the most recently published monthly production figure for U.S. bituminous coal?
   (Survey of Current Business)

10. Who is the current president of RCA?
    (Dun & Bradstreet Reference Book of Corporate Management)

11. What universities have recently published anything on labor negotiations?
    (Index of Publications of Bureaus of Business and Economic Research)

12. How many establishments were there in 1972 in industry SIC 3498 - fabricated pipes and fittings?
    (U.S. Census of Manufacturers, publication MC72 (2) 34F)

13. What doctoral dissertations, if any, have recently been written on

consumer behavior?
(*American Doctoral Dissertations* , *Dissertation Abstracts Online*, or CD-ROM *UMI Dissertation Abstracts*)

14. What is the most recently reported quarterly GNP figure for the U.S. in constant dollars?
(*Business Conditions Digest* or *Survey of Current Business*)

15. What was the output of U.S. hosiery manufacturing last year?
(*Statistical Abstract*)

16. What types of information are available by census tracts?
(*U. S. Census of Population*, Census Tract volumes)

17. What are two or three important types of information that are available on a county basis, concerning U.S. manufacturing?
(*Census of Manufacturers*, state volume)

18. What is the projected level of U.S. population for 2000?
(*U. S. Census*, P-25 series, selected publications)

19. What are two or three important types of information available at a local level concerning retail trade in the U.S.?
(*Census of Retail Trade*, state volumes)

20. What is the total amount of outstanding installment credit debt in the U.S. last year?
(*Federal Reserve Bulletin*)

21. One area which is not fully covered in Chapter 9 is the vast amount of statistical information available in published form. One can develop a class exercise that uses statistical sources only. In such an exercise use the various *Censuses of Business, Population, Housing, Manufacturing,* and *Agriculture*, as well as current economic statistics from the *Survey of Current Business, Federal Reserve Bulletin,* and the *Monthly Labor Review.* Other publications such as the *County Business Patterns,* the various Census "p" bulletins, and other monthly industrial, foreign trade, and agriculture publications are also possibilities. In such an exercise the instructor may wish to specify specific information that the students should collect and report.

3. For the final learning objective, illustrating an effective procedure for approaching a topic, one may wish to discuss briefly the various sources of information and their applicability using the flow chart in Figure 9-1 of the text as a guide. Choose some topic of interest such as "the motivation of sales people," "the use of personal computers in management," or the "outlook for the U.S. steel industry in the 1990s." It may be enough to move through the flow chart citing various sources which are likely to be useful. One may go further and assign a bibliography search project as a homework assignment; an even more ambitious project is a secondary

Chapter 9   *Secondary Data Sources*

data source project as discussed earlier in this manual.

Answers to Chapter Questions

1. This might occur when the cost in time and money is too great that only secondary sources may be used. In some cases the costs might be so great as to be prohibitive. In other cases we can not gather the data, no matter how much money and time is spent, because we do not have access to the information. For example, raw data in IRS files are not available to researchers. Also, information about historical events is available only from published sources.

    Some examples, might be:
    - A. We wish to determine the relative costs of living in every major city in the country;
    - B. We wish to study the trends in the size of family farms over the last 50 years; and
    - C. We wish to determine the relative market potential for cereal products in the 50 states.

2. There are three problems of public catalogs which tend to make the researcher's task more demanding. First, every library has limited resources and therefore does not have all of the publications which the researchers may be seeking. Secondly, it is possible for the topic to be too narrow to be a subject of a full book or pamphlet in the library collection but is contained in books with other titles. Third, the material on the subject may be in the library in one of the collections which is not listed in the public catalog. For a further discussion of these problems, consult the text section entitled Books as a Source.

3. Most companies needing such information would be involved either in marketing oriented decisions, or perhaps the location of production facilities. Companies such as retail chains, consumer goods manufacturers, and other manufacturing plants come to mind.

    - A. Retail chain - might be interested in making store location decisions. Would be interested in demographic data and family income data, and trends in these information areas. Some sources would be the various population censuses, *The County and City Data Book*, and *Sales Management Survey of Buying Power* (annual update of local area family and business statistics). In addition there might be studies prepared by local planning boards or local utilities.

    - B. Consumer goods manufacturer - might be interested in salesman territory allocation decisions and the evaluation of sales performances against some territory standards. Use the same sources as above.

    - C. Plant location decision - Need information on labor supply and conditions in the area. Also interested in such topics as transportation net-

Chapter 9　　　　　　　　　　　　　　　　　　　　　　　　　　　　　　Secondary Data Sources

works and costs, attitudes of local governments toward the promotion of industry in general, and the company's industry in particular. State Departments of Employment Security would have such information. Studies also done by local or regional growth associations, chambers of commerce, planning associations, and reports of local governmental actions in the areas of environmental control, industry subsidization, taxation, and the like.

4. This is a student project. Look for the following ideas:

   A. Set up PCs in the library with CD-ROMs and/or use terminals with modem links to on-line data bases. Services should include, but not be limited to *ABI/Inform, DIALOG, Dow Jones News/Retrieval, PTS Prompt,* and at least one of *BRS, Compuserve, ORBIT,* or *The Source.* Alternatively, or in addition, CD-ROMs should include, but not be limited to *ABI/Inform, Infotrac,* and *Newsbank.*

   B. Access can be direct, after employees complete a short educational course. If CD-ROMs are used, access would physically take place in the library at headquarters. If on-line databases are used, professionals could be authorized to access the databases and would use their desktop systems to connect.

   Alternatively, access can be provided through the corporate librarian. In this case, the librarian would respond to both one time search requests and ongoing monitoring requests. For example, if a professional needs to monitor fashion news on a monthly basis, the librarian could set up a profile to search the databases for "fashion" and "haute couture." Each month the professional would receive a listing from the librarian of references and abstracts containing the target search words.

   C. A cost benefit analysis could be done based on the costs to have outside firms provide monitoring or clipping services for headquarters versus the cost of the investment. If the firm does not currently use clipping services, then an evaluation of the market opportunities and business trends that the corporation is missing is needed.

5. In general the process to follow is that shown in Figure 9-1. The major sources would include the *Bibliographic Index,* public catalog, *Library of Congress Catalog* or *Books in Print,* CD-ROMs such as *Business Periodicals ON-DISC, CIRR on Disc,* and *ABI/Inform,* plus some periodical indexes such as *BPI, ASTI,* and *PAIS.* Other good sources would include dissertation indexes, the *Index of Publications of Bureaus of Business and Economic Research,* and a search of mathematics, personal computing, and accounting journals not cataloged in the above sources. Often these journals will have their own annual index which can be scanned for likely references.

6. There are two chief problems. One is the question of accuracy. Every study is done for some reason and we should assure ourselves that the data we use is not biased in such a way that it is unusable. In addition, there is the defi-

Chapter 9 — Secondary Data Sources

nition problem. Do we know the definitions used in the study? Are they compatible with our own?

7. This student exercise calls for the most recent copy of *Statistical Abstract*.. The question can be assigned as a short hand-in assignment. The *Statistical Abstract* has a very complete index and for most of these topics there will be substantial information.

8. In general, computerized searches are more efficient than non-computerized searches. In the authors' experience, they can be 5 to 10 times more efficient. (In 2 minutes on a computerized card catalog terminal, researchers can accomplish what takes 10 minutes with a traditional card catalog. This ratio goes up when we move to using CD-ROM or online databases versus traditional periodical indexes.) To test this, students should time their search of *Business Periodicals Index* versus *ABI/Inform* (either CD-ROM or online). Considering the fact that most libraries provide free access to CD-ROM databases, most students will find that a CD-ROM provides the least expensive search mechanism (free access, minimal researcher time). The expense comparisons of the other two alternatives, completely manual and online searches, will depend upon the rates your library uses for online searches and the proficiency with which the students use the library and database.

   A. For virtually any search, a stop at the computerized card catalog is a must. Follow this with a CD-ROM for detailed references from periodicals, newspapers, research reports, and congressional reports. Finally, use a manual search for the very latest periodicals in print (last three months) and for government documents, pamphlets, and uncataloged materials.

   B. For some specialized subjects, online databases contain the most complete information. One, for example, is *LEXIS*, the full text legal database.

   C. Manual searches should complement computerized searches, as discussed in A, above. If the subject is very narrow and only exists in one or two journals, a manual search may be just as fast and thorough as a computerized one. For example, technical comparisons of computer hardware can be found in only a handful of periodicals. In cases like this, a manual search is justified.

9. Professor or student generated project.

10. Professor or student generated project.

11. The major problem with only using a computerized search is that the researcher will miss many potential sources. The databases may not include periodicals published in the last few months. Nor will the databases include books, most government documents, reference works, association yearbooks or publications, or pamphlets. These important sources on infor-

mation should not be overlooked.

12. Below are the most likely sources for each of the eleven research needs. The list of sources in each case is not necessarily exhaustive.

   A. The public catalog, *Bibliographic Index, Books in Print. Business Periodicals Index,* CD-ROMs *Disclosure, Business Periodicals On-DISC, CIRR on Disc,* and *Newsbank,* and online sources *ABI/Inform,* and the *Dow Jones News/Retrieval* service.

   B. *United States Government Publication: Monthly Catalog,* and CD-ROM *Government Documents Catalog Service.*

   C. *American Doctoral Dissertations, Dissertation Abstracts Online,* or CD-ROM *UMI Dissertation Abstracts.*

   D. *Missouri Directory of Manufacturing and Mining.*

   E. *Dun & Bradstreet Reference Book of Corporate Management.*

   F. Check the latest volume or do an online search of *Subject Guide to Books in Print* or *Subject Guide to Forthcoming Books.*

   G. *Ayers Directory of Publications.*

   H. Vertical file at library or the *Vertical File Index: Subject and Title Index to Selected Pamphlet Materials.*

   I. *Index of Publications of Bureaus of Business and Economic Research.*

True - False Questions

T   1) Secondary sources of data can usually be found more quickly and cheaply than primary sources.

T   2) An important disadvantage of secondary information is that often it will not meet our specific needs.

F   3) The two most important secondary sources for business researchers are organization files and trade journals.

T   4) The three major uses of secondary data for research purposes. are: to find specific reference information, to serve as an integral part of a larger research study, or be used as the sole source for a research study.

T   5) One reason the *Statistical Abstract* has particular value to the business researcher is it's a very comprehensive and up-to-date compilation of statistics covering wide areas of our society.

Chapter 9 — Secondary Data Sources

T   6) The *Census of Population* taken every 10 years secures information on the population by ethnic, economic, social, and occupational characteristics.

T   7) Once the researcher has some knowledge of the research topic the development of a bibliography is typically the next step in gathering secondary data.

T   8) Even if secondary data are insufficient for the needs of the researcher, this data may be helpful in problem definition and in improving the methods by which primary data are collected.

F   9) After a problem is defined and clearly specified there is little need for secondary research.

T   10) The federal government publishes a wide variety of census data and a very large amount of statistical information which may or may not be a by product or supplement to the census reports.

T   11) "Primary Data" are the original data that a researcher collects for his/her own research purposes. This contrasts with secondary source data which have been collected for an earlier research purpose.

F   12) When searching for business periodical references if you fail to find help in the *Business Periodicals Index* or similar indexes, then there is little chance that any periodical literature on your topic exists.

T   13) Secondary data sources are usually not adequate as the sole source of information for projects.

T   14) Outlining is usually the most efficient means of recording what we want to extract from published material.

T   15) Secondary data quality depends partially on the capability of the source of the data. The source of the data being both the investigators and the measuring instrument.

F   16) Some of the most valuable sources of secondary data are newspapers.

F   17) The U.S. Government takes the *Census of Business* approximately every 10 years.

F   18) Doctoral dissertations could be a major source of secondary research information, but unfortunately there currently is no useful bibliographic referencing of them.

F   19) The major published source of statistical data for business research is books.

T   20) A good early step in a secondary data research project is to use the Bibliographic *Index*.

Chapter 9   Secondary Data Sources

F   21) The card catalog of a research library probably contains 95 per cent or more of the published materials in the library.

F   22) The best periodical index to use for a business research project is the *Readers Guide to Periodical Literature.*

F   23) While we must be aware that secondary data have been collected for purposes other than our own, this is usually not much of a problem.

T   24) There is more duplicate information about periodicals in the *Business Periodicals Index* and the *Bulletin* of the Public Affairs Information Service than any other two major periodical indexes.

T   25) The fastest growing category of published sources is that of computerized databases.

F   26) Databases contain references and sometimes full abstracts but do not contain the full text of an article or complete numeric information.

F   27) Online databases include those where a personal computer is hooked up to a CD-ROM peripheral device to get the information "online."

F   28) Because CD-ROM searches are based on computer programs, alternate spelling and synonyms are automatically included as keywords in the search.

Multiple Choice Questions

1.   Which of the following is a major disadvantage of secondary data sources?
        A) The information collection is time consuming
*   B) The information often does not fit our needs
        C) One can't gather historical data easily
        D) The process is usually more expensive than the use of primary sources

2.   In terms of research sources, published data can be classified into five major categories. Which of the following is NOT one of them?
        A) Books
        B) Periodicals
*   C) Research Reports
        D) Computerized Databases
        E) Documents

3.   The best way to learn the names of periodicals that may be published, in the United States about the stone quarry industry would be to search the:
        A) *Statistical Abstract of the United States*
*   B) *Ulrich's International Directory*
        C) *Bibliographic Index*
        D) *Business Periodicals Index*

110

Chapter 9   Secondary Data Sources

4. Probably the best quick source for articles on sales management problems would be the:
   * A) *BPI*
   B) *Readers Guide to Periodical Literature*
   C) *ASTI*
   D) *Wall Street Journal Index*

5. Suppose you were starting a research study based upon secondary sources about the use of computers for educational purposes in colleges. You should probably begin by:
   A) Going to the card catalog of the library
   B) Search *Books-in-Print* for new publications on this topic
   * C) Check the *Bibliographic Index*
   D) Since this is a new technology area, consult the appropriate *Doctoral Dissertation Abstracts* bulletins.

6. The U.S. government publishes a number of censuses. Which of the following is carried out once every ten years?
   A) Census of Manufactures
   B) Census of Business
   * C) Census of Housing

7. There are four monthly U.S. Government periodicals which provide the majority of current statistics on our economy and its operation. Which of the following is *not* one of these?
   * A) *The Economic Journal of Statistics*
   B) *The Survey of Current Business*
   C) *The Federal Reserve Bulletin*
   D) *The Business Conditions Digest*

8. You have learned that there is a serial published under the title, *Journal of Accounting Research.* You go to your library and find they do not have it. Which of the following would be most helpful to you in this situation?
   A) *Ayer's Directory of Publications*
   B) Coman's *Sources of Business Information*
   * C) *Union List of Serials*
   D) *Library of Congress Subject Catalog*

9. You are about to begin a computerized search using CD-ROM. What is your first step?
   A) Type in the search term
   B) Record all of the references that are reported
   * C) plan a research strategy
   D) select the appropriate database

10. The fastest growing area of published sources is
    A) government documents
    * B) computerized databases
    C) specialized periodicals
    D) books

111

Chapter 9   Secondary Data Sources

11. There are two types of computerized databases. They are
*
   A) reference and source
   B) reference and numerical
   C) source and full-text
   D) index and bibliographic

12. CD-ROM stands for:
   A) Compact disk, read or write material
* B) Computer disk, read only memory
   C) Compact disk, read optical memory
   D) None of the above

13. One of the disadvantages of computerized searches is
   A) a computer search can combine subject items in different ways than is possible using a manual search.
   B) computerized databases do not contain references to the most recent published periodicals.
   C) computers are hard for most people to use.
* D) computerized searches will find sources that contain the key words but the source is not related to the subject of interest.

CHAPTER 10

SURVEY METHODS

There are two learning objectives for this chapter. The first is to familiarize the student with the major survey techniques used to collect primary data. It is desirable that the student understands the features, advantages, and weaknesses of each technique. The second objective is to provide the student with a basic set of normative guides for selecting and using these techniques in ways that secure useful and appropriate information.

Class Discussion Suggestions

One class session is usually enough to cover Chapter 10. Discussion question 5 may be used to begin a discussion of when various data gathering methods are best used. Discussion of ways to improve rapport and increase participation is also interesting; questions 2, 3, and 4 are useful for this purpose. If a more limited discussion of telephone and mail survey work is desired, use questions 6 and 7.

For students without prior exposure to this material, the chapter seems a bit encyclopedic. The vignette should help bring the material down to earth. Students will often offer their own experiences with survey research and those can be used as a springboard for the chapter questions.

Inc. magazine and other business publications frequently offer survey advice to readers. In the September, 1993 issue of *Inc.*, p. 46, the Managing Director of Northwest Airlines in Bangkok discussed his efforts to improve response rates though charitable donations (a 10-15% response increase). Other suggestions were discussed in this piece which can tie nicely to the Total Design Method starting on p. 284 of the text. The Survey Research Center at the University of Michigan also publishes a newsletter that contains current examples that help to launch this chapter.

Answers to Chapter Questions

1. *Response error* occurs when the recorded data differ from the true data; such errors can come from the respondent in the editing, coding, or data entry stages.

   Interviewer error occurs when the data is corrupted by the interviewer in some fashion. This can occur as a result of inconsistent treatment of respondents or questionnaires, ineffective respondent motivation and cooperation created by the interviewer, social differences between respondent and interviewer, and cheating.

Chapter 10   *Survey Methods*

Nonresponse error occurs when the researcher had difficulty in securing interviews from respondents who have been selected into the sample, and the non-respondents differ from the respondents in a systematic way.

2. There are many ways to motivate respondents in such a case. Some methods are economic, such as cash, merchandise, or discount coupons for grocery products. Other methods are psychological, such as developing good rapport with the respondent, showing interest in the respondent's thoughts and feelings, and convincing the respondent that the research project and his participation is important and appreciated. In most cases a single method is not sufficient for adequately motivating respondents; a combination of motivational approaches is necessary.

3. Three suggestions for cutting personal interviewing costs while increasing the response rates include: developing incentive systems for efficient interviewing, using the telephone for scheduling and screening personal interviews, and using self- administered questionnaires. Improved selection of interviewers, role playing, and other forms of training are also effective ways to improve interview efficiency.

4. Many environmental conditions such as the degree of urbanization in the area, the day of the week, the time of day, the location of the interview, and the other demands being made on the respondent at the time of contact are all important factors in determining the rate of response. For example, many urban residents feel threatened in their neighborhoods and are reluctant to answer the door when a stranger calls. Likewise, in a business shopping center at dinner time it may be difficult to secure cooperation from persons rushing home.

These problems can be only partially offset. Care in the selection and training of interviewers is one of the best ways to lessen these problems. Some interviewers consistently turn in better response rates. Techniques such as varying callback times, making calls at the times of highest probability of contact, setting up interviews by phone, interviewing other members of the family (when this is acceptable), and seeking assistance from neighbors to learn the best time to call are also ways to improve performance.

5. In these examples it is often possible to use any of the three methods.

A. In this first one it is more likely that a personal interview will be used because of the compact study area and a topic which will be of high interest to participants. This is especially the case if there are a substantial number of questions and a certain degree of free form to the interview. Telephone interviewing would be the second choice.

B. Personal interview or telephone interviews for much the same reasons as above. The sampling approach probably will be a major factor. If it is going to be a convenience sample then personal interviewing at several spots on campus would be adequate. If it is a random sample it might be desirable to use telephone interviewing where possible and personal or mail surveys where telephone contact cannot be made.

C. Probably mail survey would be the most appropriate. It is possible that some written material will be sent (policy statements, etc.) and this must be handled by mail. Telephone surveys are possible if the questioning is not too complex and lengthy. Personal interviews would be the high cost alternative and probably not used unless this project had a substantial budget and was aimed as an in-depth study.

D. A mail survey would probably hold costs down and improve the chances of making contact with the special executive. One might also use a letter to inform the financial officer of the project and then call long distance at a pre-specified time to secure the answers to the questions.

E. Either telephone or mail for reasons already cited in "D" above.

6. The best way would be by random digit dialing within the exchange. There are 9,999 possible numbers from which to choose a group by using a table of random numbers or a random number generator. Record the chosen random numbers in the order in which they appear. Depending on your location (rural, suburban, or urban), use at least 70 numbers in order to have replacements for unassigned numbers, business establishment numbers, and other non- households. When a number does not answer, continue to call back up to 5-7 times at different times of day before replacing it with another numbered non-households. Continue the calling process until the sample of 40 families is achieved.

7. This can be answered in several ways. In terms of the Kanuk and Berensen review article one would suggest that follow-ups be used, that a respected sponsorship be used, that a stamped return envelope be enclosed, and that a money incentive be included. The Dillman approach is concerned more with the total design of the project. He urges concern for the improvement of all aspects of the study which could give it an aura of importance, quality, personalization, and usefulness. He addresses the problem in terms of the appearance and content of the materials as well as the process used. He stresses envelope appearance, cover letter appearance (equal to a normal business letter), careful design of cover letter content (to make a strong appeal), and the importance of the respondent's participation. He advocates multiple follow-ups and careful timing of the mail outs.

True - False Questions

T 1) Personal interviewing is a two-way purposeful conversation initiated by an interviewer to obtain information that is relevant to a research purpose.

F 2) The greatest disadvantage of personal interviewing is the possibility of bias by the interviewer.

Chapter 10   Survey Methods

T   3) The greatest advantage of personal interviewing over other data gathering methods is the volume and depth of information that can be secured by it.

F   4) The technique of stimulating respondents to answer more fully and relevantly is termed "follow up."

T   5) A probe should be neutral in nature and appear as a natural part of the conversation.

T   6) A probe is probably the best way to stimulate a respondent to answer a question more fully and relevantly.

F   7) In personal interviewing, biased results grow out of three major types of errors: sampling error, response error, and interviewer error.

T   8) Response error occurs when the data reported differ from the actual data.

T   9) Of all the advantages of telephone interviewing probably the most significant is its low cost.

F   10) Nonresponse errors are those that result when the respondents answer "don't know" when, if fact, they do know.

F   11) There is not yet a truly feasible way, in telephone interviewing, to overcome the problem of reaching unlisted numbers.

F   12) Probably the greatest advantage of the personal interview is that it enables the interviewer to find the exact person to interview.

F   13) Mail surveys are generally more economical than telephone surveys.

F   14) The major strength of a mail survey is the ease with which a random sample of responses can be secured from a population.

F   15) With mail surveys, a response rate of 10% to 20% is generally considered satisfactory.

T   16) Follow-ups, or reminders, are almost always successful in increasing the response rates of mail surveys.

T   17) The total design method (TDM) attempts to maximize the response rate in mail surveys by attending to each point in the survey process where response might break down.

Chapter 10 Survey Methods

Multiple Choice Questions

1. Which of the following would you choose as the *least* useful form of interview probing?
   A) A brief assertion of understanding like "'I see" or "uh-huh."
   * B) A question like, "will you please repeat that?"
   C) A comment like, "'anything else?"
   D) A question like, "could you tell me a little more?"

2. Research on the biasing effect of interviewers indicated that
   A) Interviewer bias is seldom a problem.
   * B) It is not really clear how big the problem is.
   C) It is somewhat of a problem, but not a major one.
   D) It is the major problem in personal interviewing.

3. The TDM approach to improving mail survey response rates depends largely on which of the following for its apparent success?
   A) A monetary incentive is included with the questionnaire.
   B) The cover letter is individually addressed.
   C) A carefully designed and tested questionnaire is developed.
   * D) Care is taken with the many details that may affect response rates.

4. Non response error occurs in survey work when
   A) The people we are interviewing refuse to answer.
   B) The responses given are not relevant.
   C) The respondents say "I don't know" when they do know.
   * D) The people we seek to interview are "not-at-home."

5. A major type of error in seeking personal household interviews is that many respondents are not-at-home. In one major study it was found that as few as about ___ % of the respondents were found on the first call.
   A) 80%
   B) 60%
   * C) 30%
   D) 10%

6. Response error occurs from all but one of the following sources. Which one is not a response error source?
   A) Processing and tabulation errors
   * B) "not-at-home" bias
   C) Interviewer bias
   D) Respondent bias

7. The major weakness of mail surveys is
   A) The impersonality of the communication.
   B) The inability to direct your message to a specific person.
   * C) The risk of a strong non-response bias.
   D) The inability to secure confidential information through this medium.

117

Chapter 10 — Survey Methods

8. Which of the following is the least important drawback to the use of telephones for conducting surveys?
   A) Such interviews need to be limited to 5 to 8 minutes.
   B) A substantial proportion of U.S. households do not have phones.
   * C) There is really no effective way to contact the many people with unlisted numbers.
   D) The medium limits the complexity of the questioning process and the use of sorting techniques.

9. Which of the following factors does research show to have the greatest positive impact on rate of returns in mail surveys?
   * A) Follow up mailings.
   B) Pre-notification of a questionnaire coming.
   C) Keeping the questionnaire relatively short.
   D) Using first class postage stamps when sending the questionnaire out.

CHAPTER 11

SURVEY INSTRUMENTS

There are three objectives for this chapter. The first is to teach instrument development by combining the question hierarchy (Chapter 3) with a logical design sequence. A connection to the running content of the vignette series is made. A second objective is to demonstrate the major considerations in developing effective survey questions. This effort explores question content, wording, structure of response, and sequence. *Bringing Research to Life* attempts to address this concern in a humorous way and prompts students to relate their experiences with survey questions to the chapter's learning points. The final objective is to explain the importance of pretesting.

For further reading, the Converse/Presser or Payne book is suggested. Payne is easy to read and a classic. The Dillman book is a another that is well worth study. Appendix B of the Selltiz, et al. text has an excellent set of rules on the construction of questions. *The Public Opinion Quarterly* is suggested for the current literature on questionnaire and survey problems.

Class Discussion Suggestions

1. The material in Chapter 11 should take at least one class session and more if the professor wishes to stress questionnaire design. We find that this material is best taught by examples, exercises, and projects rather than by lecture or discussion of principles. Students have a tendency to jump into question formation immediately without giving much consideration of what is needed. A productive way to deal with this is to stress the research hierarchy process that was covered in earlier chapters and that appears again in summary form through the Mind Writer example at the beginning of the chapter. A run through of this example is a good way to begin the class session. To reinforce this example one might use question 10 at the end of the chapter by asking what is likely to be the research objectives underlying such a questionnaire. One approach that has worked well is:

> *How well does the questionnaire from question 10 cover the desired research objectives?* We cannot be certain since no research objectives are given, but it might be useful to consider what they might be. Suppose that the research objective is: "provide information by which students may judge whether to enroll in the given course and section taught by the professor being evaluated." Given this research objective what investigative questions should be included? Those which are advanced might include the following:

A. How well does the professor perform?
   1 - communications skills in class.
   2 - technical competence in the field of study.
   3 - openness and availability to students.
   4 - fairness in student dealings.

Chapter 11 — *Survey Instruments*

        5 - ability to stimulate and motivate students.

   B. What type of class process is used?
      1 - importance of the text, lecture, and outside work in class.
      2 - degree of student active learning vs. passive learning.
      3 - use of cases, projects, and other materials.

   C. Other necessary information.
      1 - is it a required or elective course?
      2 - how important is this course to the students education?

From such a collection of investigative questions, it is a simple matter to point out where there are gaps in coverage in the questionnaire presented in question 10.

   2. The second objective in this chapter is to highlight and demonstrate the major considerations in developing effective questions. The exercise suggested above can be continued along these lines using 10 as the basis for discussion. A way to bring some variety into the class presentation is to form students into groups of 3 - 5 and ask them to work together in class to revise the questionnaire in light of the fractionation experience and their knowledge of the principles of question design. If time allows (this may take a second class period) some of the groups can present their results to the class for further evaluation. In this way it is not too difficult to drive home the point that question design is a task which calls for a "create-evaluate-revise" approach.

   3. Another approach is to propose a new problem as a homework assignment. Several assignments that have been used are:

   A. The local campus food services director wants to evaluate the general satisfaction level the students have with the food and service of the campus cafeteria. With this information s/he will try to improve the cafeteria.

   B. The U.S. Surgeon General wants to know why people continue to smoke cigarettes after the evidence suggests that smoking is injurious to health. S/he wants to take further steps to counter cigarette usage.

   C. The Dean of the School of Business wants to review his/her school's education offering and in this regard wishes to learn the career interests of his current students.

Here again it may be desirable to have some of the results presented to class, perhaps on transparencies, for evaluation and revision.

   4. The last objective, pretesting, can be woven into the above ideas or treated with a separate set of illustrations. Question 6 may be used to stimulate discussion of this objective. One of the instructor's research projects could be used to provide a different perspective.

Chapter 11 — Survey Instruments

Answers to Chapter Questions

1. A. *Direct questions* are those that the respondent should be able to answer openly and unambiguously. *Indirect questions* are those designed to provide answers through inferences from what the respondent says or does.

   B. *Open questions* allow respondents to reply with their own choice of words and concepts. *Closed questions* limit respondents to a few predetermined response possibilities.

   C. These types of questions compose three of the four levels of the research question hierarchy. *Measurement questions* are at the bottom of the hierarchy and are designed to gather specific information from research subjects. The *investigative questions* usually compose several levels of questions and are answered through the information provided by the measurement questions. The *research question* is the basic information question or questions that the researcher must answer if he/she is to contribute to the solution of the management problem. The research questions are answered through the information obtained by the investigative questions.

   D. *Questioning structure* involves the amount of structure placed on the interviewer, whereas *response structure* pertains to the amount of structure placed on the respondent. Structure limits the amount of freedom that can be practiced by the interviewer and/or the respondent when the former asks or the latter answers a question.

2. The survey technique is popular in business and social science research because so many of the research questions concern human attitudes, levels of knowledge, and other types of cognitive or affective information. Much of this information can be secured only by interrogation, or at least can be secured more efficiently by interrogation than by other means. Then, because we have spent our lives conversing with others, the thought of "asking people" comes naturally.

3. Two major problems are the frame of reference problem and the irrelevant response. The former grows out of the respondent interpreting the thrust of the question in a different way than was intended by the researcher. This can lead to unanticipated responses and event responses that appear to be acceptable but have a different meaning. For example, a question like, "What do you think of Mr. 'X' as the democratic presidential candidate in the next election?" A response of, "He is the best candidate the democrats have," might introduce a dimension that is different from the expected preference statement. Or, an answer of "great" might mean, "I prefer him because I'd like to see him be the president," or it could mean, "I'm a republican and his nomination would assure a democrat loss." An irrelevant response might be, "I think the democrats can't win, no matter who they run."

4. There are several reasons why a researcher may disguise the questioning objective. Probably the major reason would be to guard against introducing biases. The topic may be so sensitive that a direct question will elicit a re-

fusal, or the expression of socially approved statements that do not accurately reflect the respondent's views. Even if the topic is not sensitive, a question may be so uninteresting or difficult to answer adequately that the respondent replies in a stereotypical way. A third situation in which indirect questioning may be useful is when we seek information that is available from the respondent, but not at the conscious level.

5. While opinions will vary on these, four important faults of the survey instrument designer are:

   1) Failure to understand the full dimensions of the subject such that the topic is covered adequately and the information is secured in its most useful form,
   2) Failure in selecting the most appropriate communication process or combination of processes,
   3) Failure in drafting specific measurement questions without concern for each question's content, wording, and the sequence of the questions, and
   4) Failure properly to test the instrument.

6. The obvious values are that the pretests will show up deficiencies in questions, lines of questioning, and procedures of questioning. Sometimes pretests even indicate that further study is not needed or is probably not going to be useful. More specifically, the pretest should indicate which questions need revision, whether responses provide the desired information, whether the procedures are adequate, and if the questioning be done within time and cost budgets.

   Finding the best wording for a question calls for experimentation with different versions, particularly when positive and negative versions are usable. Another good guide is to follow the test-revise-retest process with all questions. These six questions are helpful.

   1. Is the question stated in terms of a shared vocabulary?
   2. Is the question clearly?
   3. Are there unstated or misleading assumptions?
   4. Is there biased wording?
   5. Is there the right degree of personalization?
   6. Are adequate alternatives presented?

   The section entitled Purposes of Pretesting provides another and more complete set of criteria.

7. The first few questions need to awaken interest and motivate the respondent to participate in the study. Often students try to achieve this by starting off with questions that have little or no information value. Another tendency they have is to ask for personal classification information at the start, normally such questions should come at the end (except when needed to qualify the respondent or fear that the percentage of completed interviews will be low). Questionnaire designers should generally begin with questions

Chapter 11 Survey Instruments

that are easy to answer and of more interest to the respondent. Ask the simpler and more general questions first, becoming more complex and specific as they progress (the funnel approach is described in the section entitled Question Sequence on page 316). It is generally advisable to deal with a single sub-topic before moving to another and there are often obvious sequences for such topics that should be considered. Finally, they should watch out for interactive questions where, for example, the answer to question 18 influences the answer later to question 25. It may be more desirable for question 25 to come first, or it may be necessary to use alternative versions to balance out the biasing effects of one question on the other.

8. Some of the major problem assumptions are:

   A. Assuming that respondents are motivated to answer every question truthfully and fully.
   B. Assuming that respondents know or understand key words or phrases.
   C. Assuming that respondents will answer the question from same frame of reference that the question is asked.
   D. Assuming that respondents will do calculations, averaging, or even diligent remembering in order to answer a question.
   E. Assuming that the development of good survey questions is a simple process.

9. None are good questions for the following reasons:

   A. It leads the respondent by asking him if he reads a prestige magazine. It will probably over-report readership. And, what is meant by "regularly"?

   B. It presents the respondent with a difficult estimation task requiring information that he is unlikely to have readily available. It is unclear whether the question is concerned with verbal requests only or any form of request.
   C. It concerns a rather trivial event in the distant past that is not likely to be remembered.

   D. The meaning of "discretionary buying power" is probably not clear. In addition, the question asks for information that is not likely to be easily available or calculable even if the term is understood.

   E. It is a simple "why" question that leaves the frame of reference open to the respondent. If the answer is of substantial importance to the research it should probably be expanded.

   F. It does not make the explicit statement alternative of "not doing a good job." It will probably bias responses in a positive direction. Also, the question is too vague and general for any purpose other than as a rough attitude indicator. Furthermore, how recent is "now"?

10. A number of criticisms may be made, but among the most likely are the following: first, there are several format problems that could be improved.

The order of questions is not bad except for putting the overall evaluation at the beginning where it is likely to influence how the individual questions are answered. A second weakness is the failure to provide adequate space for responses, especially in questions 3 and 4. It would also be wise to give some more guidance as to the form of answers sought. The various parts of question 2 apparently should be answered by yes or no, but the lack of specific indications to this effect may result in some respondents merely checking some parts and not checking others, or answering in other unexpected ways. When using what are essentially closed response questions it is wise to specify the response choices.

Question 1 - should be placed much later as a summary question. Some scale other than a good-fair-poor scale would be better since these are vague concepts. It would probably be wise to use a scale to compare the professor to other professors in the student's experience.

Question 2 - in all of these parts there should be at least "yes" and "no" response choices, it might be even better to use a more sensitive scale, say of 1 to 5 points. In 2a there is some question of the meaning of "good delivery." Does this refer to speaking delivery skills, ability to conduct class discussions, or does delivery refer to total classroom performance? Question 2b is better than most, but is "know the subject" too crude or vague in concept? A similar criticism could be made in 2c where "positive attitude" is too vague and subject to variable interpretations. "Grade fairly" (2d) and "sense of humor" (2e) are probably acceptable, but 2f is a multiple question that should be broken into several. In addition, there should be some measure of usage. In question 2g how prompt is "promptly?"

Question 3 - after providing more response space, we might improve on "strongest point." A statement asking for the professor's "greatest strength" probably clearly conveys the intentions of the writer.

Question 4 - it would improve the quality of response if more effort was made to seek that aspect of the professor's work that most "needs improvement."

Question 5 - "Kind of class" is confusing. Does this mean subject matter, type of class operation, good or bad, or what?

Question 6 - should have a yes-no specification.

Question 7 - probably could be strengthened by stressing *"voluntarily"* take another course. It might also help to give a response scale that is more sensitive than merely yes of no.

11. This letter and questionnaire is an actual example used by a master's degree candidate for thesis research at one university. The reproduction in the text does not adequately capture the flavor of the material. The letter was photocopied on one half sheet of paper with even the sender's signature photocopied. The tone of the letter is totally self-centered. No effort is made real-

ly to interest the respondent in the problem or to suggest how he/she or society might benefit from participation. The final sentence typifies this self-centered approach.

A better letter would have had some degree of personalization. It would have suggested that there is a need for such a study, offered some information about the purpose, or thanked the addressee for participation, and, in general, adopted more of a persuasive tone. The accompanying envelope should have been stamped as well as already addressed.

The questionnaire can not be fully evaluated in terms of coverage since we do not know the precise objectives of the study. On balance, however, the instrument is poorly designed and the question construction is generally bad. To begin, the heading, a single word "Questionnaire" is not very helpful. Something that identifies the project would have been better. The statement of directions is more what one would expect on some class examination or bureaucratic form rather than study that seeks voluntary cooperation. Most researchers want as much detail as possible, rather than as little. This suggests that the researcher is really not interested in his own topic, so why should the respondent be interested?

It is difficult to show the space allocation problem in this text illustration, but clearly there is insufficient room for answering most of the questions. The actual questionnaire had a similar amount of blank space for each reply. For each question the blank for response was as long as the remaining space to the right margin. Additionally, some comments can be made of each question:

Question 1 - This question assumes that all members of the ASTD are actually in the field of training while this may not be the case. The respondent does not know how the "field" is defined. Finally, the respondent may have entered the field with some organization that is not a company, e.g., university, non profit organization, or local, state, or federal government.

Question 2 - Assumes that there is a clear "field of training" definition. Also assumes that the respondent is now in the field of training while he/she may now be in a different area. In such a case does one answer by giving the total time since entering training field, or total time in that department?

Question 3 - Assumes respondent works in a company that has a training department. Like question 2, it presumes that the respondent is currently employed the field of training.

Question 4 - Gives a full line to answer, where in this case, the reply expected is something like "X years."

Question 5 - Word "department" may present problems. How does one answer if training is a part of a division? It also assumes that there is a training department.

Question 6 - Assumes that "your department" is the training department.

Question 7 - Assumes respondent is in training department, that there is a training department, and does not distinguish between what might be a relatively small branch plant of a major international company. Suppose there are three plants locally? Then how does one answer?

Question 8 - Inadequate space for persons with more than one degree.

Question 9 - "Why" question is almost impossible to answer since a full response would contain too many factors. This compound question could be handled better if broken into several questions.

Question 10 - Compound question could be handled better by breaking it up.

Note also that there are no identification or classification questions. There was a written code number on the back of the questionnaire that was never referred to.

True - False Questions

F   1) Drafting a questionnaire is a relatively simple part of the research design process.

F   2) Unstructured interview processes make it easier to develop a standard line of questioning and require less skilled interviewers.

T   3) Unstructured interviewing is particularly useful in exploratory research.

T   4) Forms of response can be classified as open or closed.

F   5) Depth interviews tend to be more structured than do normal interviews.

F   6) A focus interview is the same as a depth interview.

T   7) Researchers must occasionally disguise the objectives of a study. For example, if the study asks for a response on some topic for which the respondent may have a socially unacceptable view the question often is disguised.

F   8) A questionnaire is basically a list of investigative questions.

F   9) The problem of a question's scope has to do with whether the question leads one to a biased response or not.

Chapter 11　　　　　　　　　　　　　　　　　　　　　　　　　　　　Survey Instruments

T　　10) Closed response questions are generally preferred for large surveys.

F　　11) The three types of information normally included in a survey instrument are sought data, classification characteristic, and analysis data.

F　　12) Generally speaking, it is a good idea to ask respondent classification questions at the beginning of the questioning.

T　　13) Before a question is placed on a survey instrument, the researcher must decide if the question contributes significant information toward answering one of the investigative questions.

T　　14) If the researcher wants to secure more complete information by motivating the respondent to provide it, the first requirement is to build good rapport with the respondent.

T　　15) We can increase respondents' motivations to supply complete and truthful information by assuring them that answers are confidential.

T　　16) A major advantage of unstructured and disguised questions is the ability of this form of questioning to uncover subconscious and socially unacceptable attitudes and motives.

T　　17) Bias is the distortion of responses in one direction.

T　　18) Question content, question wording, and response structure are three major decision areas in question design.

F　　19) A question with an open response structure must specify the frame of reference for the respondent.

F　　20) Closed questions reduce the variability of response, make fewer demands on interviewer skills, are less costly to administer, and are best utilized in exploratory research.

F　　21) It is almost impossible to provide an exhaustive list of choices for most multiple choice questions. Therefore, it is typical to see a non-exhaustive list of alternatives for a question on a well-done questionnaire.

F　　22) The basic principle to guide sequence decisions is: "the nature and needs of the respondent must determine the sequence of questions but the needs of the researcher should determine the organization of the schedule."

T　　23) The interviewer's first challenge is to awaken the respondent's interest in the study and motivate participation.

F　　24) Respondents can usually be motivated to participate if the interviewer allows the respondents to talk about themselves first. For this reason, personal classification information should be obtained at the beginning of the interview.

Chapter 11 Survey Instruments

T   25) It is good practice to place simpler questions first in a survey and move progressively to more complex ones.

F   26) The reliability and validity data from a question used in one setting is easily generalized to another.

T   27) Language and idiom problems often occur when borrowing or adapting questionnaire items from other sources.

F   28) Pretests rely on colleagues rather than actual respondents for refining a measuring instrument.

T   29) Pretesting is useful to checking on respondent interest, question meaning, and question sequence.

T   30) When the researcher does not advise the respondent that the questioning is part of a pretest, the process is more likely to approach conditions of the final study.

Multiple Choice Questions

1. Which form of response is considered to be superior when you seek to discover opinions and degrees of knowledge
    * A) Open response question.
    B) Dichotomous question.
    C) Multiple choice question.
    D) No difference between them in this regard.

2. Which of the statements below best expresses of understanding of the effect and value of personalization in question design?
    A) Personalization of questions makes for superior response results.
    B) Personalization of questions makes for inferior response results.
    * C) Personalization of questions makes for different response results but we cannot say one is superior to the other.
    D) Personalization seldom gives different response results than does impersonal questions.

3. Variation in responses due to different ways of wording questions is an important design problem, but only one of several. Which of the following is more likely to be true? Variations due to differences in question wording is:
    * A) More important than bias due to compiling and methods of questionnaire administration
    B) Less important than bias due to sampling and methods of questionnaire administration
    C) About the same in importance as sampling and method of questionnaire administration
    D) Less important than sampling bias but more important than method of questionnaire administration

Chapter 11   Survey Instruments

4. Which of the following is generally considered NOT to be a matter of question content in the design of a survey instrument?
   A) Should this question be asked?
   B) Is the question of proper scope?
   * C) Does the question use a shared vocabulary?
   D) Can the respondent answer adequately?

5. Which of the following questions is least important in developing the first draft of a survey instrument?
   A) What communication mode to use?
   B) What degree of question and response structure to use?
   C) What degree of disguise to use?
   * D) What form of testing to use?

6. Which of the following sequences represent the best approach in the development of a survey research instrument?
   A) Management question - research question - measurement question - investigative question
   * B) Management question - research question - investigative question - measurement question
   C) Research question - measurement question - investigative question - management question
   D) Management question - investigative question - research question - measurement question

7. Efforts to disguise the objectives of a line of questioning are most useful when:
   * A) Respondents tend otherwise to reply with stereotyped answers.
   B) Respondents differ in some marked way from the interviewer.
   C) More than one objective is being sought in the same interview.
   D) The sponsor of the research does not wish to be identified.

8. Closed response forms of questions are the preferred type of response form when:
   A) We want to guard against respondents giving opinions they do not hold
   B) We use clearly structured question sequences
   C) We are trying to disguise our questioning objectives
   * D) We want to specify the frame of reference for the respondent.

9. In developing the question sequence in a questionnaire or interview schedule one should generally
   A) Place personal classification data first in the sequence
   B) Start with more complex questions and then break them down into sub-parts
   C) Place closed end questions before open end questions
   * D) Do none of the above suggestions

129

CHAPTER 12

OBSERVATION

This chapter is designed to introduce the student to observation as a viable form of data collection. There are two learning objectives for the chapter. The first is to familiarize the student with the major types and procedures for data gathering through observation. The second objective is to provide students with a set of guidelines that allow them to implement a research study using observation as a primary method.

Class Discussion Suggestions

The material in Chapter 12 should take one class session if the professor wishes to stress observation. Some instructors may prefer to treat observation in their overview of primary data collection methods and use the chapter for background reading. Since the use of observation does not preclude the use of other data collection methods at the same time, coverage of this topic may be combined with others. However, the potential of the observational method has been largely understated in business research and this unit offers the instructor the opportunity to rectify the impression that observation is only suitable for social scientists.

Our experience suggests that this material is enjoyed by students when it is taught with discussion, exercises, and examples, rather than by lecture. The *Bringing Research to Life* vignette and chapter Close-Up were designed to start you in that direction. In organizing a discussion, question 1 serves as a good transition from the survey unit to observation and as a preview for experimentation. Questions 3, 4, 6, and 7 offer examples to that require application of the chapter to concrete situations. Following the discussion, one of the three exercises we suggest could be used to reinforce the procedural aspects of the method and the need for preparation and training. Finally, it is desirable to cycle back to a discussion that summarizes the ethical issues that have come up during the class session.

While we are all observers, we seldom give much thought to how to carry out this process more systematically. Hence, a demonstration of the observational method can be a useful experience. Many alternatives are available, below are three:

1. Arrange either before class or at the beginning of class for about 6 students to observe what goes on in class. These students can be assigned in twos to observe the professor, the students, and the content of the session. That is, each of these topics will be assigned to two students, but it is better to have each observer work separately.

Conduct the class for about 10 minutes while the observation goes on. Then have the students summarize what they have observed on the board. The results will usually show wide differences as to what was observed, divergent perceptions of the same act, and quite different operational definitions. Discussion can bring these out and show the need for careful development of observation concepts and procedures.

2. A more elaborate exercise that has been used with good effect is to have 5 or 6 students, either by assignment or as volunteers, participate in front of the class in a discussion on some topic of interest. One topic which has been used is: "How does this school and its faculty prepare students for responsible management careers, and how can it improve its efforts?" The exercise is more interesting if you do not appoint a group leader.

Hand out a checklist (coding scheme) to the students in the audience that instructs them to carry out *only one* of the following observation assignments:

A. Who participates, how much time does each person participate, and to whom does each directs his/her comments ?

B. What is the sequence of ideas ?

C. Do leadership roles develop in the group ? Describe their impact.

D. What is the content of the suggestions, the reactions, and the degree to which they secure agreement from others ?

E. Separate observations: Observe the following pairs of panel members and record your observations using the Bales interaction classification form.

1 and 2
3 and 4
5 and 6

The discussion by the panel should be limited to about 10 minutes. After this, a few moments can be given to observers to review their notes report their findings on the board. It becomes quickly apparent that there are a variety of differences among untrained observers who have been given rather precise instructions and a limited observation task. This illustrates need for observer training. Nevertheless, the observations as a whole will have considerably more detail and affective content than a comparable survey and these differences should be pointed out when debriefing the exercise.

3. An accretion study of accumulated material serves an a interesting short exercise for illustrating unobtrusive measures. In programs where courses meet less frequently but for longer periods of time, many instructors schedule routine breaks. Students frequently wander off to a vending machine and return to the classroom with a snack and then deposit their garbage into the trash bin. Either with a confederate or by oneself, the instructor can do an inventory of the trash for several class periods before introducing the observation chapter. This inventory will likely reveal consumption patterns, brand preferences, dietary disposition, and so forth for those who have consistently consumed snacks. A confederate recorder is an asset in matching individuals to the accumulated material and thus assuring that the observations are not isolated samples but part of a pattern.

This exercise frequently raises ethical issues. In that regard, it helps to refo-

Chapter 12

cus the initial reading and discussions on ethics from the beginning of the term to the students current awareness level. By comparing the ethical dilemmas in survey research to observation and then anticipating problems with the next unit on experimentation, the role of ethics begins to coalesce for many students.

Answers to Chapter Questions

1. The observational method is a more useful method for collecting data from children, illiterate, and functionally illiterate persons. The intrusion of observation is often better accepted than questioning. Disguise and unobtrusive measures are often easier to carry out than disguised questioning. It is generally a slow, expensive process with limited opportunity to learn about the past.

    Further comparisons are found in the accompanying table. This table may be used again for question 2 of Chapter 13.

Survey	Observation	Experiment
Advantageous for discovering a person's opinions, attitudes.	Observation and recording (notes, videotape) superior to asking about it.	Superior method for establishing causality: surveys (excepts panels and other longitudinals) do not have experimental pre-post or multiple measurement advantage; observation may be longitudinal but there is little environmental control or ability ot measure change in dependent variable.
Interviewer may observe non-verbal behavior (though not with mail and limited to voice with telephone).	Primary method for non-verbal behavior analysis; has wide application for behavioral and nonbehavioral analysis.	
Structure of schedule or guide focuses attention on study purpose.	First hand observation of phenomena.	
Instruments may restrict study to previously chosen questions.	Observational instruments often lack structure (but unstructured observation offers flexibility).	Ultimate method for control of variables: smaller samples and management of extraneous factors.
	Observation may be used as exploratory front-end to survey or experiment.	Better opportunity to study change than cross-sectional surveys.
Relationship between interviewer and subject is of short duration (and promotes comparative objectivity).	Relationship between observer and subject is often extended and provides more detail (but may reduce objectivity).	Reactive effects may be caused by experimenter (also caused by survey interviewer).
Results may be product of method rather than objective reality.	Natural environmental setting lessens reactivity of subjects; results are more realistic because method is less restrictive (but there is loss of control over variables).	Laboratory settings are required for high levels of control: natural behavior is often altered or disappears. Change to natural settings reduce control options.
Good quantification potential; data are organized by the instrument and easily systematized.	Difficulties with quantification: large amounts of data, coding problems, and lower power in statistical analysis.	
Largest sampling requirements.	Smaller sample sizes	Smallest sample sizes
Anonymity/confidentiality safeguards.	Ethical questions about consent, anonymity, etc.	Ethical considerations heavily influence manipulation and control of variables.

2. Observation has the potential to involve deception (particularly with participant observation) and violate rights of privacy. With the observational method, the guarantee of anonymity is often difficult and it may not be possible to secure consent without revealing the study's objectives. Often there are safety risks for the researcher and staff. Unobtrusive measures, particularly those involving archival analysis and physical traces are less prone eth-

Chapter 12

Observation

ical dilemmas. However, garbage analysis was considered a violation to privacy rights until a Supreme Court ruling.

In addition to the Ethics Section in Part I of the book, the instructor may wish to review the following issues (they are also repeated in Chapter 13, Experimentation). Considering the four classes of observational studies (see the section entitled, The Type of Study, page 336), those which are completely structured and in a laboratory setting will resemble experiments and will produce ethical problems (for example: B, C, D, E, F, G, H, I). Unstructured observations in a natural setting may be only problematic with respect to A, H, and J.

A. Involving people in research without their knowledge or consent.
B. Coercing people to participate.
C. Withholding from the participant the true nature of the research.
D. Deceiving the participant.
E. Leading the participants to commit acts that diminish their self-respect.
F. Violating the right to self-determination: research on behavior control and character change.
G. Exposing the participant to physical or mental stress.
H. Invading the privacy of the participant.
I. Withholding benefits from participants in control groups.
J. Failing to treat participants fairly and to show them consideration and respect. [1]

3. There are three decision aspects to this question: whether to observe directly or indirectly, whether to conceal the observer or his mission in some way, and whether the observer is to participate in any functioning that goes on. Any combination of these three elements is possible, so the answer often depends upon the assumptions made and the preferences of the researcher.

A. If observer is a member of the class then direct observation in which his observation is concealed is likely, but observer participates in class activity. If observer is visitor the concealment is hardly possible and participation is unlikely.

B. This could be direct but it is not uncommon for this to be done by a video camera which takes a frame every second or so. The process of observation would probably be concealed from the customer, but the observer would probably be visible, but a nonparticipant.

C. May be direct, concealed, and nonparticipant if the client visits the scene of the focus group and observes from behind a one way mirror. Also may use a videotape and in this case it might be indirect, probably not concealed, and nonparticipant.

D. Probably direct, concealed, and participant. It is unlawful in the U.S. to "spy" on union activities on behalf of management.

Chapter 12　　　　　　　　　　　　　　　　　　　　　　　　　　　　　　　　Observation

4. This might take a variety of forms. An example similar to this is given earlier for the second observational class exercise.

5. Same as 4, above.

6. Student work experience is solicited for class discussion.

7. A. Some of the standard information items which would be noted are: sex, age, whether alone or with other adults or children, time of day, day of week, and weather conditions. Evidence of shopping activity, apparent income, race, apparent social class, and many other items might also be included, depending upon the objectives of the study.

    B. The study objectives would be a major determinant of what to observe. There would also be a number of variables that one might want to use as modifying or control variables.

    C. These would depend upon the variables used, but students should have no problem establishing reasonable operational definitions. For example, age might be separated into three or four age categories by inspection. Shopping status might be defined in terms of carrying any shopping bag or item which has apparently just been purchased.

    D. Generally the instructions should tell the observer how to act and what to do. They would include such information as to how to dress, how to conduct her/himself on the job, where to stand, how to record, and how to deal with questions or other situations which may develop. In addition, how to sample, when to conduct the observations, any special instructions as to what to observe and how to adapt to conditions which might occur.

    E. Probably there will be a time sampling such as 15 minutes of every hour, with the particular 15 minute segment being chosen originally by a random method. She/he might also be instructed to choose every 4th person passing a given point on the sidewalk, in one direction only.

8. A. *Observation* data can be collected as it occurs; it often can secure information which would have been otherwise ignored by those present. It is possible to capture the total event, it is often less obtrusive than surveys, and often information can be secured only by observation. On the other hand observation is slow and expensive to conduct, is limited to overt action information, the observer often has to be at the scene of the event to secure the information, and for many types of historical information the method is not usable.

    On the other hand, *questioning* enables one to gather more information about the past, about future expectations, and to gather information such as attitudes and expectations which are not reflected in overt behavior. Information can be gathered with less cost and from long distance by phone and mail.

B. *Nonverbal analysis* is one form of behavior analysis in which body movements, motor expressions and the like are of major concern. *Linguistic analysis* is the analysis of speaking behavior, including how and what is said and to whom. *Extra-linguistic analysis* includes voice pitch and loudness, rate of speaking, duration, rhythm, interactions including tendencies to interrupt, dominate, etc., and verbal styles including vocabulary use, pronunciation, dialect, and the like.

C. *Factual observation* is restricted to those manifest events, actions, and conditions which are reported as they occur or fail to occur. *Inferential observation* calls for the observer to interpret events and actions by drawing conclusions about latent factors that are at work, or reasons why one reacts in a certain way. Evaluations of performance is an example of inferential observation.

True - False Questions

T   1) Observation is a slow and expensive process which requires either human observers or some type of surveillance equipment.

T   2) Records analysis is one of the most prevalent forms of observation.

F   3) Process or activity studies such as traffic flows in a distribution system or paperwork from in an office are forms of behavioral observation.

T   4) The observational study of human nonverbal behavior is the most prevalent form of behavioral observation.

F   5) An observer who is well trained can usually do a good job of observing several different activities at the same time.

T   6) Direct observation is usually considered to involve more bias than indirect observation.

T   7) In the partial concealment approach, the presence of the observer is not concealed, but the objectives of the study are concealed.

T   8) Systematic observation employs standardized procedures, training of observers, schedules for recording, and other devices to control the observer and sometimes even the subject.

T   9) In event sampling, the researcher records selected behaviors that answer the investigative questions.

T   10) An example of inferential observation would involve the observation of the degree of enthusiasm exhibited by a participant in an exercise.

Chapter 12 — Observation

F   11) In observation studies a natural setting is still said to exist when no controls are placed on the subject although some changes may be introduced by the observer in a disguised way.

F   12) The design of an observation study follows the same general procedures as other research.

T   13) Unobtrusive measures encourage creative applications of indirect observation, archival searches, and variations on simple and contrived observation.

F   14) There are two types of observation studies, structured and unstructured.

Multiple Choice Questions

1. Which of the following is an example of observation at an inferential level?
    A) Count of cars passing an intersection.
    B) Number of agreement comments made in a small group session.
    C) Number of efforts made to interrupt a dialogue.
    * D) Number of times an argument was effectively rebutted in a debate.

2. Which of the following would normally qualify as an observation "act," depending on the nature of the study
    A) A single expressed thought
    B) A facial expression
    C) A type of behavior
    * D) A, B, and C

3. Which of the following states well the status of researcher bias in observation research?
    A) Observer bias is as pronounced as interviewer bias and sometimes even more.
    B) Observer bias can be eliminated only by observer concealment.
    C) There is very little observer bias since the observer plays a background role in the research situation.
    * D) None of the above states the status of observation bias very well.

4. The observational study of body movements and motor expressions are examples of
    A) Physical process analysis
    * B) Nonverbal behavior analysis
    C) Spatial analysis
    D) Extra-linguistic behavior analysis

Chapter 12

5.*   Which of the following is a major weakness of the observation method
   A) The observer generally must be on the scene when an event occurs or it is lost.
   B) Observation is more intrusive than is questioning.
   C) Observation is of limited value in behavior studies.
   D) It is almost impossible to observe without the subject being influenced by the observation process.

Notes

1. Louise H. Kidder and Charles M. Judd, *Research Methods in Social Relations,* 5th ed. (New York: CBS College Publishing, 1986), p. 461.

Chapter 13 *Experimentation*

CHAPTER 13

EXPERIMENTATION

There are three learning objectives for this chapter. The first is for the student to understand the nature of experimentation and the elements which are essential for conducting an experiment. The second objective is to produce a comprehension of the threats to internal and external validity. The third objective is for the student to be able to identify the major variations of experimental designs and to choose among designs for specific experimental purposes. The thread of ethical responsibility is woven throughout this chapter starting with the vignette. There are many opportunities to continue this discussion.

For a detailed discussion of the classification of experimental design types and their problems of validity, the instructor should refer to the Cook and Campbell or the Campbell and Stanley references at the end of the chapter. The Edwards book is excellent on the problems and techniques of experimental design. Green and Tull provide a marketing perspective.

Class Discussion Suggestions

One class period should be allocated for the topic of experimentation. In part this is possible because some of the introductory material has already been covered in Chapter 5, Testing Causal Hypotheses, while the testing of experiment results is deferred until Chapters 15 and 17. If one day is used for this subject, the instructor needs to concentrate on the threats to validity (internal and external) and how various designs treat these threats. The section entitled Conducting an Experiment serves as a good review to begin the discussion or lecture.

The concepts of experimentation may be discussed using the questions at the end of the chapter. In particular, questions 1, 3, 5, 6, and 7 deal with specific definitional and usage concerns. Questions 7 and 8 allow exploration of few design types: from pre-experiments to quasi-experiments and on to true experiments. Questions 8 and 9 address some situations which dictate the use of one type of design over another. Question 4 addresses ethical issues and serves well for closure.

If the instructor wishes to expand the coverage of experimentation, the analysis of variance material from Chapters 15 and 17 may be assigned so that there is connecting coverage of statistical tests. We recommend an extended recapitulation of ethics in research.

Answers to Chapter Questions

1. A. *Internal validity* was called simply "validity" in Chapter 6. It involves the question of whether we are measuring what we think we are, i.e., is the experimental treatment the real cause of the result we find in the experimental group? *External validity* concerns the degree to which the experiment

can be generalized across persons, times, or settings. That is, can the experiment be viewed as an accurate sample of some more general conditions.

B. *Pre-experiment designs* are the crudest forms of "experimentation" because they fail to control extraneous variables and they often omit the basic process of comparison. History, maturation, and instrumentation problems often plague these designs. *Quasi-experiment designs* are more sophisticated than pre-experiment designs, but they too do not qualify as true experiments. These designs are used when the researcher can control only some of the variables. In the quasi-experiment the researcher cannot establish equivalent experimental and control groups through random assignment, and often he/she cannot determine when or to whom to expose the experimental variable. On the other hand, researchers can often determine when and whom to measure.

C. Both are problems of internal validity. *History effects* represent specific events that occur during a study which can influence the IV-DV relationship. *Maturity effects* occur purely as a function of time passage and are not specific to a given event or condition.

D. *Random Sampling* (Chapter 8) is the special case of the probability sample where each population element has an equal chance of selection. Randomization and matching are both useful devices by which one can improve the equivalency of control and experimental groups. Neither method is perfect, but *randomization* is the basic method because it is the primary means of assuring compatibility within some known error interval. Subjects are randomly assigned to groups by probability sampling, the type depending on the nature of the experimental design. *Matching*, which employs a nonprobability quota sampling approach, is a way to supplement random assignment and can improve the equivalence of test and control groups.

E. *Active factors* are those variables which an experimenter can manipulate by causing various subjects to receive more or less of the factor. *Blocking factors* are those which a subject has in some degree and can not be changed by the experimenter. The experimenter can only identify and classify subjects on these blocking factors.

2. See table in Chapter 12, question 1.

3. Students should operationally define the following variables: performance differences, microcomputers, local area network, minicomputer, terminals. There are permissible differences in the definitions. Below, some alternatives are covered.

Performance Differences - Define performance as the speed at which the system completes a task. Several tasks could be measured and combined in a weighted average to come up with a scaler number which represents the performance of each of the two computer setups in a particular customer environment. For example, the following tasks could be included: time to retrieve client information from a database; time to update a database, time to complete a calculation, time to check the spelling of a document, time to print a document. Since the research question involves more than one "workstation," the tasks should be measured with varying numbers of people doing the tasks (i.e., 1, 5, and 10). The performance differences are represented by the difference between the time it takes the first system to complete the tasks and the time it takes the second system to complete the tasks.

Microcomputers - A microcomputer should be defined as a personal computer containing a microprocessor with a specific speed and hard disk of specific size and speed. It may include a monitor and specific audio options. For example, it may be an IBM compatible personal computer with a 486 processor running at 66 MHz and a 270 MB hard disk having a 12 msec access time. Or it may be an Apple with a PowerPC processor running at 50 MHz and a 510 MB hard disk having a 13 msec access time.

Local area network (LAN) - A local area network is defined as a set of microcomputers connected together by cabling, able to share data, programs, printers, scanners, and etc. Several types of LANs are available and the type of LAN will effect the performance. Therefore, LANs should be further operationally defined to be token ring or ethernet and the speed at which it runs should be defined (4 or 16 Mb/sec for token ring, 10Mb/sec for ethernet).

Minicomputer - Any of a number of midrange computer systems, like Digital's VAX machine. These systems operate only through terminals or microcomputers that are attached directly or via a modem. They have more complex software, faster processors, and larger hard disk storage than microcomputers. They support anywhere from several to more than one hundred terminals.

Terminals - Includes a keyboard and a screen that connects to a computer. A terminal has no "intelligence" (processor) to do computing on its own and depends on the computer to which it is linked for data storage as well.

4. (See the Ethics Section in Part I of the book). In the past there has often been too little concern among researchers for this problem. Clearly subjects in experiments have rights that can be violated easily, especially in research involving students who may not feel free to refuse participation. The federal government has promulgated regulations concerning the use of humans as subjects in research and many universities and colleges have formed committees to monitor faculty research projects in this respect. Student-run projects have generally not been monitored but there would appear to be no compelling reason why they should not.

The discussion of this point should consider the degree to which the following ten items are pertinent to the experimental method:

A. Involving people in research without their knowledge or consent.
B. Coercing people to participate.

Chapter 13 — Experimentation

    C. Withholding from the participant the true nature of the research.
    D. Deceiving the participant.
    E. Leading the participants to commit acts that diminish their self-respect.
    F. Violating the right to self-determination: research on behavior control and character change.
    G. Exposing the participant to physical or mental stress.
    H. Invading the privacy of the participant.
    I. Withholding benefits from participants in control groups.
    J. Failing to treat participants fairly and to show them consideration and respect.[1]

5. He is saying that the model of experimental design is the most powerful basis we have for determining causation and that we should seek, in research efforts, to approach this ideal model as closely as possible.

6. The major characteristic of the true experiment is the achievement of equivalency between experimental and comparison groups through the use of random assignment. In this way we can enhance internal validity.

7. The question can be answered in many ways and each may be tested with several designs. Some examples might be:

1. *(Marketing)* An experimental design in a supermarket in which the objective is to test to what degree the increase in the number of shelf facings of a canned food product will result in greater sales of that item. The sales rate of several different brands of a product could be observed: then a random choice can be made to increase the facings of one of the brands. Observation of sales could then be continued for a period of time. This is an example of the pretest-posttest control group design.

2. *(Marketing)* Design a sales test using video tape machines as a selling device. Randomly separate customers into two groups, one to receive the regular sales presentation which uses printed material to tell the sales story and the other group to receive the supplemental assistance from the video tape presentation. This is a posttest only design.

8.   A. Completely randomized design -

        A = no incentive   R   A 0_1

        B = $1 Incentive   R   B 0_2

        C = $3 incentive   R   C 0_3

    B. Randomized block design -

Assume that there are strong reasons to believe that the experiment should be blocked on political affiliation and that the three political classifications

Chapter 13　　　　　　　　　　　　　　　　　　　　　　　　　　　Experimentation

are:

		Democrat	Independent	Republican
No Incentives	R	A	A	A
$1	R	B	B	B
$3	R	C	C	C

C. Latin square -

Assume that a second extraneous factor, age, is believed to have an important effect. We divide all respondents into young, middle age, and old groups.

Age	Democrat	Independent	Republican
Young	A	C	B
Middle	B	A	C
Old	C	B	A

D. Factorial design -

Assume that we wish to test the effect of the sex of the interviewer at the same time we test the incentives. The factorial design might be:

Interviewer	No incentive	$1	$3
	(A)	(B)	(C)
Male (M)	MA	MB	MC
Female (F)	FA	FB	FC

With the information given it is not possible to determine which design to use. If there is no apparent reason to use a more complex design, one might use the completely randomized design. If there is a useful basis on which to block, this would normally increase the precision of results as this type of stratified sampling is typically more statistically efficient than simple random sampling. With a total sample of 300 one might prefer a design with only a few cells.

9. A. Probably the most appropriate design is a quasi-experiment called the nonequivalent control group. One might assume that there are three different factories (e.g. assembly plants) and each one will use a different compensation method. While the specific method assigned to each plant could be done randomly, this limited randomization does not give much equivalency assurance. The use of the same compensation system within each plant would at least partially guard against the contamination effect that might be found if one were to try three experimental patterns within the same plant.

B. This case calls for a factorial design since there are two variables which are being tested simultaneously. This project might call for setting up the experiment in several cities so as to achieve different levels of advertising.

C. This research situation calls for a quasi-experiment known as the separate sample pretest-posttest design. In this two random samples of persons could be set up prior to the announcement and one of them surveyed just before the profit and bonus announcements, immediately after the announcements the other sample would be surveyed.

D. Several different designs might be suggested here. Some will suggest a time series quasi-experiment design in which various time periods will be control periods (i.e., no music) while others will be experimental periods. In this case each time period is a unit of observation.

Another approach might be to use a randomized block design in which blocking is done on time periods with different traffic levels since this may affect shopping speed. Individuals entering the store during either control or experimental study periods would be timed.

True-False Questions

T   1) Experimentation is used to determine whether and in what manner variables are related to each other.

F   2) The overwhelming advantage of experimentation is that no other method approaches its power to determine statistical relationships among variables.

F   3) When we are concerned about whether a demonstrated statistical relationship implies cause we are dealing with an external validity issue.

F   4) Among the threats to the internal validity of every experiment are maturation, selection, and the interaction of sitting and treatment.

T   5) Instrumentation results in a threat to internal validity when changes are made, between observations, in the measuring instrument or observers.

T   6) To the extent that subjects do not perceive deviations from their everyday routines, an experiment cannot be justly criticized as "artificial."

T   7) External validity is largely a question of generalization from a study to other persons, settings, and times.

F   8) We typically seek external validity while trying to secure as much internal validity as is compatible with external validity requirements.

F   9) The history threat to validity occurs when members of a control group differ in background from members in an experimental group.

T   10) There are two types of independent variables which may be found in experiments. They are the so-called active factors and blocking factors.

F   11) Randomization, when used to eliminate selection bias in experimental designs, works best when the groups being compared are small.

F   12) The one-shot case study fails to provide control over extraneous variables but careful effort to make accurate measurements can compensate for its lack of controls.

T   13) The one-group pretest-posttest design is not a true experimental design and should be used only when nothing better is possible.

T   14) The major deficiency of pre-experimental designs is that they fail to provide truly equivalent comparison groups.

T   15) Matching is a useful device for making improvements in equivalency, but random assignment is the basic safeguard.

F   16) In all single group time-series designs there is a single temporary treatment that is preceded and followed by measurements at specified intervals.

T   17) The pretest-posttest control group design controls for all seven internal validity factors.

T   18) An example of a two level blocking factor is the sex of the participant.

F   19) When there are two major sources of extraneous variation the randomized block design is to be preferred.

F   20) A major advantage of the Latin square design is that there is no interaction between treatment and blocking factors.

F   21) The Latin square may be used whenever there are an even number of blocking factors if the researcher has large computational facilities available.

T   22) Factorial designs are capable of testing two or more variables at the same time, determining the main effects of each variable, and measuring the interaction effects of the variables.

T   23) In the quasi-experiment we cannot determine when or to whom we can expose the experimental variable, but usually we can determine when and whom we measure.

F   24) In quasi-experiments we can usually establish equivalent experimental and control groups through random assignment.

Chapter 13 Experimentation

T   25) If comparison of pretest results between experimental and control groups shows a similarity between groups, there is more reason to believe that internal validity of the experiment is good.

T   26) The major internal validity problem for the group time-series design is not mortality but history.

Multiple-Choice Questions

1. In experimental design the critical safeguard to assure equivalency is
   * A) Random assignment.
   B) Random selection.
   C) Matching.
   D) Covariance analysis.

2. The critical difference between an experiment and a quasi-experiment is the difference in
   A) Degree of design sophistication.
   B) Versatility of design.
   C) Relative cost of the two methods.
   * D) Ability to control variables.

3. The Latin square experimental design is
   A) Probably the most powerful discussed in the text.
   B) A form of quasi-experiment.
   * C) Useful when there are two extraneous variables.
   D) A form of the Solomon four-group design.

4. Validity which is concerned with the generalization of a finding across other persons' settings and times is known as
   A) Internal validity.
   * B) External validity.
   C) Statistical conclusion validity.
   D) Construct validity.

5. The basic form of true experiment is the
   A) Randomized block design.
   * B) Completely randomized design.
   C) Latin square design.
   D) Factorial design.

6. Which of the following is not a type of problem encountered in internal validity considerations?
   A) Maturation.
   B) Statistical regression.
   C) Experiment mortality.
   * D) Interaction of testing and treatment.
   E) All of the above are encountered in internal validity.

Chapter 13 Experimentation

7. One threat to validity is the history threat. Which of the following best illustrates this threat?
   A) Members of experimental and control groups with different religious backgrounds.
   B) The act of pretesting sensitizes subjects to the research topic.
   * C) Some extraneous variable influences experimental results during the study.
   D) Older subjects will typically react differently from younger subjects.

8. The major advantage of experimentation over other research designs is that it is
   A) The most economical way to determine causal relationships.
   B) The easiest way to determine causal relationships.
   * C) The most powerful way to determine causal relationships.
   D) The most widely used way to determine causal relationships.

9. You have been asked to measure the relative effect of three types of persuasive messages on employees in a company. You have reason to believe that your results might easily be confounded by the sex of the subject so you use the following experimental design.

			Sex	
Message			M	F
A	R		X_1	X_1
B	R		X_2	X_2
C	R		X_3	X_3

What type of design is this?
   A) Latin square.
   B) Factorial.
   * C) Randomized block.
   D) Completely randomized.
   E) None of the above.

10. Which of the following research designs is a quasi-experiment design?
    A) Static-group comparison.
    B) Posttest only control group design.
    C) Latin square design.
    * D) Nonequivalent control group design.
    E) None of the above.

11. The major way that experimentation differs from ex post facto research is that in the former the researcher:
    A) Uses both independent and dependent variables and in the latter does not.
    * B) Uses variable manipulation but not in the latter.
    C) Uses control groups but not in the latter.
    D) Is interested in causal relationships but not in the latter.

147

12. In the typical experiment we can often control for extraneous variables through blocking. It is also possible to apply some degree of indirect statistical control on one or more variables through
    A) Analysis of covariance.
    B) Analysis of variance.
    C) Omission of before measurement.
    D) Analyses of internal validity.
    E) Use of the intact equivalent design.

13. The group Time-Series Design is
    A) A form of pre-experiment.
    B) Superior to a true experimental design.
    C) Known for random assignment of experimental and control groups.
    D) Susceptible to history threats.

Notes

1. Louise H. Kidder and Charles M. Judd, *Research Methods in Social Relations*, 5th ed. (New York: CBS College Publishing, 1986), p. 461.

CHAPTER 14

DATA PREPARATION AND PRELIMINARY ANALYSIS

There are three learning objectives for this chapter. One is to develop student understanding of data preparation activities such as editing, coding, data entry, and handling don't know answers. These topics are critical to a project's accuracy but are not intellectually stimulating. However, their importance needs to be stressed, especially the need for planning standardized procedures. A hands-on exposure to computerized data entry is also essential.

The second learning objective is to develop student insight and ability with preliminary analysis. A first pass at any data set requires the ability to use descriptive statistics to summarize a variable's characteristics. We have gone one step further by introducing exploratory data analysis. This topic does not require much more than basic statistical knowledge. EDA tools are valuable for visualizing distributions, diagnosing problems with outliers, and locating errors in the data. The section on Techniques for Displaying and Examining Distributions offers several techniques to help students understand the characteristics of their data and prepare descriptive reports. For some studies this may be sufficient. If time permits, it would be appropriate to introduce this topic with computer applications. Most software programs offer both exploratory and diagnostic procedures.

Students are hesitant when asked to interpret data in cross tabulation. When a third variable is added their difficulties are compounded. Thus, the third objective is to get them sufficiently familiar with tables, their configuration, and percentage analysis so that when statistical tests are added in the next chapter, they will have a thorough grounding. Some attention in class to specific examples can be an effective way to improve these skills.

The suggested readings are highly recommended for the preparation of explanatory materials to augment the text and discussion questions.

Class Discussion Suggestions

This chapter is one of the longest in the book -- which makes it appear foreboding for students. Although it has been shorten in this edition, we recommend breaking it up into three parts: data preparation, preliminary analysis, and crosstabulation. Normally, two sessions will be sufficient. Depending on the level of students, some follow up may be required.

1. Data Preparation

    A. If the student projects have progressed to the point where it is appropriate to precode instruments, use a portion of the period to help each group trouble shoot. Examples may be solicited in advance for illustration and suggestions from other student teams will produce involvement.

Chapter 14 — Data Preparation and Preliminary Analysis

    B. The classification of open-ended responses is an exercise much needed by most students. Question 3 at the end of the chapter is a good assignment to be brought to class. At the beginning of class ask several students to put their classification schemes on the blackboard for review. A variation is to call for the assignments, quickly inspect them, and choose several that provide a variety of approaches. These can then be put up on the board for discussion. In evaluating the various classification schemes concentrate on such questions as: How well does each system meet the four rules for establishing category sets? To what degree is information lost by a particular classification scheme? Actually classify several of the responses by each system and then discuss what new categorization system might better capture the information in the responses.

    C. If a computer lab is close by or it is possible to bring a portable PC with projection capability to the classroom, the section on data entry can be nicely illustrated. You may wish to augment this presentation with a guest lecture. For example, a local research firm that specializes in telephone interviewing may be willing to demonstrate its approach to direct data entry.

2. The unit on preliminary analysis is best taught with examples and exercises. Questions 4 through 8 provide some materials for assignment and in-class work which may be done by hand and/or with a computer. The notion of exploration may be somewhat foreign to students who have been taught that one does not muck about in the data before hypothesis testing as it ruins ones objectivity. <u>These impressions are easily unlearned when examples are provided that show how various hypothesis testing techniques would have been improperly applied had it not been for diagnostics and exploratory data analysis.</u> Finally, the point needs to be made that EDA is *not* a form of data snooping; the null and alternative hypotheses should never be formulated *after* we have examined the data -- not only because it is dishonest but also because it reduces the power of rejecting any null hypothesis.

3. The third unit is devoted to crosstabulation.

    A. An understanding of how variables are related through cross tabulation is an important entry level skill. After introducing this topic, discuss the direction in which percentages in a cross tabulation should flow. Question 10 at the end of the chapter is useful here. Other relationships which might be used for discussion of correlation and the direction of table percentages are the following:
      1. Age and political membership
      2. Occupation and education
      3. Opinions regarding product "X" and frequency of its use
      4. Family income and purchase of common stocks

B. It is helpful to begin the coverage of elaboration by going through the examples shown in the chapter to point out the nature and function of each type of relationship. Try organizing the discussion around the following purposes of the test factors:

Objective	Relationship
1. Avoid accepting false relationships	Extraneous factors or distorter factors
2. Avoid rejecting true relationships	Suppressor or distorter factors
3. Give more precise and specific explanation of the "cause"	Component factors
4. Give a more complete explanation of the chain of connection between the IV and DV.	Intervening factors
5. Give more information on the background on the IV which is relevant to the IV-DV relationship	Antecedent factors

Once these different factors have been discussed one might use questions 12 and 13 at the end of the chapter to give students some practice in elaboration and table interpretation. In each case students might answer the following questions: (1) What is the type of asymmetrical relationship? (2) What does the elaboration tell us in each case? (3) What type of factor testing is illustrated?

Answers to Chapter Questions

1. A. *Coding rules* govern the establishment of category sets. There are four; categories should be: (1) appropriate to the research problem or purpose, (2) exhaustive, (3) mutually exclusive, and (4) derived from only one classificatory principle.

    B. *Spreadsheet data entry* uses personal computer software for spreadsheet computation as a data entry device. Preliminary analysis, data manipulation, summary statistics, and graphics are frequently available in this medium.

    C. *Control or test variables in elaboration*. The addition of one or more variables to a two-variable contingency table is used to further the explanation or the circumstances under which the original relationship may hold.

    D. *Alphanumeric variables* contain a combination of letters and numbers to designate an appropriate range of responses.

    E. *Precoded instruments* anticipate responses to questions and assign numerals or other symbols for those responses in advance.

F. *Nonresistant statistics* (e.g., the mean and standard deviation) are influenced by outlying values in a distribution and may change significantly in response to a small change in the data set.

G. *Measures of shape* include skewness and kurtosis which describe departures from symmetry and the relative flatness (or peakedness) of a distribution, respectively.

H. *The five-number summary* consists of the median, upper and lower quartiles, and largest and smallest observations in a distribution.

I. *Notched boxplots* are a variation on boxplot design to show a confidence interval that may be used to visualize a test of equality of group medians.

J. *Spread-and-level plots* examine the relationship of the average value (level) of a variable and its variability (spread) using the log of the median and the log of the interquartile range. From the slope, a power transformation can be estimated that will eliminate or lessen the relationship.

2. There are several ways to handle these answers. If there are only a few they might be left as a separate category and included in the findings. Another approach is to eliminate them. In doing this we are assuming that they have no particular bearing on the pattern of answers we are getting. In cases where we suspect that they may be a disguise for some other answer, we may attempt to correlate the DK answers with these other answers. Comparing answers to other questions and checking with the interviewer may at times also help interpret these replies.

3. Note: *Items labeled a - n are not separate questions but 14 representative responses for coding this problem.* These responses may be categorized in a number of ways. This example is taken from one in which more than 30 replies were used. In the longer exercise, the following classification system was the best that resulted from the efforts of the student team involved.

		Mention	Not Mention
A. Buying practices			
1. Less advance buying		___	___
2. Careful requirements planning		___	___
3. Buy closeouts, etc.		___	___
4. Better or more careful buying		___	___
5. Buy for cash		___	___
B. Product selection			
1. Less style emphasis		___	___
2. Fewer resources/lines		___	___
3. Concentrate on known brands		___	___
4. Reduce item duplication		___	___

Chapter 14 *Data Preparation and Preliminary Analysis*

        5.   Concentrate on in-stock shoes   _____   _____
        6.   Eliminate fringe items   _____   _____

    C.   Price reduction

        1.   Small early markdowns   _____   _____
        2.   Markdowns at season end   _____   _____
        3.   Do not markdown staples   _____   _____

    D.   Sales effort intensification

        1.   P.M.s   _____   _____
        2.   Push slow movers   _____   _____
        3.   Sales   _____   _____
        4.   Better sales work   _____   _____

    E.   Inventory control

        1.   Careful checking   _____   _____
        2.   Keep stock low   _____   _____

4.   A.   Histograms are less helpful for error detection than frequency tables, stem-and-leaf displays, or boxplots. A histogram of family size that had and unexpected code , such as a midpoint at 20, might reveal a coding error or alert the analyst to a potential outlier.

    B.   Stem-and-leaf displays present data values in condensed form facilitating inspection of questionable observations. These, in turn, may be linked back to the data file and to the respondent that produced them.

    C.   Boxplots through whiskers and outlier identification call attention to values that extend beyond the main body of the data. Since extreme values have a substantial influence on numerical summaries, errors in this area are often detected early.

    D.   The presence or absence of unexpected categories or frequency counts in crosstab cells alerts the analyst to a potential coding problem.

5.   A.   The main body of the data is between the upper and lower hinges labeled "H" in Exhibit 14 - 1, below. This area represents 50% of the observed values.

Chapter 14   Data Preparation and Preliminary Analysis

Exhibit 14-1 Stem-and-Leaf Display for Net Profit Variable*

```
Minimum:        251.00
Lower hinge:    807.60
Median:        1084.35
Upper Hinge:   1723.80
Maximum:       4224.30

          0     2
          0     4555
          0     66777
          0  H  8888888999999
          1  M  00011
          1     22233
          1     45
          1  H  667
          1     89
          2
          2
          2     444
          2     6
          2     99
       ***Outside values***
          3     789
          4     2
```

*Fastat Statistics for the Mac

B. The upper and lower "inner fences" are plus or minus 1.5 IQRs from the hinges. The IQR is 1406.36. Since the lower hinge is 807.6 and the minimum value in the distribution is 251, there are no lower outside values. The upper "inner fence" would be 3130.16 (1723.80 + 1406.36) and the last observed value inside that fence is 2975. Thus, four values are outside: 3758, 3825, 3939, and 4224.3 . (See Exhibit 14 - 1.)

6.   A.   The five-number summary is shown at the top of Exhibit 14 - 2.

       B.   See the boxplot in Exhibit 14 - 2.

Exhibit 14-2 Five-Number Summary and Boxplot for Sales Variable*

```
Minimum:      7492.0        Skewness    2.5639
Lower hinge: 11990.0        Kurtosis    7.1644
Median:      17478.5        IQR        13932.0000
Upper hinge: 25922.0
Maximum:    126932.0
```

```
150000. +
         |
         |
         |
         |      (E) Case 2
         |
         |
100000. +
         |      (E) Case 6
         |      (E) Case 4
         |
         |
         |      (O) Case 5
         |      (O) Case 11,3
 50000. +      (O) Case 9
         |       ┌─┐
         |       │ │
         |       │*│
         |       │ │
         |       └─┘
     0. +
         └────────────────────────────────
         Symbol Key:    * Median    (O) Outlier    (E) Extreme

Valid cases:    50.0    Missing cases: 0   Percent missing: 0
```

*SPSS Release 4.0 for Macintosh

C. The upper "inner fence," 1.5 IQRs from the end of the rectangular box, is 46820. Seven observed values lie beyond this point, each of which is designated by a case number in the exhibit and has a corresponding subject number in the Data Table for this problem. This distribution is positively skewed and somewhat peaked. Extreme values are primarily from the following sectors: Durable - Capital Equipment, Energy, and Hi - Tech.

Chapter 14   *Data Preparation and Preliminary Analysis*

Exhibit 14-3   Histogram of Market Value in 5000 Unit Intervals *

```
Count   Midpoint    One symbol equals approximately .40 occurrences
  13     6391.00
   9    11391.00
  12    16391.00
   4    21391.00
   6    26391.00
   1    31391.00
   1    36391.00
   0    41391.00
   1    46391.00
   0    51391.00
   2    56391.00
   1    60345.00
            0        4        8       12       16       20
                         Histogram frequency
```

Mean	18472.020	Std err	1891.506	Median	16151.500
Mode	3891.000	Std dev	13374.969	Variance	178889785
Kurtosis	3.023	S E Kurt	.662	Skewness	1.720
S E Skew	.337	Range	56454.000	Minimum	3891.000
Maximum	60345.000	Sum	923601.000		

*SPSS Release 4.0 for Macintosh

7.   A.   The histograms for this problem are shown is Exhibit 14 - 3 (1000 unit), 14 - 4 (2000 unit), and 14 - 5 (5000 unit increments). There is considerably less information in the the 1000 and 2000 interval histogram than in the 5000 unit version. Extreme values and outliers are apparent in all examples but the 2000 and 5000 display them best. The 5000 provides a clear picture of gaps in the main body of the distribution but not sufficiently more so to justify its size.

      B.   The 1000 or 2000 unit version would be the most desirable for a management report based on the tradeoffs of size, clarity, and completeness of information.

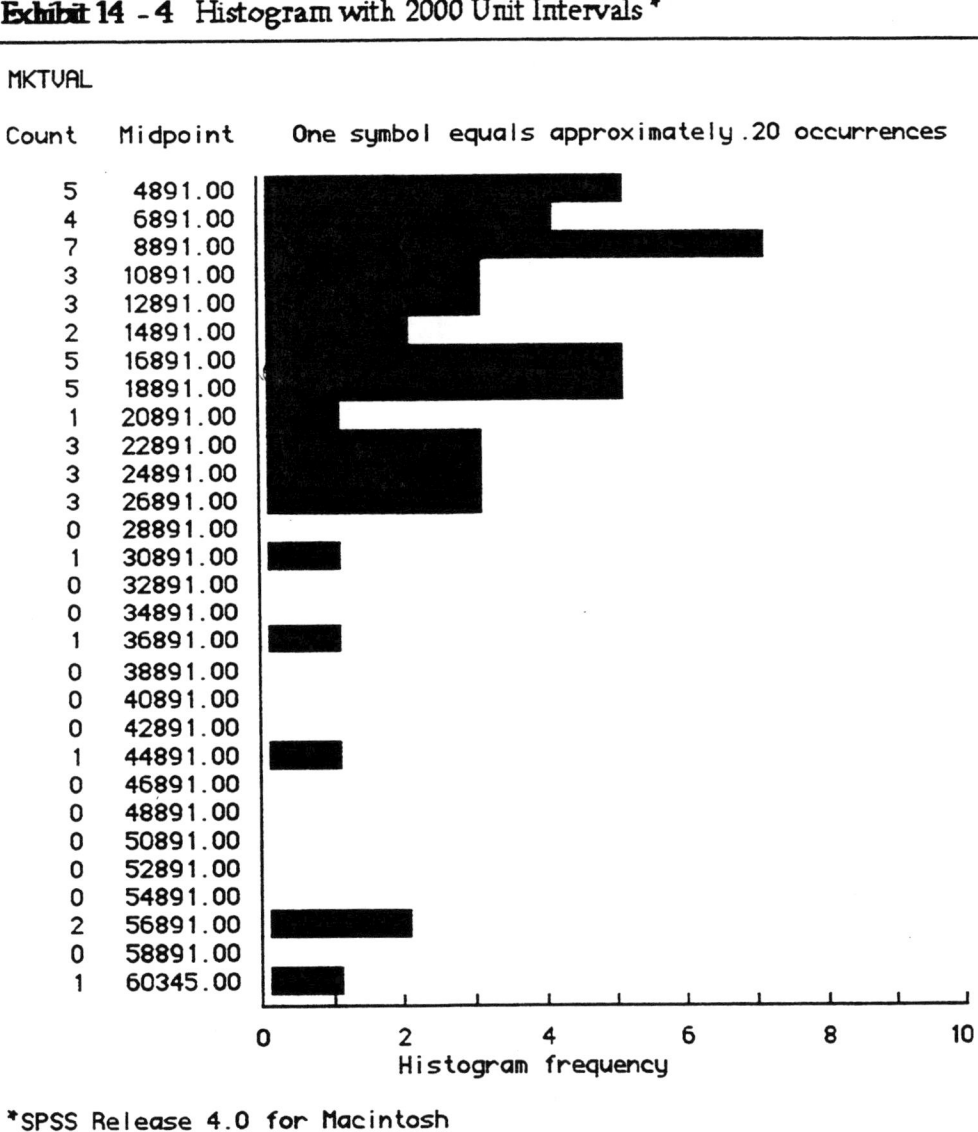

Exhibit 14 - 4 Histogram with 2000 Unit Intervals *

MKTVAL

Count   Midpoint   One symbol equals approximately .20 occurrences

Count	Midpoint
5	4891.00
4	6891.00
7	8891.00
3	10891.00
3	12891.00
2	14891.00
5	16891.00
5	18891.00
1	20891.00
3	22891.00
3	24891.00
3	26891.00
0	28891.00
1	30891.00
0	32891.00
0	34891.00
1	36891.00
0	38891.00
0	40891.00
0	42891.00
1	44891.00
0	46891.00
0	48891.00
0	50891.00
0	52891.00
0	54891.00
2	56891.00
0	58891.00
1	60345.00

Histogram frequency: 0 2 4 6 8 10

*SPSS Release 4.0 for Macintosh

C. Several factors make this distribution one where transformation is considered. It is stretched to the right by outliers and its peakedness in the vicinity of the mean and median is more pronounced than expected under the normal distribution (see overlay of normal in Exhibit 14 - 3). Dispersion statistics have also been affected by extreme scores.

D. Exhibit 14 - 6 shows a spread-and-level plot for this data. At the bottom is a recommended transformation of .445. Rounding up, our first transformation attempt would use the square root.

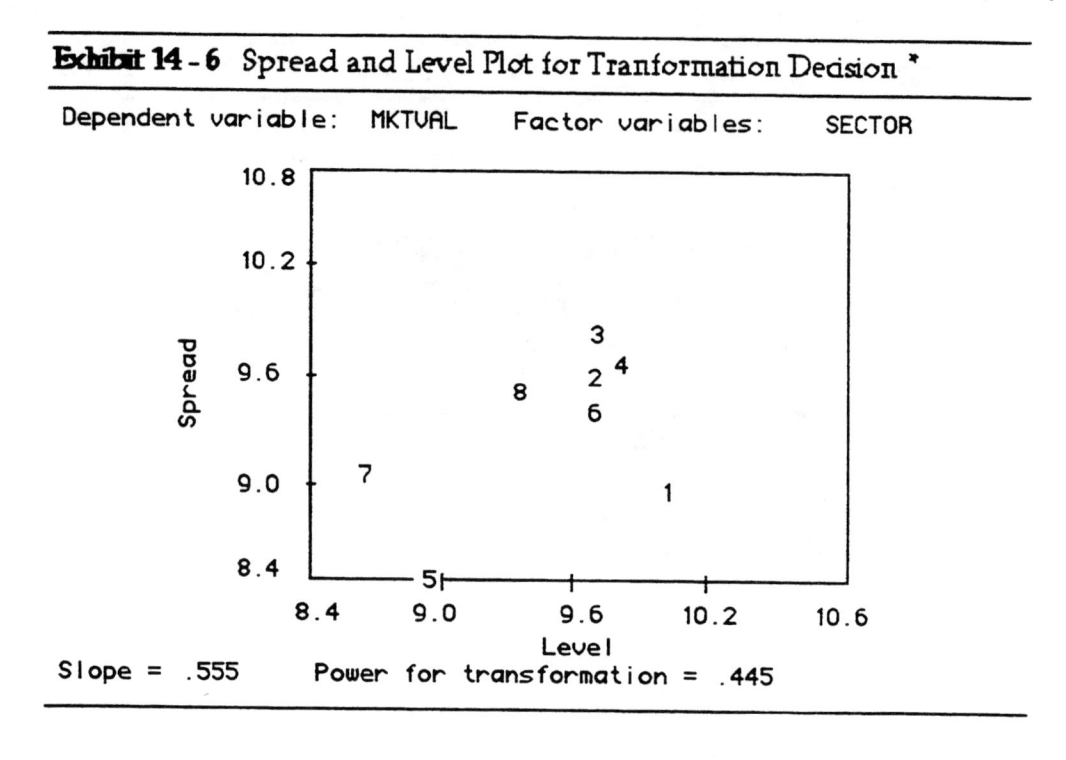

Chapter 14 — Data Preparation and Preliminary Analysis

Exhibit 14-6 Spread and Level Plot for Tranformation Decision *

Dependent variable: MKTVAL   Factor variables: SECTOR

[Scatter plot with Spread on y-axis (8.4 to 10.8) and Level on x-axis (8.4 to 10.6), showing points labeled 1–8]

Slope = .555   Power for transformation = .445

8. See Exhibit 14 - 7.

9. This question requires student collected data. Any of the following units may be used to analyze this data: syntactical, referential, propositional, or thematic. One might use syntactical units (word counts) for specific mention of position, activity, goal structure (immediate or deferred), or strategy. A propositional approach (e.g., actor, action, action object) might mention goal attainment through family, school colleagues, mentoring, or personal environmental scanning.

Exhibit 14-7 Recoded Crosstab: Sector by Sales *

```
Recode sales (7492 thru 25099 = 1) (25922 thru 126932 = 2).
Recode sector (1 = 1)(4 = 2)(5 =3)(7 = 4) (10 = 5).
Crosstabs / variables sales (1,2) sector (1,5)
 /tables= sales by sector/ cells count row column total.
```

	Count Row Pct Col Pct Tot Pct	SECTOR C-M 1	Energy 2	Fin 3	HiTech 4	Other 5	Row Total
SALES							
7492–25099	1	2 6.1 100.0 4.3	11 33.3 61.1 23.9	6 18.2 66.7 13.0	12 36.4 80.0 26.1	2 6.1 100.0 4.3	33 71.7
25922–126932	2		7 53.8 38.9 15.2	3 23.1 33.3 6.5	3 23.1 20.0 6.5		13 28.3
	Column Total	2 4.3	18 39.1	9 19.6	15 32.6	2 4.3	46 100.0

*SPSS Release 4.0 for Macintosh

10. The standard rule in determining which direction to compute percentage totals in a cross tabulation is to compute them in the direction of the causal factor, following this rule: (a) the age variable would total 100%, (b) family income would total 100%, (c) marital status would total 100%, and (d) unemployment would total 100%

    However, some may point out that there are circumstances where it would be useful to run the percentages in the other direction. Consider, for example, the relationship between age and consumption of breakfast food, a property-behavior relationship. One would not suggest that cereal changes cause age changes, but a cereal manufacturer might still find it to be very informative to have an age profile of the users of each of its cereal products. In like manner we might be very interested, in an economic survey, to know the family income patterns of the optimists and pessimists regarding their family futures.

11. At first glance it would appear that students on aid have a higher tendency to drop out of school than do students on no aid. The remainder of the data, in which aid grants are cross tabulated with drop out by nearness of the student's home to school, indicates that the original aid/drop out relationship is reversed. That is, when adjusted for nearness of home to school, the aid students tend to be retained in school better than the non-aid students. This

occurs because a much higher percentage of the "home far" students are on aid than is the case with the "home near" students. The table shown would have resulted if the absolute numbers involved were as follows:

	Home near		Home far	
	Aid	No aid	Aid	No aid
Drop out	5	60	120	40
Stay	95	340	280	60
Total	100	400	400	100

12. A. Appeal A is superior.

B. Working class members respond better than do middle class.

C. One would conclude that both social class and appeal type are important variables, but that working class is stronger, perhaps by 50% or so. This can be shown by comparing the WC/B to MC/A cell response rates.
Percent replies:

Response	Middle class	Working class
A	20	40
B	15	30

Why use these cells rather than the MC/B vs. WC/A? To compare the joint effects we compare mixed pairs of categories (mixed in the sense that each pair contains one better and one worse category). Since working class is the better and appeal B is the worst, the intersection of these two factors is compared to the other worse-better cell (MC/A).

13. Part A indicates that salaried employees have a generally lower turnover than wage earners. There is also evidence that persons from rural origins have less turnover than persons from urban backgrounds (but only in salaried positions). When education level is included we see that is a very important factor in the relationship.

	Salaried			Wage		
	Hi Ed.	Lo Ed.	H-L	Hi Ed	Lo Ed.	H-L
Rural	6	18	-12	14	18	-14
Urban	10	19	- 9	12	20	- 8
R-U	- 4	- 1		2	- 2	

It seems to be several times stronger than the rural/urban origin. In fact, along wage earners the rural/urban difference becomes confused and is probably immaterial. When rural/urban origin is "held constant" it appears that education is perhaps twice as important as job type, and even more so among those of urban origin.

	Rural			Urban		
	Hi Ed.	Lo Ed.	H-L	Hi Ed	Lo Ed.	H-L
Salary	6	18	-12	10	19	- 9
Wage	14	18	- 4	12	20	- 8
S-W	- 8	0		- 2	- 1	

Chapter 14 — Data Preparation and Preliminary Analysis

True - False Questions

T   1) Analysis involves breaking down and rearranging data into more meaningful groups to aid the search for significant relationships.

T   2) The normal first step in analysis is the editing of the collected raw data.

F   3) Field editing is usually not recommended because it can encourage interviewers to revise the responses they have collected in such a way as to bias them.

T   4) In central editing, it is preferable for each editor to edit all of a particular portion of a questionnaire.

T   5) The coding process consists of assigning numerals or other symbols to answers so as to enable the responses to be grouped into a limited number of categories.

F   6) The rule on exhaustiveness states that there must be one and only one category for a data item.

F   7) Precoding of questionnaires typically is unwise because it fails to give adequate consideration to responses which are not anticipated by the researcher.

F   8) A "don't know" response is seldom a legitimate response and is almost always a failure of the questioning process.

T   9) The use of percentages facilitates relative comparisons by translating the data into a standard form.

F   10) When two dimensional tables are used the total number of cases in each category of the dependent variable should be the base for calculating the percentages.

F   11) One advantage to using percentages is that they can be averaged in either a simple or weighted fashion.

T   12) When using percentages one should always state the data base from which the computations were made.

F   13) The two most important statistical measures of central tendency are the mean and the mode.

T   14) Numeric data reduced to a manageable number of classifications form a set known as a frequency distribution.

T   15) Frequency distributions are summarized through measures of central tendency and dispersion.

Chapter 14 — Data Preparation and Preliminary Analysis

F   16) Keypunch data entry remains one of the faster methods for getting coded information into a data file.

T   17) A data field contains numeric, alphabetic or symbolic information.

F   18) Exploratory data analysis and descriptive analysis using numerical summaries involve the same approach.

T   19) A distribution's shape is just as important as its location and spread.

F   20) The median is the most frequently occurring value.

F   21) The range is a measure of shape used with nominal data.

T   22) Resistant statistics are relatively unaffected by outlying values.

T   23) Histograms are constructed with bars or asterisks that represent data values where each values occupies an equal amount of space within the enclosed area.

F   24) Piecharts are pictorial devices for displaying interval variables.

T   25) A column of depths to the left of the stem in a stem-and-leaf display is used to identify summary values.

F   26) The five number summary consists of the median, mode, and quartiles.

T   27) Transformation is the reexpression of data on a new scale using a single mathematical function.

F   28) Z-scores are used to reexpress nonlinear data.

T   29) Crosstabulation is a technique for comparison of two classification variables, such as sex and race.

T   30) Descriptive analysis is largely the study of distributions of one variable or, in other words, a one-dimensional analysis.

T   31) Each time we introduce what appears to be a relevant third variable and find the original two variable relationship remains. the more confidence we can have in the original relationship.

T   32) When an original IV-DV relation between age and absenteeism among workers holds up when we introduce a third variable - education - we say that the latter is an extraneous variable.

F   33) Suppressor variables are those which, when accounted for, reveal that the correct interpretation is the reverse of that suggested by that original data.

Chapter 14 — Data Preparation and Preliminary Analysis

T   34) Elaboration may keep the researcher from becoming misled as well as providing a more precise understanding of a two-variable relationship.

T   35) Conditional relationships represent a situation where we wish to specify the conditions under which the original relationship is strengthened or weakened.

Multiple Choice Questions

1. Suppose you cross classify consumption rates with income and find no apparent relationship. When age is introduced you find that there is a relationship between consumption and income within age groups. This is an example of a(n) _____ variable at work.
   A) Antecedent
   B) Component
   C) Extraneous
   D) Intervening
   * E) Suppressor

2. The requirement(s) for coding are that category sets should be:
   A) Exhaustive
   B) Appropriate
   C) Mutually exclusive
   D) Defined in terms of a single dimension
   * E) All of the above

3. It is proposed that income changes affect saving motivation which, in turn, affects actual saving. The motivation variable in this case is
   A) A dependent variable
   B) An independent variable
   C) A component variable
   D) An extraneous variable
   * E) An intervening variable

4. Which of the following is an incorrect instruction for survey editors?
   A) Make all entries on a schedule in a distinctive color
   * B) When correcting schedules erase the original entry completely to avoid later confusion
   C) Place initials and date of editing on each schedule completed
   D) Initial all entries changed or supplied

5. There are a number of rules for the correct use of percentages in statistical reports. Which of the following is not a good rule?
   * A) Use only simple averages of percentages
   B) Do not use big percentages such as 1000%
   C) Do not use small number bases for calculating percentages
   D) When calculating percentage decreases always use the higher number as the base

Chapter 14   Data Preparation and Preliminary Analysis

6. All of the following are exploratory data analysis tools except:
   A) Frequency tables
   B) Barcharts and Piecharts
   C) Histograms
   * D) None of the above

7. Stem-and -leaf displays:
   A) Are related to histograms.
   B) Consist of a stem containing the leading digits and leaves containing the trailing digits.
   C) Are more versatile in summarizing distributions than frequency tables.
   * D) All of the above.

8. Boxplots are said to incorporate resistant statistics because:
   * A) They are constructed with a five-number summary.
   B) Do not contain weak measures of central tendency like the median.
   C) Are based on a new type of dispersion statistics.
   D) Use whiskers to represent quartiles.

9. Marginals are the totals of row and/or column variables in a:
   A) Piechart
   B) Barchart
   * C) Cross-classification table
   D) Frequency table.

10. When a test factor is added to a 2-way relationship we may find that the impact of the test factor affects one subgroup more than another. This is an example of a
    A) Distorted relationship
    * B) Conditional relationship
    C) Interlocking relationship
    D) Variable relationship
    E) Causal relationship

11. Which of the following is the *least* desirable way to handle "DK" answers?
    A) Do a better job of designing questions at the design stage
    B) If they are legitimate "DK" answers keep them as a separate category
    C) Keep them as a separate category
    * D) Assume they occur more or less randomly, so prorate them or exclude them from the tabulation

12. Which of the following is the most true about calculating percentages in a two dimension table?
    A) Calculate percentages on the vertical dimension
    B) Calculate percentages in the direction of the dependent variable
    * C) Calculate percentages in the direction of the independent variable
    D) Calculate percentages on both dimensions

13. The process by which we introduce a third variable into a two-way statistical association to test the relationship between the two variables is called
   A) Asymmetrical analysis
   B) Cross classification
 * C) Elaboration
   D) Multidimensional analysis
   E) Significance testing

CHAPTER 15

HYPOTHESIS TESTING

The primary learning objectives for this chapter are an understanding of (1) hypothesis testing, (2) test selection, and (3) the ability to perform simple tests. To do this the student must understand the logic of testing, comprehend the scope and application of the tests available, and be able to perform them.

Class Discussion Suggestions

Students usually find this to be one of the most difficult chapters in the book. It is impossible for them if they are undergraduates without prior statistics exposure! Although we counsel users in the Preface and in Chapter 14 of our assumptions in writing these chapters, our admonitions are not often heeded. Thus, you should be prepared for trouble when your students have not had the necessary preparation.

Even with more advanced students, it may be necessary to spend a couple class sessions on this material. It is probably wise to concentrate on only a few tests. For this reason, many of the nonparametric tests are placed in Appendix E.

1. The first task should be to assure that the students clearly understand the logic of classical hypothesis testing. Emphasize that:

A. We set up a hypothesis of *no difference* between the sample and population figures except that which comes from sampling error. We then determine whether we can reject this hypothesis or fail to reject it. There is a subtle difference here in that if we *fail to reject* we do not therefore accept. Although we often use the easier, "accept a null hypothesis," it actually means that the sample figure and the population figure are the same, while to fail to reject is to say that "we can't say they are different."

B. Significance testing assumes random sampling and addresses only the question of sampling error. Many people who are unfamiliar with the theory of hypothesis testing use the term *statistically significant* as a magic label to bless those numbers associated with it. There are situations where the findings are statistically significant and still of little practical value for decision making.

C. In discussing the meaning of hypothesis testing one should discuss testing logic, Type I and Type II errors, and testing procedures. Discussion questions 1 to 3 and 6 to 8 serve as good warm ups for discussion.

2. The next step is to acquaint the students with various types of significance tests and their use. In going through the the section on Tests of Significance, it is helpful to repeat the six step testing process. Class discussion should also concern at least the following:

Chapter 15 *Hypothesis Testing*

A. Point out the factors which influence the choice of test. Figure 15-5 (p. 445) or some of the software programs available to assist with decisions can be used effectively to approach this topic from different perspectives. The nature of assumptions and the diagnostics to confirm choices may be also illustrated. Questions 8, 12, and 13 provide examples for ANOVA. Similar diagnostics may be used for other parametric tests. The examples in the chapter and Appendix E can be used to explain when and why each test is chosen.

B. Once students are comfortable in choosing the appropriate test the next step is application. Chi-square, *t*, and ANOVA tests are worth review if it has been some time since your students have had a statistics course. If there is time, add the two-way or repeated measures ANOVA or selected nonparametric tests.

1. Another approach to test applications uses examples of previous student projects (which you may have saved as models). It is interesting for students to be shown how correct choices were made by their peers or how better alternatives could have improved the findings.

2. This can be followed up with the problems at the end of the chapter. These may be assigned either as homework or introduced into class discussion. Questions 4 - 5 and 9 - 11 may be done by hand; 12 - 18 offer an opportunity to practice with a computer package such as BMDP, Minitab, SPSS, SYSTAT, SAS, or other program your school may prefer.

Answers to Chapter Questions

1. A. Both parametric or nonparametric tests assume random probability sampling. Recall also that significance testing is concerned only with possible sampling errors, and tells us nothing about the many other types of error which might exist. *Parametric tests* assume that the measurement is at least interval in nature, while *nonparametric* testing assumes only nominal or ordinal scales depending on the test. Many parametric tests also assume:

    1. Independent observations.
    2. Observations from a normally distributed population.
    3. Populations which have equal variances.

Nonparametric tests typically have fewer and less restrictive assumptions than parametric tests. The particular assumptions vary from test to test, but nonparametric tests are often referred to as '"distribution-free tests." While this is an exaggeration, they usually do have few distribution requirements.

B. When testing a null hypothesis we have two choices: we can reject the null hypothesis, or we can fail to reject it (loosely, we refer to this as *accepting the null* but this is not technically correct). We also find that two circumstances may exist - either the null hypothesis is true or it is false. This combination of states of nature (i.e.. null hypothesis is true or false) and decisions (i.e., reject or not reject the null) gives us four conditional outcomes, two of which are correct and two of which are not. They may be displayed as follows:

	Null hypothesis is:	
Decision is:	True	False
Do not reject null hypothesis	Correct decision Probability $p = 1 - \alpha$	Incorrect decision Type II error $p = \beta$
Reject null hypothesis	Incorrect decision Type I error $p = \alpha$	Correct decision power of test $p = 1 - \beta$

Type I error is measured by a which we set in our hypothesis testing. It is the probability (or significance) level at which we will risk rejecting the null hypothesis. We define it by choosing some critical value beyond which the occurrence of a sample value leads us to conclude that the null hypothesis is false. Given such a critical value, we then compute the probability that we will incorrectly fail to reject the null hypothesis when it is false. This is *Type II error* or beta (β) error. It is not difficult to compute this arithmetically, but it is sometimes difficult to explain conceptually. The b error depends upon what assumptions we make as to how far the population parameter may have changed. For example, if the parameter was originally 50 and changes to 52 we get a different b than if it changes only to 51.

C. The *null* is a hypothesis of no change or no difference. More specifically, we conclude that a population value has not changed from one time to another, or that a sample statistic does not vary significantly from an assumed population parameter. In other cases we use the null hypothesis to state that one sample distribution does not differ from another (i.e., that they both are from the same population). The *alternative hypothesis* holds that there is a difference between sample statistics or between a sample statistic and population parameter.

D. The *acceptance region* delineates the area in a distribution where the occurrence of a sample statistic value leads us to fail to reject the null hypothesis. The *rejection region* is that portion of the distribution where we have agreed to reject the null hypothesis. The "critical value" divides these two areas.

E. A *two-tailed test* is a significance test in which the alternative hypothesis specifies no direction of difference from the population parameter value such as m. Equal rejection regions are in both tails of the distribution. In a *one-tailed test* we specify a "less than" or "greater-than" direction to the alternative hypothesis, placing all of a rejection region in one tail, or differing amounts of rejection region in each tail.

F. The probability that we will incorrectly fail to reject the null hypothesis when it is false is a *Type II error* or β error. The *power of the test* is cal-

Chapter 15 — Hypothesis Testing

culated as 1- β and is the probability with which we will correctly reject the false null hypothesis (see Figure 15 - 3, p. 440).

2. The tradeoffs between Type I and Type II errors have a practical dimension as defined by the costs incurred for each error. Often a change in the status quo is associated with great cost (e.g., gambling the future of a firm on a new technology, an acquisition, a sizable investment in equipment, etc.). Since the change must be beneficial, the risks associated with α should be kept very low. However, if it was essential to detect changes from a hypothesized mean, the risk of a β error would be paramount. Thus, we would choose a higher, less critical level for α.

3. A. We can reduce the probability of a Type I error by moving our critical values farther from the expected mean, i.e., expand our region of acceptance and reduce our area of rejection. A second way is to hold our same critical value but increase the size of sample. A third way is to shift from a statistically inefficient sample design to one more efficient, keeping the same sample size.

Type II error can be reduced, given an assumed population mean, by increasing the size of sample. A second way is to increase our α risk by moving our critical value closer to the original mean. A third way to reduce Type II error is to use a one tailed distribution. That is, place the entire region of rejection in the tail of the distribution in the direction of concern.

B. Statistical significance is concerned with whether there is truly a difference or not. Practical significance concerns whether the difference, even if it exists, is of any useful value for decision making.

C. Yes. This is obviously the case since a census of both groups was taken. Whether the difference has any real meaning or practical value is another question.

4. (1) The null hypothesis is that there is no difference between the long run average of 3.0 and the current year's average of 3.2 other than what is expected by sampling variations. It would seem appropriate here to use a one tailed test since we are concerned only with whether the sampling variation could have gone as high as 3.2.

(2) The proper test is the parametric test involving one sample results being compared to a population value. Use the t test.

(3) The desired level of significance is set at $\alpha = .05$

(4) Calculated value:

$$t = \frac{\overline{X} - \mu}{\sigma_{\overline{X}}} = \frac{3.2 - 3.0}{.4/\sqrt{25}} = \frac{.20}{.08} = 2.5$$

169

Chapter 15   Hypothesis Testing

(5) Enter Table F - 2 with 24 degrees of freedom. We find a critical value (one tailed test) of 1.711 for α = .05.

(6) Since the calculated value 2.50 > critical value (1.711) the null hypothesis is rejected.

The question also asks: "At what α level would it be significant?" Checking Table F-2, again we find that the critical value of 2.492 is found for an α of .01.

5. (1) The null hypothesis would be that there is no difference between the degree of conservatism of professors and students, and that the differences found are due to sampling variations only.

(2) This is a case of two independent samples involving proportions. The appropriate test is parametric. Using the t test.

(3) The desired level of significance is again set at α = .05

(4) Calculated value:

$$t = \frac{p_1 - p_2}{\sigma_{p_1 - p_2}} = \frac{.5 - .3}{\sqrt{\frac{.25}{20} + \frac{.21}{20}}} = \frac{.200}{.152} = 1.32$$

(5) Critical value from Table F-2 using 38 df is 1.69 for one-tailed test and 2.03 for two-tailed test.

(6) Calculated values of 1.32 < either critical value, so null hypotheses is not rejected. That is, the differences found between professors and students could be due to sampling errors only.

6. There are six relatively well-defined steps: (1) State the null hypothesis; (2) Choose the statistical test; (3) Select the desired level of significance; (4) Compute the calculated difference value; (5) Obtain the critical test value; and (6) Make the decision to accept or reject the null.

7. The Mean Square $_{between}$ is the result of the between-groups sum of squares divided by the between-groups degrees of freedom (number of groups minus one). This calculation represents the effect of the treatment condition. The Mean Square $_{within}$, calculated by dividing the within-groups sum of squares by the within-groups degrees of freedom (total observations minus number of groups), represents the error due to sampling and random fluctuations. When MS_b is divided by MS_w, the F ratio results. If the null hy-

pothesis is accepted, the ratio reflects the fact that there is relatively little difference between the presumed treatment (numerator) and error variance (denominator).

8. The required assumptions for ANOVA are: (1) independent random samples from each of the represented populations, (2) normal distribution of the represented populations, and (3) equal variances of said populations. Assumptions 2 and 3 are checked with diagnostic procedures. Measures of location, shape, and spread were discussed in Chapter 14 along with graphic techniques for examining distributions for normality. In addition, Figure 15 - 4 provides an example of normal probability plotting and detrended probability plotting for examining normality. With respect to equal variance, there are a number of homogeneity of variance tests -- many of which are dependent on the normality of the sample. For this reason we have referred to the Levene test in both Chapters 14 and 15. It is less dependent on the assumption of normality and, when using the SPSS Procedure EXAMINE, is nested within a spread-and-level plot which also serves to determine whether the data should be transformed.

9. (1) Null hypothesis. H_0: There is no difference between average annual starting salaries of the graduates at the two universities. H_A: Graduates of Eastern University received higher starting salaries than graduates of Western University.

    (2) Statistical test. The t test is chosen because the data are at least interval in form and the samples are independent in a two test situation.

    (3) Significance level. $\alpha = .05$ (one-tailed test; the alternate hypothesis states direction)

    (4) Calculated value:

    $$t = \frac{(18800 - 18000) - 0}{\sqrt{\frac{36(1000)^2 + 40(1000)^2}{(36+40)-2}\left(\frac{1}{36}+\frac{1}{40}\right)}} = \frac{800}{232.8179} = 3.436$$

    (5) Critical test value = 1.66. d.f. = 74, one-tailed test. $\alpha = .05$.

    (6) Decision. Since the calculated value is larger than the critical value (3.44 > 1.66), reject the null hypothesis and conclude that graduates of Eastern University secured higher average annual starting salaries.

    B. Random samples from normal populations with the same variance.

Chapter 15 — Hypothesis Testing

10.

	Number Interviewed	Percent	Favorable (2) × 270	Neutral (2) × 220	Unfavorable (2) × 310
Freshmen	220	.275	100(74.25)	50(60.5)	70(85.25)
Sophomores	210	.2625	80(70.88)	60(57.75)	70(81.38)
Juniors	180	.225	50(60.75)	50(49.5)	80(69.75)
Seniors	190	.2375	40(64.12)	60(52.25)	90(73.62)
	800	1.000	270	220	310

Frequencies: O_i (E_i)

O_i = observed E_i = expected

(1) Null hypothesis. H_0: $O_i = E_i$. That is, the attitudes toward corporations in the population is independent of college class. H_A: $O_i \neq E_i$. That is, the attitudes toward corporations in the population do vary by class.

(2) Statistical test. Choose the k sample χ^2 test to compare the observed distribution to a hypothesized distribution. The χ^2 test is used because the responses are classified into nominal categories and there are sufficient observations in each cell.

(3) Significance level. Let $\alpha = .05$.

(4) Calculated value:

$$\chi^2 = \sum_{i=1}^{k} \frac{(O_i - E_i)^2}{E_i}$$

$$\chi^2 = \frac{(25.75)^2}{74.25} + \frac{(9.12)^2}{70.88} + \frac{(-10.75)^2}{60.75} + \frac{(-24.12)^2}{64.12} + \ldots + \frac{(16.38)^2}{73.62}$$

$$\chi^2 = 33.6$$

(5) Critical test value = 12.59. $\alpha = .05$, df = 6 (Appendix Table F-3)

(6) Decision. The calculated value is greater than the critical value, so reject the null hypothesis and conclude that there is a significant difference among the classes as to attitude toward corporations.

11. (1) Null hypothesis. H_0: There is no difference in readership rates between business school and liberal arts students. H_A: Readership rates differ between business and liberal arts students.

(2) Statistical test. Use t test of two independent samples.

(3) Significance level. α = .05, two-tailed test (alternative hypothesis is not directional).

(4) Calculated value:

$$t = \frac{(5.6 - 4.5) - 0}{\sqrt{\frac{100(2.0)^2 + 100(1.5)^2}{(100+100)-2}\left(\frac{1}{100}+\frac{1}{100}\right)}} = \frac{1.1}{.251} = 4.378$$

(5) Critical value = 1.96. α = .05, two-tailed test, d.f. = 198. Consult Table F-2.

(6) Calculated value of 4.4 > critical value (1.96). Reject the null hypothesis.

12. (1) Null hypothesis. H_0: There are no durability differences among the three products. H_A: There are durability differences between the three products.

(2) Statistical test. We use the F test with one-way analysis of variance because the data are ratio scales. There are k independent samples, and we accept the assumptions underlying this parameter test.

(3) Significance level. α = .05.

(4) Calculated value: See Exhibit 15-1.

(5) Critical test value for F = 3.89, α = .05, d.f. = (2,12)

(6) Decision. Since the calculated value is greater than the critical value (5.49 > 3.89) we reject the null hypothesis.

Exhibit 15-1 Analysis of Variance Results for Question 12

```
- - - - - - - - - - - - - - - - - - O N E W A Y - - - - - - - - - - - -
     Variable   SCRUBS
     By Variable   TYPE

                          ANALYSIS OF VARIANCE

                          SUM OF        MEAN         F        F
     SOURCE      D.F.    SQUARES       SQUARES     RATIO    PROB.

BETWEEN GROUPS     2    212.1333      106.0667    5.4957   .0202
WITHIN GROUPS     12    231.6000       19.3000
TOTAL             14    443.7333
```

In the continuation of this exhibit, a post hoc comparison of the three paints using the Scheffe procedure shows that the significant differences are between One-Koat and Competitor B (groups 1 and 3).

Exhibit 15-1 continued   Multiple Comparison Test for Question 12 *

SCHEFFE PROCEDURE
RANGES FOR THE 0.050 LEVEL -

   3.94   3.94

THE RANGES ABOVE ARE TABLE RANGES.
THE VALUE ACTUALLY COMPARED WITH MEAN(J)-MEAN(I) IS..
    3.1064 * RANGE * DSQRT(1/N(I) + 1/N(J))

(*) DENOTES PAIRS OF GROUPS SIGNIFICANTLY DIFFERENT AT THE
    0.050 LEVEL

```
                                   G G G
                                   r r r
                                   p p p

             Mean       Group      3 2 1

            22.4000     Grp 3
            26.6000     Grp 2
            31.6000     Grp 1      *
```

*SPSS Release 4.0 for Macintosh

---

13. Two diagnostics appear in Exhibit 15-2. All of the homogeneity of variances tests in the top of the exhibit indicate that we cannot reject the null hypothesis that the group means are equal. Note that those that are dependent on the normality assumption have higher probabilities than the Levene test.

Exhibit 15-2 Diagnostic Checks of Assumptions *

Tests for Homogeneity of Variances

```
                                                          Significance
   Cochrans C = Max. Variance/Sum(Variances) =  .6615    .144 (Approx.)
   Bartlett-Box F =                             1.640    .196
   Maximum Variance / Minimum Variance          7.226

   df1     df2
    2       12       Levene Statistic          2.9278    .0921
```

Three normal probability plots are presented for each of the three products. The points have fallen more or less on a straight line and we cannot reject the hypothesis of normality. The Wilks-Shapiro test, generally more versatile than the K-S (Lilliefors), was used because means and variances were known.

Exhibit 15-2 continued Diagnostic Checks of Assumptions *

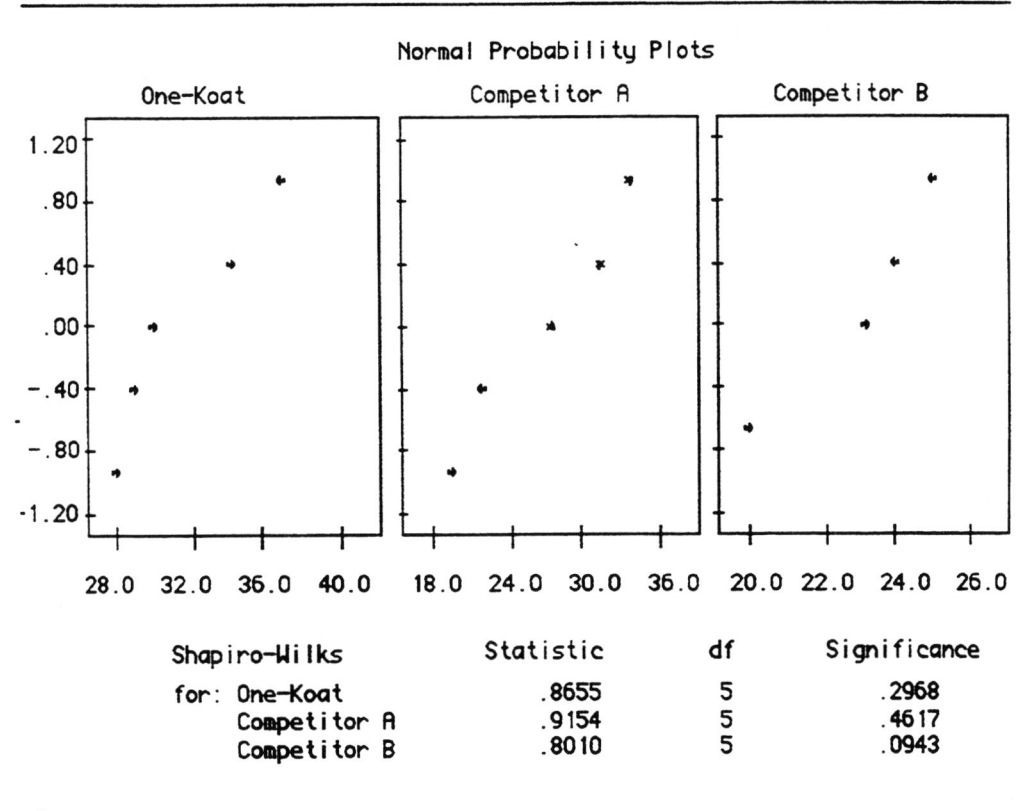

Normal Probability Plots

	One-Koat	Competitor A	Competitor B

Shapiro-Wilks for:	Statistic	df	Significance
One-Koat	.8655	5	.2968
Competitor A	.9154	5	.4617
Competitor B	.8010	5	.0943

* SPSS Release 4.0 for Macintosh

14. (1) Null hypothesis. H_0: There are no differences between the means of the two groups relative to flight service ratings.

(2) This is a case of two independent samples. The appropriate test is parametric because the data are interval. Use the t test.

(3) The desired level of significance is again set at $\alpha = .05$

(4) Calculated value: See Exhibit 15 - 3.

Exhibit 15-3 *t*-Test Table for Question 14

```
t-tests for independent samples of Flight Service Rating 2

GROUP 1 - GPS  EQ    2.00
GROUP 2 - GPS  EQ    3.00
```

Variable	Number of Cases	Mean	Standard Deviation	Standard Error
RATING2				
GROUP 1	20	72.2500	10.572	2.364
GROUP 2	20	79.8000	11.265	2.519

		Pooled Variance Estimate			Separate Variance Estimate		
F Value	2-tail Prob.	t Value	Degrees of Freedom	2-tail Prob.	t Value	Degrees of Freedom	2-tail Prob.
1.14	.785	-2.19	38	.035	-2.19	37.85	.035

*SPSS Release 4.0 for Macintosh

(5) Critical value from Table F-2 using 38 d.f. is 2.03 for two-tailed test. The F test on the left of the exhibit indicates that we cannot reject the hypothesis of equality of means; thus we interpret the pooled variance estimate section.

(6) Calculated values (absolute values) of |-2.19| > critical value(|2.03|). The null hypotheses is rejected. That is, there is a significant difference found between the two groups with respect to the service rating.

15. (1) Null hypothesis. H_0: There are no differences among the three sales strategies (as represented by store types).

(2) Statistical test. We use the F test with one-way analysis of variance because the data are ratio scales. There are k independent samples, and we accept the assumptions underlying this parameter test.

(3) Significance level. $\alpha = .05$.

(4) Calculated value: See Exhibit 15 - 4.

Exhibit 15-4 Analysis of Variance Results for Question 15 *

```
- - - - - - -  - - - - - - - - - O N E W A Y - - - - - - - - - - - - - - -
      Variable  SALES
   By Variable  STYPE

                          ANALYSIS OF VARIANCE

                              SUM OF      MEAN       F        F
         SOURCE      D.F.    SQUARES    SQUARES    RATIO    PROB.

   BETWEEN GROUPS     2      28.9333    14.4667   5.4250    .0210
   WITHIN GROUPS     12      32.0000     2.6667
   TOTAL             14      60.9333

                            SCHEFFE PROCEDURE

   RANGES FOR THE 0.050 LEVEL -

        3.94    3.94

   THE RANGES ABOVE ARE TABLE RANGES.
   THE VALUE ACTUALLY COMPARED WITH MEAN(J)-MEAN(I) IS..
        1.1547 * RANGE * DSQRT(1/N(I) + 1/N(J))

   (*) DENOTES PAIRS OF GROUPS SIGNIFICANTLY DIFFERENT AT THE 0.050 LEVEL

                                         G G G
                                         r r r
                                         p p p

                      Mean     Group     1 3 2

                     3.6000    Grp 1
                     5.2000    Grp 3
                     7.0000    Grp 2       *
```

*SPSS Release 4.0 for Macintosh

(5) Critical test value for $F = 3.89$, $\alpha = .05$, d.f. = (2, 12) Appendix Table F-9.

(6) Decision. Since the calculated value is greater than the critical value (5.43 > 3.89) we reject the null hypothesis. A post hoc comparison of the three store types using the Scheffe procedure shows that the significant differences are between the electronics store and the department store (groups 1 and 2).

16. A test for related samples should be used since the data are collected on the same firms and are paired for the one year interval.

(1) Null hypothesis. H_0: There is no difference between the profits in the two periods of the utility companies. H_A: The profits are higher in the second year.

(2) Statistical test. The related samples t test is chosen because the data are ratio and the samples are dependent.

(3) Significance level. $\alpha = .05$

(4) Calculated value: See Exhibit 15 - 5.

Exhibit 15 - 5 Test of Related Samples t-Test for Question 16 *

--- t-tests for paired samples ---

Variable	Number of Cases	Mean	Standard Deviation	Standard Error
P89	11	181.2545	121.720	36.700
P88	11	160.7545	109.265	32.944

(Difference) Mean	Standard Deviation	Standard Error	2-tail Corr. Prob.		t Value	Degrees of Freedom	2-tail Prob.
20.5000	44.297	13.356	.932	.000	1.53	10	.156

*SPSS Release 4.0 for Macintosh

(5) Critical test value = 1.81. d.f. =10, one-tailed test. $\alpha = .05$.

(6) Decision. Since the calculated value is smaller than the critical value (1.53 < 1.81, we fail to reject the null hypothesis and conclude that there are no differences between profits of the two years.

17. (1) Null hypothesis. $H_0: p_1 = p_2$, the proportion removed by Anti-V is equal to the proportion removed by Q-Cure. $H_A: p_1 \neq p_2$

(2) Statistical test. The McNemar test is chosen because the groups have been matched according to the control characteristic-- standard number of viruses that each antivirus product is presumed to remove. Although nominal measurements were used, the chi-square test of independence is not appropriate.

(3) Significance level. $\alpha = .05$ (two-tailed test)

(4) Calculated value: (see table)

	Removed by Q-Cure?	
Removed by Anti-V?	Yes	No
Yes	A 45	B 33
No	C 58	D 20

$$Z = \frac{B - C}{\sqrt{B + C}}$$

$$Z = \frac{33 - 58}{\sqrt{33 + 58}} = \frac{-25}{\sqrt{91}} = -2.62$$

(5) Critical test value = ± 1.96, $\alpha = .05$.

(6) Decision. Since the (absolute value) calculated value is larger than the critical value ($|-2.62| > |\pm 1.96|$), reject the null hypothesis and conclude that the proportion removed by Anti-V is not equal to the proportion removed by Q-Cure.

Note: the other approach to McNemar, a modified chi-square which was illustrated in the text, produced a χ^2 value of 6.86. With 1 d.f. at $\alpha = .05$, the critical value is 3.84. We reject the null. (The square root of 6.84 is the Z result of 2.62.)

18. A. Test of hypothesis:

(1) Null hypothesis. H_0: $O_i = E_i$. That is, the styling preferences are independent of buyer behavior. H_A: $O_i \neq E_i$.

(2) Statistical test. Choose the two independent sample χ^2 test to compare the observed distribution to a hypothesized distribution. The χ^2 test is used because the responses are classified into nominal categories and there are sufficient observations in each cell.

(3) Significance level. Let $\alpha = .05$.

(4) Calculated value: See Exhibit 15 - 6.

(5) Critical test value = 3.84. $\alpha = .05$, d.f. = 1

(6) Decision. The calculated value (20.94) is greater than the critical value, (3.84) so reject the null hypothesis and conclude that styling preference is not independent of buyer characteristic.

B. Many analysts would apply the correction for continuity since the sample size is larger than 40 and a 2 x 2 table is used. In this case, the calculated value drops only slightly to 19.11 and we continue to reject the null hypothesis.

Exhibit 15-6   Contingency Table for Question 18 *

Styling Preference

Count	European	Japanese	Row Total
Repeat	40	20	60 / 60.0
First time	8	32	40 / 40.0
Column Total	48 / 48.0	52 / 52.0	100 / 100.0

Chi-Square	Value	DF	Significance
Pearson	20.94017	1	.00000
Continuity Correction	19.11225	1	.00001
Likelihood Ratio	22.05550	1	.00000

Minimum Expected Frequency -   19.200

True - False Questions

T   1) Statistical inference and descriptive statistics are the two major categories of statistical procedures.

T   2) The Bayesian approach to hypothesis testing is an extension of the classical approach in that it also uses sampling data for decision making. However, it goes beyond this to incorporate other information that is available to the decision maker.

F   3) According to the null hypothesis any observed difference found between the parameter and the statistic being compared to it is due to real differences in the population.

T   4) An alternative hypothesis can be a one-tailed or a two-tailed type of hypothesis.

F   5) In the case of a Type I error (a) we accept a false null hypothesis.

Chapter 15 — Hypothesis Testing

T 6) An increase in the alpha error (α) will cause a decrease in beta (β) if other things remain the same.

F 7) Alpha error and beta error are complementary and must add to one.

T 8) The significance level is normally set by the researcher at a somewhat arbitrary level on the basis of how confident he/she wishes to be in the results.

F 9) Non-parametric tests are more powerful than the parametric and are generally the tests of choice if their use assumptions are reasonably met.

T 10) Testing for a significant difference between some sample statistic and its population parameter is an example of a one sample case of hypothesis testing.

F 11) The *t* test is particularly useful in tests involving nominal data but it can be used for higher scales.

F 12) When the calculated *t* value is less than the critical *t* value we reject the null hypothesis.

T 13) The binomial test is appropriate when the measurement scale is nominal and the population is viewed as only two classes, such as male or female.

T 14) There is a different chi-square distribution for each value of degrees of freedom.

T 15) A chi-square test compares the deviations of the actual frequencies per category with the hypothesized frequencies. The greater the difference between them, the less the probability that these differences can be attributed to chance.

F 16) The chi-square is a test of goodness-of-fit in which we specify the cumulative frequency distribution which would occur under the theoretical distribution and compare that with the observed cumulative frequency distribution.

T 17) One of the *t* test's basic assumptions is that observations are independent.

F 18) The alternative hypothesis in the two sample case is that any difference between the sample statistics of the two sample distributions is due to random sampling fluctuations only.

T 19) A one-way ANOVA is used with simple random samples to compare the impact of a single independent variable on a dependent variable.

Chapter 15 — Hypothesis Testing

T   20) The *k* sample chi-square test is merely an extension of the two independent sample case.

T   21) It is the objective of ANOVA to break total variance down into its component parts thereby accounting for each and allowing evaluation of its effect.

Multiple Choice Questions

1. In an attitude survey, using an ordinal scale, you test the differences in results between a sample of college students and noncollegiate people of college age. You test for statistical significance using the chi-square test. Which of the following is the most correct statement?
   A) It is the most appropriate test to use in this situation.
   B) It is an inappropriate test to use in this situation.
   C) It is acceptable in this case, but not as good as the Wilcoxon test.
   * D) It is acceptable, but wastes information.

2. Which of the following is *not* one of the rules we should use to choose the proper significance test?
   A) Is the measurement scale nominal, ratio, interval or ordinal?
   B) Are the samples related or independent?
   C) Does the test involve one sample, two samples, or *k* samples?
   * D) Is the case one-tailed or two-tailed?

3. Which is the more correct statement?
   A) Type II error occurs when one rejects a true hypothesis.
   B) Type II error is also known as alpha error.
   C) Type II error is measured by the portion of the original distribution which falls into the region of rejection.
   * D) Type II error depends upon the size of the alpha error we specify

4. * Which of the following is *not* an assumption of parametric tests?
   A) Observations should be related.
   B) Observations should be drawn from normal distribution.
   C) Populations should have equal variances.
   D) Measurement scales should be at least interval.

5. You are setting up an experiment to test 3 levels of selling effort to three types of customers and you wish to test the statistical significance of the results. They are stated in dollar sales terms. Which test would you use?
   A) Chi-Square
   * B) ANOVA
   C) KS
   D) Wilcoxon
   E) Walsh-Ward

6. The probability of a Type I error is shown in a distribution in terms of
   A) A null hypothesis
  * B) A region of rejection
   C) A region of acceptance
   D) Bayesian statistical analysis

Appendix E True-False Questions

T   E1) The value D in a KS test is the point of greatest divergence between the observed and theoretical distributions.

F   E2) The McNemar test is a parametric test which may be used with nominal or ordinal data.

T   E3) The Sign test is used with matched pairs when the only information we have is the identification of the pair member that is larger or smaller or has more or less of some characteristic.

F   E4) If we can determine both direction and magnitude of the difference between carefully matched pairs we can use the KS two-sample test.

T   E5) The Kolmogorov-Smirnov (KS) test is preferred to the chi-square test when the data are ordinally scaled.

F   E6) In the Kruskal-Wallis k sample test the total variance is broken into two components called the "between column" variance and the "within column" variance.

CHAPTER 16

MEASURES OF ASSOCIATION

There are three learning objectives for Chapter 16: (1) to understand the fundamentals of bivariate correlation analysis, (2) to extend that knowledge to bivariate regression analysis, and (3) to become acquainted with the wide array of nonparametric measures of association and their applications.

Class Discussion Suggestions

One or two class sessions should be sufficient to cover this chapter, depending on *the background of your students* and your emphasis. We have followed the organization of the last chapter by presenting parametric topics first then nonparametric. The regression unit builds upon correlation; comparisons to correlation are made at the outset of that section. We also provide an overview of most of the measures of association at the beginning of the chapter. Thus, if extended coverage is desired, it can be related to the whole.

1. Discussion questions 2 and 4 are useful for beginning a review of the nature of correlation and the importance of diagnostics. This ties into the section entitled Scatterplots for Exploring Relationships. Question 6 may be used to discuss the role of matrices and introduce low level computer applications. The fact that Spearman's rho is a Pearson correlation for ranked data is illustrated in question 7. This notion can be extended by creating interval values for the ranks in Table 16 - 11 of the text.

2. Discussion questions 3 and 10 are good transitions into bivariate regression. In conjunction with the definitions in question 1, the linkage between correlation begins to emerge for some students. Testing the goodness of fit may be handled as a review of ANOVA principles and *t* tests from the last chapter. Question 5 is good in this regard. In preparation for multiple regression, question 12 provides an assessment of regression assumptions and a good orientation for computer applications. Although we use SPSS illustrations, most major packages provide diagnostics.

3. An introduction to nonparametrics should not be neglected in business research. Many of our variables have nonparametric characteristics and the proper measure should be applied. Our overview of this topic in the chapter is fairly extensive and the following chapter questions may be used to guide discussion and instruction: 8, 9, and 11. Contingency tables are repeated in the text and manual so that connections to chi-square (from the last chapter) may be made.

Answers to Chapter Questions

1. A. A *regression coefficient* is the value which expresses how much of a dependent variable's value is estimated to change with the change of one

Chapter 16   Measures of Association

unit in the independent variable. A *correlation coefficient r* is a measure of the association between one or more independent variables and a dependent variable. The correlation coefficient can range from -1.0 to +1.0.

B. Both $r = 0$ and $p = 0$ state that there is no relationship between the X and Y variables. The index r represents the sample data whereas p represents the population correlation.

C. The test of the slope ($\beta_1 = 0$) is a very important test in bivariate linear regression. If the true slope is found to be zero, there is no linear relationship between the X and Y variables. The test of the intercept is only to determine if the regression line goes through the origin. The test of $r^2 = 0$ is similar to the test of the slope with a slightly different interpretation. As a goodness of fit test, r^2 tells us how well the regression line fits the data. By partitioning the sum of squares in the dependent variable, we discover the proportion of variation in the dependent variable explained by the model.

D. The coefficient of correlation, r, describes the relationship between the two measured variables. The coefficient of determination is r^2. It shows the degree to which the variables in question share common variance. If r is found to be .90, r^2 is equal to .81; that is, 81% of the variance in X is explained by Y and vice versa.

E. A slope of 0 is represented by a horizontal line in bivariate linear regression and an infinite slope is represented by a vertical line. The meaning of a zero slope may be based on several conditions: (1) Y is completely unrelated to X and no systematic pattern is evident, (2) there are constant values of Y for every value of X, or (3) the data are related but nonlinear.

F. In bivariate regression, a test of goodness of fit uses t. In multiple regression, the F test is used to check the entire model and individual t tests evaluate each independent variable separately. The F test, when applied to bivariate regression, produces the same result result as t^2.

2. The interpretation of the four plots is as follows: (A) No relationship, (B) Positive relationship, (C) Nonlinear relationship, (D) Negative relationship.

3. (A) See Exhibit 16 - 1   (B) Y = 4.8 + 1.067 X   (C) See Exhibit 16 - 1

    (D) If X = 10, Y = 15.5
        X = 17, Y = 22.9

Chapter 16   *Measures of Association*

Exhibit 16 - 1 Scatter plot for Question 3

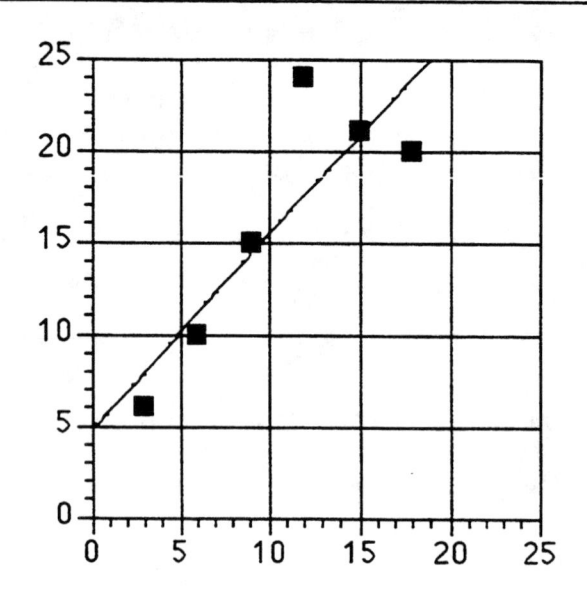

4.   A.   See Exhibit 16 - 2.

Exhibit 16 - 2 Scatter plot for Question 4

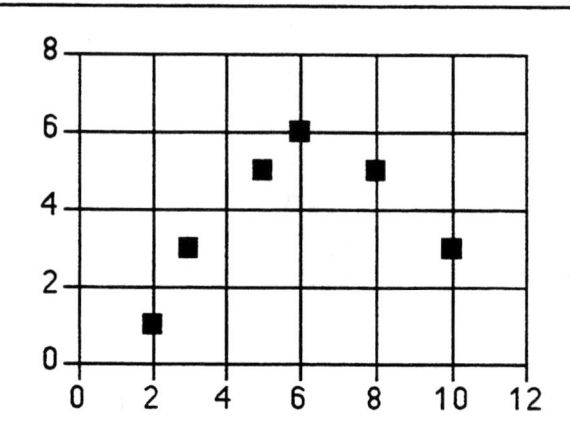

B.   Eta may be used for nonlinear data.

5.   See Exhibit 16 - 3.

A. With d.f. (1,8) the critical value of F is 5.32. In this table, the calculated value is 95.75 (found from the mean squares once the student fills in the df and sum of squares by subtraction). We reject the null hypothesis, β = 0.

B. The t value (9.79) is the square root of F. It is the primary test of the slope for bivariate regression.

Chapter 16　　　　　　　　　　　　　　　　　　　　　　　　　　　　　　　　Measures of Association

Exhibit 16-3 ANOVA Summary Table

	DF	Sum of Squares	Mean Square	F
Regression	1	11116995.47	11116995.47	95.75
Error	8	928837.03	116104.63	
Total	9	12045832.50		

6.

Exhibit 16-4 Correlation Matrix for Question 6[1]

	ASSETS	SALES	MKTVAL	NETPROF	CASHFLOW	EMPLOY
ASSETS	1.0000	.5791*	.4835	.6224*	.4393	.1229
SALES	.5791*	1.0000	.8617**	.8249**	.8213**	.5069
MKTVAL	.4835	.8617**	1.0000	.9607**	.9704**	.2824
NETPROF	.6224*	.8249**	.9607**	1.0000	.9298**	.3082
CASHFLOW	.4393	.8213**	.9704**	.9298**	1.0000	.1494
EMPLOY	.1229	.5069	.2824	.3082	.1494	1.0000

* Signif. ≤ .05　　** Signif. ≤ .01　　(1-tailed)

[1] SPSS Release 4.0 for Macintosh

7. The largest Pearson coefficient is .9704, the relationship between cash flow and market value. The Spearman rank order correlation is found to be .9758. Normally we would expect the Spearman to display a lower coefficient since the ratio data is lost when each data point is converted to a rank. In this case, the order preserved the relationship with precision.

```
CASH                .9758
           N(    10)
           SIG  .000

                    MKT
```

8.　A.　Gamma is found to be .886 - as per computer calculation in Exhibit 16-5.

　　B.　Kendall's Tau $_b$ and Tau $_c$ are .707 and .70, respectively.

　　C.　Gamma is based on a comparison of concordant and discordant pairs of scores. It treats variables symmetrically in calculation: no independent or dependent variable is designated. Both versions of tau are refinements of gamma which considers that not all pairs of variables are concordant or discordant; some observations may be tied on variable X, Y, or both. Like gamma, the range for tau is -1.0 to +1.0 and larger coefficients imply

Chapter 16   *Measures of Association*

stronger relationships between the variables. Technically, tau $_b$ can only obtain this range for a square table if no marginal frequency is equal to 0. Tau $_c$ better approaches the outer limits of the range for tables of any row by column configuration.

D. A large value for gamma often occurs when a more appropriate measure of the variables would produce a smaller coefficient. In this sense, gamma is often inflated. Since all the coefficients would be approximately the same if their were no tied pairs, it appears prudent to consider this effect and the greater stability of tau across different situations. For this data, either tau would be suitable although tau $_c$ would be the more conservative choice.

9. See Exhibit 16 - 5. Somers' *d* symmetric is .707 and asymmetric, with opinion dependent, is .70. The symmetric coefficient results from averaging the two asymmetric coefficients. Somers' is extension of gamma that considers the number of pairs not tied on the independent variable. The magnitude of the coefficients is quite similar to the tau results. We would assume that education influences opinion on the tax and that the asymmetric coefficient with opinion dependent is the most appropriate one to interpret. We conclude from this problem that there is a relatively strong positive relationship between education and opinion about a tax on stock and bond transactions.

Chapter 16 Measures of Association

Exhibit 16-5 Contingency Table for Measures of Association *

	Count	Education H.S. 1	College 2	MBA 3	Row Total
Opinion					
Favorable	1	15	5	0	20 / 33.3
Undecided	2	10	8	2	20 / 33.3
Unfavorable	3	0	2	18	20 / 33.3
Column Total		25 / 41.7	15 / 25.0	20 / 33.3	60 / 100.0

Chi-Square	Value	DF	Significance
Pearson	46.80000	4	.00000

Minimum Expected Frequency -   5.000

Statistic	Value	ASE1	T-value
Kendall's Tau-b	.70741	.06302	11.20498
Kendall's Tau-c	.70000	.06247	11.20498
Gamma	.88608	.05293	11.20498
Somers' D :			
symmetric	.70737	.06301	11.20498
with ED dependent	.71489	.06495	11.20498
with OPIN dependent	.70000	.06247	11.20498

*SPSS Release 4.0 for Macintosh

10. A. The relationship between X and Y is shown as - .84 in Exhibit 16 - 6.

B. The sign of the correlation is negative; they vary in opposition.

C. The square of the correlation, r^2, is equal to .71; that is 71% of X is explained by Y, and vice versa.

Exhibit 16-6 Correlation Results for Question 10 *

```
- - Correlation Coefficients - -

                    X              Y
        X        1.0000         -.8438**
        Y        -.8438**        1.0000

      ** Signif. ≤ .01        (2-tailed)
```

D. The equation is: Y = 31.64 - 1.04 X. The line is plotted as shown:

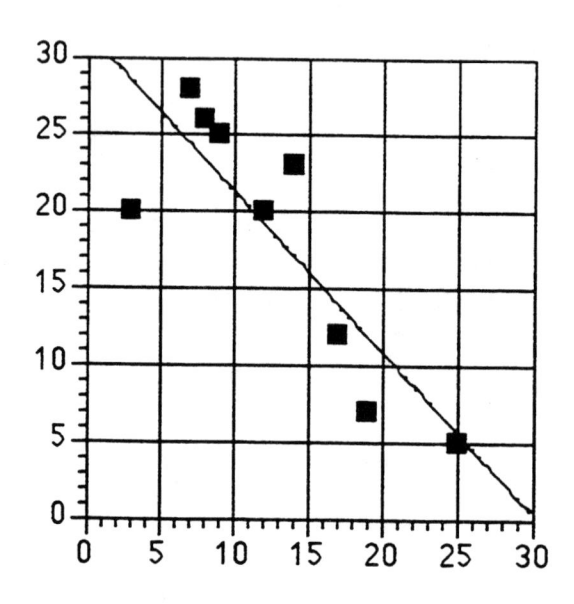

E. Refer to Exhibit 16-6. The test of the slope ($\beta = 0$) was rejected below our conventional $\alpha = .05$, with a t value of -4.16 and significance of .0042. The test for the significance of the correlation coefficient was determined by a two-tailed t test as shown in the top of the exhibit. This null was rejected at .01. Finally, the F test of the regression model was equal to t^2 (17.3).

Chapter 16 *Measures of Association*

Exhibit 16-6 continued Regression Results for Question 10 *

```
Multiple R          .84379
R Square            .71198
Adjusted R Square   .67084
Standard Error     4.84374

Analysis of Variance
              DF      Sum of Squares    Mean Square
Regression     1         405.98960       405.98960
Residual       7         164.23262        23.46180

F =    17.30428      Signif F =  .0042
```
------------------ Variables in the Equation ------------------

```
Variable           B          SE B        Beta          T     Sig T

X             -1.041889     .250464    -.843792     -4.160   .0042
(Constant)    31.641711    3.559759                  8.889   .0000
End Block Number   1   All requested variables entered.
```

*SPSS Release 4.0 for Macintosh

---

11. We have computed four measures of association in Exhibit 16-7. Of the four, phi is the most appropriate because the table in question is 2 x 2. As noted elsewhere, Cramer's V simplifies to phi for 2 x 2 tables. The Pearson contingency coefficient C is problematic because of its upper limit and comparability to other measures. All of these three are based on the chi-square. Lambda, on the other hand, offers a PRE interpretation. Given the information in the problem, it would be difficult to identify a predictor variable for lambda in that it could be argued that one's position on taxes in general is just as good a predictor of party affiliation as party affiliation would be for predicting favorableness on a specific position.

Exhibit 16-7 Contingency Table and Correlations for Question 11*

```
             Tax Proposal
   Count   Favor   Against
                              Row
              1       2       Total
Party     ┌───────┬───────┐
          │  50   │  80   │   130
Demo   1  │       │       │   50.0
          ├───────┼───────┤
          │  90   │  40   │   130
Repub  2  │       │       │   50.0
          └───────┴───────┘
  Column     140     120       260
  Total      53.8    46.2      100.0
```

Chi-Square	Value	DF	Significance
Pearson	24.76190	1	.00000
Continuity Correction	23.53929	1	.00000

Minimum Expected Frequency - 60.000

Statistic	Value	ASE1	T-value	Approximate Significance (Chi-Square Probability)
Phi	.30861			.00000
Cramer's V	.30861			.00000
Contingency Coefficient	.29488			.00000
Lambda :				
symmetric	.28000	.06936	3.73551	
with PARTY dependent	.30769	.07573	3.45746	
with TAX dependent	.25000	.08229	2.66692	

*SPSS Release 4.0 for Macintosh

12. The variables selected for illustration were net profits and market value. The regression appears in Exhibit 16-8. The R^2 is .92 and a t value for the slope is 9.79. The null hypothesis was rejected at the .00005 level.

The following assumptions were examined: linearity, equality of variance, independence of error, and normality. In addition, residuals were examined for outliers.

Exhibit 16 - 8   Regression Results and ANOVA Summary for Question 12*

```
* * * *   M U L T I P L E   R E G R E S S I O N   * * * *
```

Dependent Variable..   MKT VALUE

Variable(s) Entered on Step Number
   1..   NET PROFIT

Multiple R   .96067
R Square   .92289
Adjusted R Square   .91325
Standard Error   340.74129

Analysis of Variance
              DF   Sum of Squares   Mean Square
Regression   1   11116995.47080   11116995.47080
Residual   8   928837.02920   116104.62865

F =   95.74980   Signif F =   .0000
------------------ Variables in the Equation ------------------

Variable   B   SE B   Beta   T   Sig T

NET   8.961790   .915853   .960672   9.785   .0000
(Constant) 214.281797   194.223578   1.103   .3020
End Block Number   1   All requested variables entered.

       0 Outliers found.   No casewise plot produced.

*SPSS Release 4.0 for Macintosh

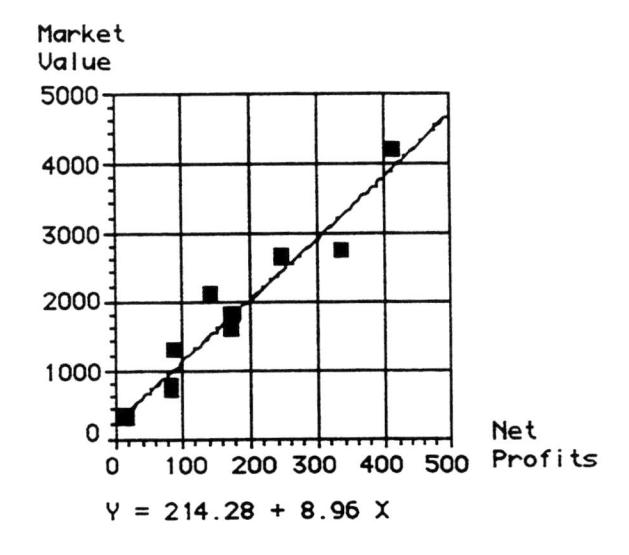

Y = 214.28 + 8.96 X

Chapter 16 *Measures of Association*

Linearity: The scatterplot on the previous page graphs the relationship of the X and Y variables. There is little doubt that the function is linear and that a straight line fits the data.

Equality of Variance: The assumption of equality of variance may be checked with the plot shown in Exhibit 16 - 9. There is some spread of the residuals with increases in predicted values. Even with this small sample size, we should be cautious about this assumption.

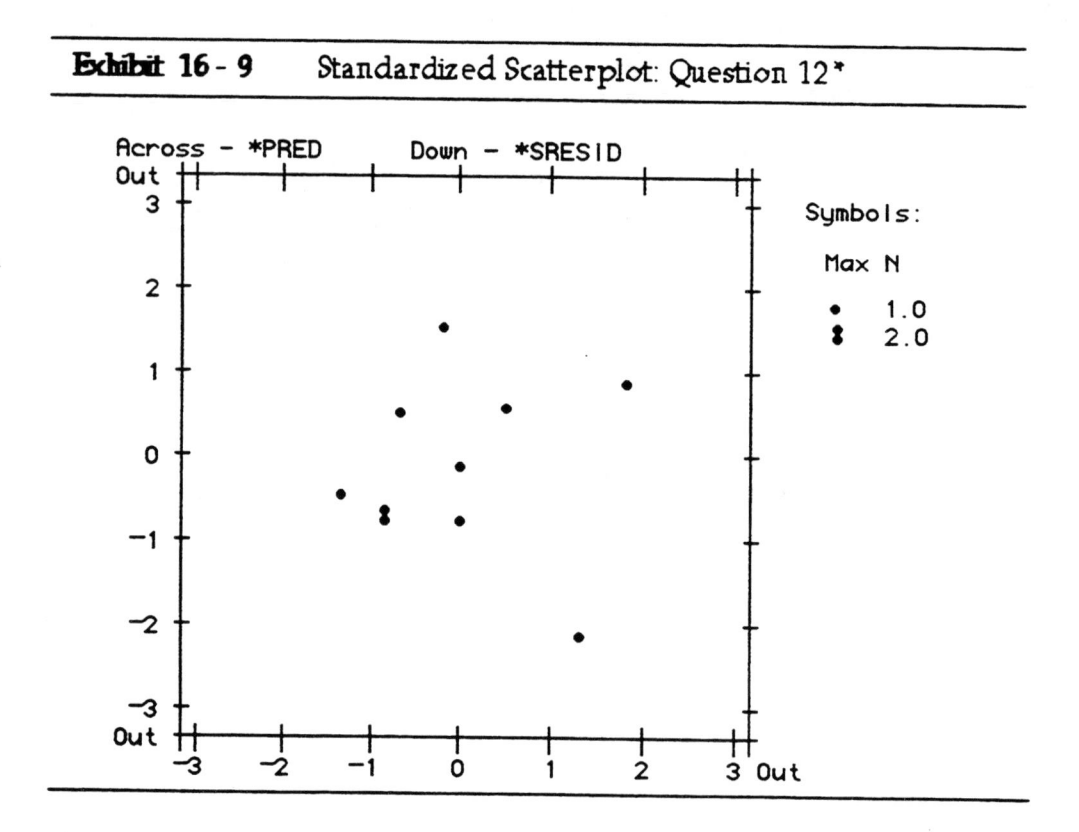

Exhibit 16 - 9 Standardized Scatterplot: Question 12*

```
Across - *PRED      Down - *SRESID
Out
 3                                          Symbols:
 2                                          Max N
 1                                           •    1.0
 0                                           ⁑    2.0
-1
-2
-3
Out
    -3  -2  -1   0   1   2   3 Out
```

Independence of Error: The collection and recording of data was a computer generated random sample. There is no reason to suspect sequential values. As shown at the bottom of Exhibit 16 - 8, no casewise plot was produced for this examination because no outliers were found.

Residuals: The summary of residual statistics in Exhibits 16 - 10 and 16 - 11 does not seem to indicate that the ranges (in the -1.6 to 1.7 range for standardized values) would not be a cause for concern.

Exhibit 16 - 10 Residual Statistics for Question 12*

Residuals Statistics:

	Min	Max	Mean	Std Dev	N
*PRED	376.4902	3919.9819	1795.5000	1111.4053	10
*ZPRED	-1.2768	1.9115	.0000	1.0000	10
*SEPRED	107.7526	242.3802	146.8297	42.9723	10
*ADJPRED	409.9225	3685.4070	1793.0375	1089.1759	10
*RESID	-532.0935	579.0892	.0000	321.2540	10
*ZRESID	-1.5616	1.6995	.0000	.9428	10
*SRESID	-1.8493	1.7982	.0006	1.0641	10
*DRESID	-746.2096	648.3182	2.4625	415.2544	10
*SDRESID	-2.2862	2.1792	-.0011	1.2174	10
*MAHAL	.0000	3.6539	.9000	1.1429	10
*COOK D	.0000	.6881	.1589	.2332	10
*LEVER	.0000	.4060	.1000	.1270	10

Exhibit 16 - 11 Standardized Residuals by Case Number: Question 12*

Outliers - Standardized Residual

Case #	*ZRESID
8	1.69950
7	-1.56158
2	.76046
1	-.75578
5	.67212
10	.59976
4	-.58648
9	-.55199
6	-.25089
3	-.02511

Normality: The histogram of studentized residuals in Exhibit 16 - 12 does not (as we know from prior checks) reveal any residuals beyond ± 3.16. For a sample of 10, the Expected N conforms reasonably well to the observed N. Although there are some of departures from a strictly normal histogram, we are dealing with residuals and nonconstant variance and therefore expect that normality will show some effects. The normal probability plot of standardized residuals in Exhibit 16 - 13 also provides some indication of departures from normality but not in a patterned way.

Exhibit 16 - 12 Histogram of Standardized Residuals: Question 12 *

```
N Exp N       (* = 1 Cases,     . : = Normal Curve)
0  .01   Out
0  .02   3.00
0  .04   2.67
0  .09   2.33
0  .18   2.00
1  .33   1.67  *
0  .55   1.33  .
0  .81   1.00  .
3 1.06    .67  :**
0 1.25    .33  .
1 1.32    .00  ·
1 1.25   -.33  :
3 1.06   -.67  :**
0  .81  -1.00  .
0  .55  -1.33  .
1  .33  -1.67  *
0  .18  -2.00
0  .09  -2.33
0  .04  -2.67
0  .02  -3.00
0  .01   Out
```

Recommendations: Generally, the diagnostics suggest that this small random sample from Forbes 500 data conforms rather well to regression assumptions. Equality of variance could be improved with transformation and that would be our next step in this problem. Otherwise, the departures are relatively minor.

Chapter 16 Measures of Association

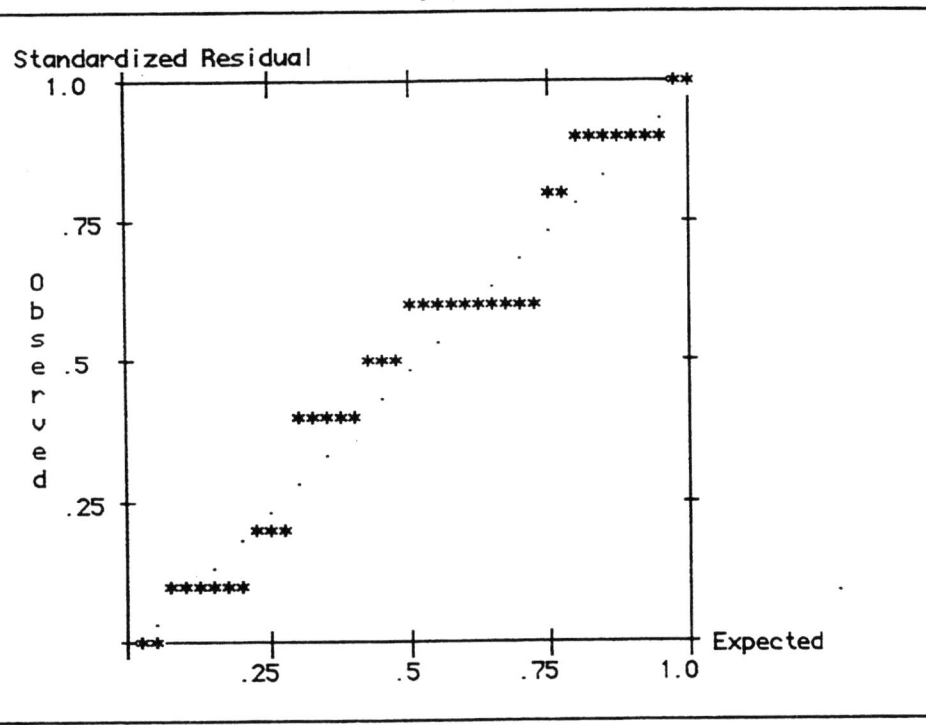

Exhibit 16-13 Normal Probability (P-P) Plot: Question 12*

```
Standardized Residual
    1.0 ┤                                        **
        │                                  *******
        │                                     .
        │                               **  .
    .75 ┤                             .
  O     │                          .
  b     │                      **********
  s     │                       .
  e  .5 ┤                    ***
  r     │                  ******
  v     │                .
  e     │              .
  d .25 ┤           ***
        │        ******
        │     .
        │ ***─┬──────┬──────┬──────┬──────── Expected
              .25    .5    .75    1.0
```

True - False Questions

F   1) When we use our knowledge of one variable to estimate a second one we call these methods correlation analysis.

T   2) Parametric correlation requires two continuous variables.

T   3) Bivariate correlation analysis distinguish between independent and dependent variables.

F   4) The magnitude and the direction of a correlation are essentially the same thing.

F   5) It is possible to determine if two variables are linear from examining the coefficient of correlation.

F   6) A bivariate normal distribution is a necessary assumption for nonparametric correlation.

F   7) If a correlation is statistically significant, it is also practically significant.

F   8) There is no way of determining whether a correlation is statistically significant.

Chapter 16 — Measures of Association

T 9) The coefficient of determination help to explain the proportion of shared variance between to variables.

T 10) A correlation matrix may be used for bivariate and multivariate purposes.

T 11) Bivariate regression is used to predict Y values from X values.

F 12) There are three regression coefficients: the slope, the intercept, and the error term.

T 13) The intercept is the value of the linear function when it crosses the Y axis.

F 14) The method of least squares is used to maximize errors in order to find the best fitting line.

T 15) A residual is what remains after the line is fit in a regression model.

F 16) The t test is used to test the overall model in multiple regression.

F 17) Lambda is a chi-square based measure of association.

F 18) Cramer's V and phi may be applied without regard to table size.

T 19) The Goodman and Kruskal Tau statistic incorporates marginals to improve prediction.

F 20) Gamma, Kendall's tau, Spearman's rho are frequently used measures for nominal data.

T 21) Lambda and Somer's d are alike in their provision for asymmetry and different in the level of data they may handle.

T 22) In correlation analysis we calculate a coefficient by which to measure the closeness of association between variables.

T 23) In regression analysis we develop an estimating equation in which we use data from one or more independent variables to estimate values for a dependent variable.

F 24) Confidence and prediction bands are identical in regression analysis.

F 25) The range of values for Cramer's statistic for nominal data is from zero to one. When the row totals give a frequency distribution identical to the column totals there is no association and Cramer's statistic equals zero.

T 26) The coefficient Lambda (l) is based on how well the frequencies of one nominal variable offer predictive evidence about the frequency of the second nominal variable.

Chapter 16 — Measures of Association

T   27) The Pearson product-moment coefficient r is the summary statistic which represents the linear relationship between two sets of variables.

F   28) Multiple correlation can be defined as a set of statistical techniques which focus upon the structure of simultaneous relationships among three or more phenomena.

Multiple Choice Questions

1. If you wish to correlate two sets of rank order data which of the following measures would be the most appropriate?
   A) Cramer's Statistic
   B) Pearson's product moment correlation
   C) Cochran's Q
   * D) Spearman's rho

2. Suppose you calculate a correlation between age of head of household and household income. You find an r of .55. Approximately what percent of income is "explained" by age?
   A) About 74%
   B) About 55%
   * C) About 30%
   D) Can not tell from information given

3. Which of the following is NOT a measure of association used with nominal data?
   A) Contingency coefficient
   B) Cramer's statistic
   C) Lambda
   * D) Kendall Tau
   E) All of the above are used with nominal data.

4. Which of the following are *not* important attributes of a Pearson product moment correlation?
   A) Linearity
   * B) Concordance
   C) Magnitude
   D) Direction

5. In examining a scatterplots of a correlation with a positive coefficient, which of the following are we *least* likely to find:
   * A) A set of points in the shape of a ball.
   B) A wide band of points trending from upper right to lower left.
   C) A narrow band of points from upper right to lower left.
   D) A curvilinear pattern.

199

Chapter 16 — Measures of Association

6. The best index of shared variance among variables is:
   A) r
   * B) r^2
   C) Multiple R
   D) $Y = \beta_0 + \beta_1 X_1$
   E) t

7. Which of the following does *not* define the characteristics of bivariate regression:
   A) The measurement scale is interval or ratio.
   B) The variables are continuous and linearly related.
   * C) X and Y are symmetric.
   D) The proportion of variability in X is explained by its least squares regression on Y.

8. The unexplained variation, that which cannot be explained by the regression relationship, is evaluated statistically as:
   A) The total sum of squares.
   B) t^2
   * C) The sum of squares error.
   D) The F ratio.
   E) None of the above.

CHAPTER 17

MULTIVARIATE ANALYSIS: AN OVERVIEW

The primary objective of this chapter is to *expose* the student to the types and applications of multivariate analysis. The student should be able to explain the basic concepts of each method discussed.

Class Discussion Suggestions

Class time committed to this chapter usually does not exceed one period depending on the background of the students. *It is possible that you may not want to assign this chapter because of the nature of your curriculum.* However, if you have time for this unit, you will discover that our approach is more verbal than mathematical and the illustrations virtually carry the individual topics.

Figure 17-1 provides a starting point for an overview of techniques and applications. The section on Selecting a Multivariate Technique takes the student through a couple examples to improve familiarity with the guide and the decisions that must be made. You may wish to highlight these or add some of your own.

If your course emphasis is very quantitative, it would be appropriate to develop the theory of multivariate normal distributions and the technical relationships between the methods at this point. The chapter does not provide this, for obvious reasons, but the suggested readings have several references.

Instructors who wish to cover this material at the level of the objectives -- an overview or exposure to topics-- may proceed with discussion questions 1, 2, and 6 for definition, comparison, and application to situations. Question 3 helps the student begin to see the connections between techniques and how, under different circumstances, one technique may be used as a front-end device and in another situation, a confirmation device. The questions are based on specific applications.

Answers to Chapter Questions

1. A. *Multidimensional Scaling* uses a spatial map to describe perceptions. Usually respondents rate or rank objects (or people, places, constructs, etc.) with the smallest value applying to objects that are perceived to be most similar and the largest applying to objects that are perceived to be least similar. Often, the respondent is instructed on the criteria to use in judging similarity. The researcher decides on the number of axes used to display the spatial map. Two to three dimensions are most useful. The map shows the most similar pair as closest to each other and the least similar pair as furthest away from each other.

   B. In contrast to MDS which spatially shows similarities and dissimilarities, *cluster analysis* groups objects by similarities. Whereas MDS is used mainly for perceptions, cluster analysis is used for any set of attributes. Its algorithm is defined to maximize membership in mutually exclusive clusters which are homogeneous. Both techniques use a graphical presentation; cluster analysis puts the objects into distinct groups and MDS does not.

C. *Factor analysis* like cluster analysis is a grouping technique. However, whereas cluster analysis requires members to be in one group only, variables can load on more than one factor in varying amounts. Whereas cluster analysis groups similar members together into a cluster, factor analysis attempts to explain (or describe) latent constructs by creating new factors to replace the original variables.

2. Dependency and interdependency identify the two types of interrelationships among variables. In the *dependency* situation the concern is with the "effect" that independent variables have on a dependent variable. In the *interdependency* situation there is no designated dependent variable. Rather, the interrelations among variables are studied.

A dependency technique would be chosen when one or more variables can be classified as dependent.

3. If a MANOVA problem has two factor levels and several dependent variables, the position of the variables could be reversed and treated with discriminant analysis. The two levels of the factor, already a technically nominal classification, become the dependent variable in the discriminant equation with the several dependent variables (from the MANOVA) becoming the predictors. In this way, the degree to which each dependent contributed to a linear equation predicting the correct classification could be assessed.

4. There are a variety of possibilities here about which your students will quite possibly have some expertise. Some of the factors and levels that could be considered for are:

Factor	Levels
Brands	3 (required)
Number of wheels	2 (3 or 4 wheels)
Hardness of shocks	3 (soft/medium/hard)
Gearing	2 (low/high)
Weight	2 (light/heavy)
Tire size	3 (car/truck/other)
Tread type	3 (highway/off-road/other)
Number of seats	3 (1/2/4)

If we use the <u>first 5 factors</u> of the list, we have a 3 x 3 x 2 x 2 x 2 design or a 72-option full concept design.

5. The R^2 value indicates that the four independent variables statistically account for 92 percent of the variation in the annual sales. The standard error of estimate is a measure of the precision of the Y estimates. This value of 11.9 million dollars indicates that two out of three times the equation esti-

mates of company sales were within a plus or minus 11.9 million of the true sales figure.

The regression coefficients indicate that:

1. Y = 49.85 million dollars when all the IVs are zero.
2. Y is lower by $68,000 for each increase of a million annual marriages. This is illogical and suggests that the estimating equation might be improved by substituting another variable. All other regression coefficients show the effects on Y of a change in one unit of the independent variable.

6. A. Probably a discriminant analysis. The problem involves a dependency relationship in which the dependent (or criterion) variable is nonmetric (i.e.. applicants either choose to attend or not attend). We are not sure about the measurement scales of the independent (predictor) variables but it is assumed that they are metric. Another possibility is multiple classification analysis with a 0-1 dependent variable.

B. This situation also involves the dependency relationships and presents a metric dependent variable and at least some independent variables which are metric. The appropriate multivariate technique is multiple regression, perhaps with some dummy (0-1) independent variables.

C. A multiple regression equation for the reasons of dependency plus metric predictor and criterion variables.

D. This appears to call for a statistical technique which relates the various test results and extracts a fewer number of latent variables or dimensions which "explain" sales success. This would suggest factor analysis.

7. One way to judge the predictive value of a discriminant analysis is to determine the percent of correctly classified dependent variable cases. In this problem, 210 of 280 or 75 percent of the cases were correctly classified. From the detailed data we see that the best record was in predicting which persons would take alternative A.

8. A. Factor loadings are correlation coefficients between the factor in question and the variables from which the factor is derived. For example, in Table 17-9 there is a correlation of .41 between factor 1 and financial accounting grades, but only a correlation coefficient of .01 between factor 1 and managerial accounting grades.

B. The communality value of .11 on Table 17-9 indicates that 11 percent of the variance in grades in the human behavior course is explained by the three factors.

C. One interpretation is that the three factors which have emerged are an artifact of the statistical analysis, resulting largely from the number of factors chosen, the small size of sample used, and the type of rotation scheme

Chapter 17   *Multivariate Analysis: An Overview*

used. Another interpretation is that the factors reflect teaching styles and approaches of the few professors involved rather than student "types."

True - False Questions

T   1) In regression analysis we develop an estimating equation in which we use data from one or more independent variables to estimate values for a dependent variable.

F   2) Factor analysis is the best known and most widely used of the multivariate statistical methods.

F   3) A dummy variable is one which is left blank in a regression calculation because the data are unavailable.

T   4) One use of multiple regression as a descriptive tool is to explicate causal theories.

T   5) Multicollinearity is the situation where some of the independent variables in multiple regression are highly correlated.

T   6) The objective of discriminant analysis is to minimize the misclassifications in a set of unordered categories (nominal scale).

T   7) Discriminant analysis may be used to analyze known groups to determine the relative influence of specific factors in determining into which group various cases fall.

F   8) The correlation coefficients in factor analysis are called principal components.

T   9) In factor analysis the factors are the new set of composite variables which are uncorrelated with each other.

F   10) The interpretation of factor loadings is guided by a clearly defined set of objective criteria.

F   11) The multiple regression coefficient is also known as r.

F   12) Discriminant analysis can only be used where there are two groups which make up the dependent variable.

T   13) In factor analysis the purpose of rotation is to illuminate the constructs underlying the factors.

F   14) An eigenvalue and a communality are essentially the same thing in factor analysis.

Chapter 17 — Multivariate Analysis: An Overview

T 15) Multivariate analysis assesses the relationships between more than two variables.

F 16) If variables are interrelated without the assumption that some are criterion and some are predictor, then there is an assumption of dependence.

T 17) MANOVA assesses the relationship between two or more dependent variables and a group of independent variables or factors.

F 18) MANOVA tests all of the variables and their interrelationships in a sequential fashion, much like running consecutive ANOVAs.

T 19) MANOVA tests for similarity or differences among the multivariate means or centroids of several populations.

F 20) LISREL, has two parts: a discriminating model and a regression model.

T 21) In LISREL, since the hypothetical constructs cannot be measured directly, the measurement model is used to relate the observed, recorded, or measured variables to the latent variables.

T 22) Conjoint analysis interviewing or questionnaire techniques require respondents to make tradeoffs on preferences which mimic those made in an actual buying situation.

F 23) Principal components analysis is similar to factor analysis in that both techniques discover the set of components which account for variation in multivariate data and reduce the numbers of variables a researcher handles by concentrating on the most important components.

T 24) Cluster analysis is set of techniques for grouping similar objects or people.

T 25) LISREL allows researchers to analyze complex covariance structures. Latent, interdependent, and reciprocally causal variables are easily handled within the measurement and structural equation models.

T 26) Conjoint analysis is a technique which typically uses input from nonmetric independent variables.

T 27) Multidimensional scaling is a technique which facilitates the description of a respondent's perception about a product, service, or other object of interest, in a spatial manner.

F 28) The objective of canonical analysis is to secure *part-worths* or utility scores that represent the importance of each aspect of a product or service in the subjects' overall preference ratings.

Chapter 17

Multiple Choice Questions

1. In multiple regression equations, when the regression coefficients are expressed in standard deviation units:
   A) The regression coefficients are called betas.
   B) The regression's y intercept falls to zero.
   C) The regression coefficient values will indicate the relative importance of their independent variables.
   D) A and C are correct
   * E) A, B, and C are correct.

2. Which of the following variables is more likely to be the dependent variable in a discriminant analysis problem?
   * A) What is one's political party?
   B) What is the family's after tax income?
   C) What is the average high temperature in January.
   D) What is one's ranking in a tennis tournament?

3. Which of the following multivariate techniques does *not* have an assumption of dependence?
   * A) Factor analysis
   B) MANOVA
   C) Multiple regression
   D) Discriminant application

4. MANOVA is similar to the univariate ANOVA with the added ability to handle:
   A) Multiple independent variables
   * B) Multiple dependent variables
   C) More than one F test
   D) SSCP matrices

5. Which techniques allows the researcher to develop a decision rule that describes the relationship of several independent variables on one dependent variable?
   A) Canonical analysis
   B) Factor analysis
   C) MANOVA
   * D) Conjoint analysis

6. One of the first steps in a conjoint study is to:
   A) Complete a principal components analysis.
   B) Decide on scaling terms.
   * C) Select the factors.
   D) Select the structural equation model.

206

7. What technique is best used when a researcher is interested in explaining a set of several dependent variables?
   A) Conjoint analysis
   B) Multiple regression
   * C) Canonical analysis
   D) Factor analysis

8. Some techniques require variables to be independent and not correlated. Which of the following techniques is sometimes used beforehand, to create uncorrelated variables?
   A) Multidimensional Scaling
   B) LISREL
   * C) Principal Components Analysis
   D) MANOVA

9. Suppose that you are planning a study involving conjoint analysis. You plan to test three prices, three brands, three speeds, two levels of educational values, two categories for games, and two categories for work assistance. This means that you have
   * A) A 216 full-option model.
   B) An impossible task since respondents cannot order that many variations of products in a consistent way.
   C) A 108 full option model.
   D) A requirement to start with for Principal Components Analysis (PCA) to reduce the number of variables.

10. With Multidimensional Scaling, items which are perceived to be similar will
    A) be far apart in multidimensional space.
    B) be in different clusters or groups.
    C) be in the same cluster or group.
    * D) fall close together in multidimensional space.

11. Which of the following can be an important problem in using multiple regression?
    A) Interpreting the meaning of the equation.
    B) Needing to use dummy variables.
    C) Getting negative regression coefficients.
    * D) Failing to test for multicollinearity.
    E) Stating regression coefficients in standardized form.

CHAPTER 18

PRESENTING RESULTS: WRITTEN AND ORAL REPORTS

The first objective for this chapter is for the student to learn the rudiments of writing an acceptable research report, including format and presentation specifics. The second objective is for the student to know what makes for an acceptable oral presentation of research findings.

Class Discussion Suggestions

Class time committed to this chapter usually does not exceed one period and sometimes the chapter is assigned without discussion. Depending on the level of the class, you may want to assign the chapter early in the semester and then review parts of it as students approach various stages in their assignments.

For example, before the first briefings are presented one might review the materials in that section. The authors have tried the approach of demonstrating what is obviously a poor oral briefing and then attempted to show the same material in a better presentation. This can be done with a 5 minute presentation followed by a discussion of deficiencies. Then we present the improved version. Students respond well to this in class and it appears to have a marked effect on their own attention to presentation technique.

As students move into the early stages of writing their reports, a portion of a class may be used to review the major principles of good report writing. It is most helpful if one can present actual examples of well written reports as well as poor ones. Students will follow good models when they see them. William Zinsser's book, *On Writing Well* (Harper & Row) is a good review for instructors preparing this material for the first time.

Answers to Chapter Questions

1. A. A *speaker-centered* presentation is one where the focus (generally resulting from the speakers sense of inadequacy) relies on memorization of the manuscript. The style of delivery reflects a preoccupation with the memorized message to the detriment of establishing rapport with and adapting to the needs of the audience. It is considered self or speaker-centered because it is strictly one-way communication. In contrast, an *extemporaneous presentation* replaces a script with an organized set of ideas that may be presented from notes or an outline. This approach takes into consideration the need for adaptability to the occasion, flexible response to audience feedback, and a conversational delivery of the message.

    B. *Technical reports* not only include a full presentation of the analysis but also sufficient procedural information to permit another researcher to replicate the study. The report structure follows the steps of the research study itself: prefatory items, introduction, methodology, findings, conclusions, appendixes, and bibliography. The appendixes contain detailed information such as instrumentation, data analysis methods, and instructions for the field personnel.

Management reports are written for the nontechnical client. They minimize methodological details. Conclusions are presented before the findings that support them. A liberal use of graphics are used to enhance comprehension. The appendix is short compared to the technical report and the bibliographic references are often omitted.

C. The *topic outline* is a format in which only a key word or two are used for each item. *Sentence outlines* express the essential thoughts associated with the specific topic. Brief sentences are used in the sentence outline.

2. A. It is important to include a balanced and thoughtful but fair expression of the conceptual and implementation limits that the reader should keep in mind when drawing inferences from a report's findings. It is a mark of the true professional. In student reports, one sometimes sees an extensive listing of faults, which may be justifiably true, but detract from the report.

    B. Complex tables should be avoided except in an appendix. The opposite is desired. That is, we should make a special effort to simplify tables so that they are easily understood by readers. The best way to achieve such simplicity is to restrict each table to one or two specific points. In place of tables, use charts and graphs whenever possible.

    C. The physical presentation of the report is critical to its comprehension. It is especially important to design the report to fit its audience and to deal adequately with the knowledge gap that may exist between the writer and reader. The particular form of the report should be appropriate to the audience, occasion, and importance of the subject.

    D. "Pace" concerns the problem of how quickly concepts are developed and how deeply they are explained. The pace tends to be slow and the depth limited if the topic is complex and the audience unsophisticated. If the topic is complex, but the audience is sophisticated, the writer can assume a certain depth of knowledge and move quickly and deeply into the subject.

3. A. A short report, informational in nature, most likely a memo. Costs, reimbursement amounts, and employee satisfaction with the health plan are comparative aspects which may be included in graphical form.

    B. A technical report which follows the suggested format of the journal in question.

    C. A short report: memorandum or letter style, informational in nature.

    D. A long report. A technical report would be mandatory, a management report may also be presented to supplement the technical report.

4. Some likely requirements for statistical materials are:

A. Statistical data should usually be presented in small doses.

B. All tables should be labeled adequately to insure that the reader can understand their contents.

C. Writers should seldom put more than several statistical numbers in the body of text. When there are more than this they should go into tables or semi-tabular presentations.

D. Whenever possible, salient points should be emphasized by means of a powerful graphic. For time series data, bar charts and stratum/area charts are good choices. For percentage data, a pie chart can be used. For distributions, consider the histogram or box plot.

E. Writers should recognize that charts and graphs represent visual comparisons which have more impact than the labels on the data. For example, the omission of a zero base line may give a wrong visual impression even though the scales may be labeled correctly.

F. Statistical data from which findings are drawn should be adjacent to those findings.

5. A. Written report problems include the following:

   1. Reports are badly organized.
   2. Lack of headings and subheadings to show the organization of the report. Paragraphs that are too long, rather than short, one-topic expositions.
   3. Padding of the report with extra verbiage.
   4. Too much dependence on traditional essay style rather than the more telegraphic research reporting style.
   5. Careless spelling.
   6. Failure to revise; the first draft is the only draft.
   7. Assignment of sections of report to different writers, making for uneven writing.
   8. Badly designed tables, charts, and graphics. Tables too often include too much material.
   9. Failure to locate charts and tables contiguous to the first reference to them.
   10. Too small margins and too little white space.
   11. Too much space given to chronology of the project.

   B. Oral Briefing problems include the following:

   1. Failure to keep within time constraints.
   2. Lack of eye contact with audience members.

3. Distracting physical actions such as change rattling, hands in pockets or on hips, repetitive movements, pen clicking, and etc.
4. Distracting verbal actions such as "ah" and "you know."
5. Poor verbal delivery, e.g., halting and/or slow delivery, very fast speech, or monotones.
6. Poor or unclear organization of presentation.
7. Overdependence on notes.
8. Too few visuals and poor handling of visuals.

6. A self analysis question for students.

7. This can be a good exercise to have students prepare in advance and then have several shown on chalkboard or via transparencies. One suggested outline for the first assignment is given below. Answers to parts B and C depend on the circumstances at the time.

    I. Prewriting Considerations
        A. Purpose of report
        B. Define audience
        C. Circumstances and limitations
        D. How will it be used?

    II. Report Choice
        A. Informational or research?
        B. Long or short?
        C. Management or technical?
        D. Format?

    III. Draft body of report
        A. Analysis of data
        B. Select important findings
        C. Statistical tests
        D. Draft conclusions
        E. Draft recommendations
        F. Review and revise
            1. by self
            2. by others

    IV. Writing report
        A. Outline body of report
        B. How to present data
            1. draft tables
            2. set up charts
            3. develop graphics
        C. Introduction
        D. Appendix
        E. Synopsis
        F. First draft - total report
        G. Review and revise
            1. by self
            2. by others

Chapter 18 *Written and Oral Reports*

        H. Final printing and finishing touches

    V. Submit the report

8. Several different graphic forms are acceptable for each of the cases mentioned.

    A. If the intent is to show yearly data for the decade it is probably wise to use a line diagram on a semilog chart because semilog scales show rates of relative change much better than do arithmetic scales. If one is showing only the percentage change between annual income in 1985 and 1995 then an arithmetic line scale diagram may be used if 1985 for each country is set at 100 and 1995 is expressed as a ratio to 1985. A better choice would be to use a multiple variable bar chart, with both countries listed above the years, 1985 and 1995. The raw data and the percentage change can thus be shown on the same chart, using numbers to augment the graphic.

    B. There are several ways to show this data, depending on the message being delivered. If there is a desire to only compare percentages of income spent on items, it would probably be best to use a horizontal bar chart of the 100% component type. This is the best way to show comparable allocations among subparts. A vertical version of the same type of chart is often found and is also acceptable. If, on the other hand, the absolute dollar comparisons are desired, a vertical stacked bar chart would be a good choice. Other possibilities include a set of pie charts (for percentagesonly), a 3-D column chart if the data has been collected for more than one year, or a stratum chart.

    C. This could be the two-way percent change horizontal bar chart. It is an ideal way for comparing percent changes between two points for a limited number of entities, especially when one or more may be negative percent changes. Alternatively, a multiple variable vertical bar chart could be used to graphically show the changes from year to year. This would be best done with the years 1993 and 1994 as the variables and the six firms as the heading for the groups of bars. A third possibility is to use a line chart with each firms' price shown as a different line.

True - False Questions

F   1) The research report should contain findings, analysis of these findings, interpretations, and conclusions but not recommendations.

T   2) Whether the researcher uses the technical or the management type of long report depends chiefly on the audience and the researcher's objective.

T   3) In order to guard against including nonessential material in a technical report, a good guideline is that sufficient information of a procedural nature should be included to enable others to replicate the study.

Chapter 18   *Written and Oral Reports*

T   4) The management report is the best design when the readers of a long report are less concerned with the methodological details but more interested in learning quickly the major findings and conclusions.

F   5) In the management format for a long report the introductory information covering the purpose of the study, methodology, and limitations is followed by the findings.

T   6) The executive summary in a research report may serve as a "report in miniature" or as little more than a review of the major conclusions.

F   7) Study limitations are usually included as part of the executive summary.

T   8) It is often useful to present one item per page in the findings section of the report with the quantitative data supporting the finding in a small table or chart on the same page.

F   9) The summary is a brief restatement of the recommendations.

F   10) A management report is usually presented in a logical order.

T   11) Probably no single element detracts more from a report's quality image than spelling errors.

F   12) Tables facilitate quantitative comparisons and surely provide the most concise and efficient way to present numerical data and general quantitative values.

F   13) Compared to a graphs, tables show only a few pieces of information and the values are only approximate.

T   14) One good way to achieve accurate visual impressions of values on a graph is to include a zero base line on the scale on which the curves are plotted.

T   15) One problem with line diagrams occurs when we try to compare relative and absolute changes among two or more sets of data. A good rule is to use a semilogarithmic scale when interested primarily in rates of growth.

F   16) In drafting histograms one should generally leave a space between bars equal to one half or more of the width of a bar.

T   17) The opening of a "briefing" should be direct, attention arresting, and indicate the nature of the discussion to follow.

F   18) Memorization of a speech is time-consuming but provides the best presentation with the least risk of mishap.

Chapter 18 — Written and Oral Reports

Multiple Choice Questions

1. Good writing should have proper "pace." This is best defined as follows:
   A) it is writing in simple plain terms rather than in the more elegant style of nonbusiness writers.
   * B) it is neither overcrowding nor presenting too sparse a volume of concepts per page.
   C) it is organizing the flow of concepts so that those mentioned first are the foundations for those that come later.
   D) it is writing in a linear style which limits the amount of "referencing back" needed.
   E) it is none of the above.

2. Which of the following would probably be the best way to show a comparison of 10 year growth rates between the economies of the U.S.A. and China?
   A) Pie chart
   B) Line diagram with arithmetic scale
   * C) Line diagram with semilog scale
   D) 100% component bar chart

3. Which of the following is probably the one single element which detracts as much or more than any other from a report's quality image?
   A) Poor report appearance
   * B) Incorrect spelling and punctuation
   C) Overcrowding of the text
   D) Use of listings rather than text
   E) Writing that is difficult for the reader

4. The Executive Summary section of a research report
   A) Should be an introduction to the research problem.
   B) Should include only the major findings and conclusions.
   * C) Should include facts, conclusions, and recommendations.
   D) Is also known as the Synopsis.
   E) Is not well described by any of the above.

5. Which of the following statements is most correct concerning the contents of the introduction section of a research report?
   A) Methodology, including copies of measurement instruments should be placed in the introduction.
   B) Statements of limitations should usually be placed in the findings section rather than the introduction.
   C) The Executive Summary is generally a part of the introduction section.
   * D) Operational definitions of critical variables should be included in the introduction.
   E) More than one of the above statements is correct.

Chapter 18 Written and Oral Reports

6. A college textbook which is written at the appropriate level, according to the Gunning fog index, should have a score of about
   A) 45
   B) 60
   C) 7.5
   D) 10
   * E) 12.5

7. There are some general considerations that the report writer should deal with before beginning to write the report. Which of the following best expresses these considerations?
   A) First ask, "What is the purpose of this report?"
   B) Ask, "Who will read the report?"
   C) Ask, "How will the report be used?"
   * D) Ask three of the above.

8. When using tables in a research report, which of the following is the best guide to follow?
   * A) Use small simple tables, although this may mean using many tables.
   B) Try to keep the number of tables small, although this means more complex tables.
   C) Try to keep most tables in the Appendix.
   D) Where at all possible, place quantitative data within text discussions rather than in tables.
   E) Don't use any of the above suggestions as a guide.

9. Every research report should include a statement on the study's limitations. Where in the report is the most appropriate place to locate this?
   A) Synopsis
   * B) Methodology
   C) Findings
   D) Summary and conclusions
   E) Appendix

10. Which of the following best expresses the majority view on the use of visual aids in conducting business research briefings?
    A) It is easy to use too many visuals, turning the briefing into a "side show."
    B) They are very useful, but largely to express numeric data which cannot be conveyed well orally.
    C) Whether to use them or not is largely an unresolved question.
    * D) Even visual aids consisting totally of words can be very valuable.
    E) Probably the best visual aid to use consists of handout materials.

IRWIN

Instructor's Manual to accompany *BUSINESS RESEARCH METHODS*, Fifth Edition
by Donald R. Cooper

Please use this postage-paid form to report any errors that you find in this material. Be as complete as possible noting specifically which changes should be made. We will address them in subsequent printings and future editions. Thank You.

Attention: R. T. Hercher

Name _____   School _____

Office Phone _____

Please fold and seal so that our address is visible.

BUSINESS REPLY MAIL
FIRST CLASS MAIL   PERMIT NO. 17   HOMEWOOD, IL

POSTAGE WILL BE PAID BY ADDRESSEE

RICHARD D. IRWIN

1333 Burr Ridge Pky.
Burr Ridge, IL 60521-0084

ATTENTION: R. Hercher

NO POSTAGE
NECESSARY
IF MAILED
IN THE
UNITED STATES

(fold)

(fold)